PRAISE FOR *EVE SPONSORSHIP A FUNDRAISING*

'In the ever-changing and burgeoning world of live experiences, this publication manages to step back and take a firm grasp of the vital discussions and dynamics around sponsorship and fundraising events. For a marketing channel that has, rather frustratingly, traditionally been less associated with strategy and meticulous communications planning, it's particularly refreshing to see the diversity and depth to which the subject has been explored.' **Nick Adams, Founder and Managing Director, Sense**

'Writing a book that will be useful for practitioners yet also appeal to an academic audience is difficult. Tom Lunt and Eva Nicotra have pulled it off. I have no doubt that their book will be adopted widely for use in event management degree programmes because it is very well informed, analytical and grounded in practice. Its nuanced (and often critical) reflections on current ways of doing things and its accessible style should also make it popular with thoughtful practitioners. By writing this book, the authors also demonstrate how academics in vocational fields such as event management might contribute to the improvement of practice.' **Professor Rhodri Thomas, Dean, School of Events, Tourism and Hospitality Management, Leeds Beckett University**

'Event sponsorship and fundraising are critical to the success of any event delivered in today's highly volatile and politicized world. Lunt and Nicotra present an extremely important text examining the challenging and innovative world of sponsorship and it is a welcome addition to the event management literature. The book adopts an informative and accessible approach effortlessly combining theory and practice. The use of practical templates makes it an excellent resource for students and event managers alike. An extremely diverse range of case studies and professional and research insights support the theoretical underpinning and make for interesting and engaging reading!' **Dr Jane Ali-Knight, Professor in Festival and Event Management, Edinburgh Napier University**

'This book will make a great contribution to the teaching of events management for both undergraduate and postgraduate students. Knowledge of this area is essential for graduates, and this is one of the first texts to address finance, fundraising and sponsorship issues in a way that is immediately relevant to events managers. The mixture of research insights, professional insights and industry case studies means that this book will be equally valued by teachers and students.' **Dr James Kennell, Principal Lecturer and Programme Leader for Events Management, University of Greenwich, UK**

Event Sponsorship and Fundraising

An advanced guide

Tom Lunt and Eva Nicotra

KoganPage

First published in Great Britain and the United States in 2019 by Kogan Page Limited

2nd Floor, 45 Gee Street	c/o Martin P Hill Consulting	4737/23 Ansari Road
London	122 W 27th St, 10th Floor	Daryaganj
EC1V 3RS	New York NY 10001	New Delhi 110002
United Kingdom	USA	India
www.koganpage.com		

© Tom Lunt, Eva Nicotra, 2019

The right of Tom Lunt and Eva Nicotra to be identified as the authors of this work has been asserted by them in accordance with the Copyright, Designs and Patents Act 1988.

ISBN   978 0 7494 8092 9
E-ISBN   978 0 7494 8093 6

British Library Cataloguing-in-Publication Data

A CIP record for this book is available from the British Library.

Library of Congress Cataloging-in-Publication Data

A CIP record for this book is available from the Library of Congress.

Typeset by Integra Software Services, Pondicherry
Print production managed by Jellyfish
Printed and bound by CPI Group (UK) Ltd, Croydon, CR0 4YY

This book is dedicated to all those who work in the events industry and event education, colleagues and students, especially those that the authors have had the pleasure of working with. The following passage, spoken by Ulysses to his crew as he sets out on his final voyage, is by way of encouragement to you (young or old!) for your next project.

> [...] you and I are old;
> Old age hath yet his honour and his toil;
> Death closes all: but something ere the end,
> Some work of noble note, may yet be done,
> Not unbecoming men that strove with Gods.
> The lights begin to twinkle from the rocks:
> The long day wanes: the slow moon climbs; the deep
> Moans round with many voices. Come, my friends,
> 'Tis not too late to seek a newer world.

('Ulysses', Alfred, Lord Tennyson)

CONTENTS

Online resources

To support teaching and learning on this module, the following downloadable material is available at www.koganpage.com/event-sponsorship:

- lecture slides;
- seminar and activity sheets;
- sample lesson plans.

FIGURES AND TABLES

Figures

Tables

CASE STUDIES AND INSIGHTS

Case studies

Fundraising insights

Professional insights

Research insights

Sponsorship insights

ABOUT THE AUTHORS

Tom Lunt is a Senior Teaching Fellow at the University of Surrey. He has also lectured in events management; first at London Metropolitan University and then at the University of Greenwich. Prior to his academic career Tom worked in fundraising events; first at the Royal Star & Garter home for disabled servicemen and women and then at Christian Aid, where he was Events and Community Fundraising Manager. He has managed a wide range of events, including exclusive black-tie dinners, overseas challenge events, and sponsored cycles and walks. Tom completed his doctoral thesis in 2016 and has published research and presented at conferences in both the event management and education fields, where his interests focus on social media, experiential event management and event design.

Eva Nicotra is Senior Lecturer in Creative Industries Management at London Metropolitan University where she is Course Leader for the BA Events Management and teaches modules including event planning, marketing and sponsorship of events, and live music events promotion. She is an accomplished events and music industry professional and previously was a director of an events company which organized concerts and charity events. Within the subject area her academic interests include events marketing, live music events and festivals management, and the night time economy.

FOREWORD

More than ever, present day special events are exhaustively mined to illustrate ongoing industry change. The increasingly pivotal role of sponsorship and fundraising, to both wider cultural production and individual events' own development and survival, is becoming clear. This engagement with the commercial and funding world is meticulously explored in this insightful book. The authors have gone to great lengths to research and collect first-hand accounts of the intricate, subtle and creative practices that are leveraged to persuade governments, brands and individuals to invest in events. From the arts to business, from festivals to fetes, and from gala dinners to sport, all are in one way or another connected to the relationships and marketing channels that sponsorship and fundraising catalyses.

2018 saw the UK gripped by a heat wave, with one of the hottest summers on record since the long, hot, hazy days of 1976. Spontaneous summer parties and celebrations were plentiful; despite Glastonbury's brief recess year, the world's greatest sporting event, the FIFA World Cup, finished with jubilation in France. Mere weeks later, that most iconic of sports events, the Tour de France, concluded with a maiden victory for Geraint Thomas, and the sixth in seven years for his Sky-sponsored team. While the World Cup is backed by state funding, whether held in Brazil, Russia or Qatar, it also generates millions through ticket sales, global commercial benefits and sponsorship deals, amongst others. By contrast, the Tour de France sells no spectator tickets, has more localized commercial activity and is contested not by national teams, as in the World Cup, but by sponsored trade teams. Indeed, without the latter there would be no Tour and no professional road cycling. The participation of national teams in the World Cup is a by-product of its format but participation of teams at the Tour is a constant revolving door as the teams depend upon commercial sponsors to operate. In 2018, the big-name sponsored teams aside from Sky were UAE Emirates, Movistar, Bahrain-Merida and AG2R. From head to toe the professional cyclist is a monument to modern sponsorship and fundraising practices that fund everything, from their kit and equipment, to transport and management. Without this income stream, the stark reality is that there would be no professional cyclists, no teams and ultimately no events. The turnover of sponsors who constantly leave is relatively high and there is constant pressure on team owners/managers to maintain commercial networks, develop relationships, source opportunities, present pitches and demonstrate the value of road cycling to potential investors. This book unpacks and explains this process through several case studies. Once the sponsorship is secured, it must then be managed so that the team and the cyclists become central to the brand campaigns at both micro and macro level. Cycling has to offer a platform for brand media exposure and experiential activation that is critical to all stakeholders. The Tour itself requires cash injections to survive, not only from headline sponsors, but also from towns and cities paying for the privilege to host a stage or part thereof. Leveraging the impact exposure of the teams and the economic benefit of a town hosting a stage is essential for the sustainability of the teams, the event and the sport. The complex and competing demands of relationship management in events, epitomized within professional road cycling, is expertly captured in this book by Tom Lunt and Eva Nicotra. The authors unravel an often mysterious yet compelling environment that trades cash and services for brand exposure, or raises finances through intensely personal and emotional bonds. The strategies and techniques for achieving success in this industry require constant, persistent attention to detail, and never has this been better expressed than in the section 'What's in the goody bag?'. Innocuous but haphazard placement of mementos and 'goodies' is no longer enough; they must mean something to the recipients, the chapter suggests – authenticity is key, otherwise it is just another pointless and wasteful freebie. The endeavour to create emotional experience and connection between brand and audience is a constant thread throughout the book, providing a valuable anchor for readers new to the field of sponsorship and funding or for those looking to enhance their expertise.

Dr Graham Berridge
Principal Teaching Fellow
School of Hospitality and Tourism Management, Surrey University, UK

PREFACE

The events industry is a diverse and fast-moving sector that plays an important role in the arts, business, culture, education, entertainment and sport sectors. While those working in event management have experienced many changes in recent years, the need for sponsorship and fundraising income remains a vital factor that will often be the difference between an event project's success and failure.

Competition for sponsorship and other funding has increased as the number of events increases in some sectors, such as music festivals. At the same time, the demands of sponsors and funders for more rigorous evaluation to justify their investment have also become more stringent.

In writing *Event Sponsorship and Fundraising: An advanced guide*, the authors seek to respond to these demands and equip the reader with an understanding of how to:

- research prospective sponsors and other sources of funding;
- write excellent sponsorship proposals that will attract sponsors and funding bodies to invest in their events;
- develop and manage relationships with sponsors and funders;
- oversee the implementation of a sponsorship campaign or funding programme at an event;
- evaluate the results of a sponsorship campaign or funding programme.

The book also offers guidance on how to build a career to those who are new to sponsorship and fundraising.

Purpose and approach of the book

Our aim in this book is twofold. We have focused on writing a management-based 'how to' guide that will enable event managers to develop sponsorship and fundraising strategies that will sustain their events. At the same time, we have developed an analysis of current practice that asks questions, takes alternative perspectives and provides suggestions for new approaches to the practice of sponsorship and fundraising in event management.

This book is the first of its kind to offer a critical analysis alongside a practical guide to sponsorship and fundraising. In doing so it:

- offers the reader a significant range of academic and practical literature, providing a foundation of knowledge on which to develop both tactical and strategic planning;
- engages with leading practitioners in live music, experiential marketing and sporting events to give valuable up-to-date insights into current practice;
- asks questions of the reader to encourage reflection and action on their current activities, aims and objectives.

The book discusses significant concepts, such as 'expectancy', 'relevancy' and 'fit' in sponsorship. At the same time, sponsorship is located within the integrated marketing communications mix and its relationship with experiential marketing is assessed. Alongside these central topics, particular attention is paid to notions of authenticity and the postmodern consumer, and their implications for sponsorship of events.

Readership of the book

This book has been written with the following groups of people in mind:

- Students studying event management, business and marketing related degrees will find this book helpful in understanding how sponsorship and fundraising relate to other core business activities.
- Teachers in higher education who are developing courses will find this book an invaluable resource for preparing stimulating learning experiences for their students on a very important subject area of event management.
- Professionals working in event sponsorship and fundraising will find fresh perspectives and insights that will help to develop their approach.
- Academics will find this book a useful resource in this specialist area.

How to use this book

Event Sponsorship and Fundraising: An advanced guide has been written to give the reader a multi-layered insight. Each chapter incorporates a range of components including:

- Professional insights – Interviews with leading event sponsorship professionals.

- Research insights – Summaries of recent academic research related to topics in the chapter.

- Case studies – Real-world examples illustrating how the concepts and topics are applied in practice.

- Recommendations for further reading – Each chapter ends with a set of readings, such as academic journal articles, books and websites, that provide additional perspectives and insights on the topics covered in the chapter. These are primarily for students looking to engage with a range of literature.

- Questions for discussion – At the end of each chapter a set of questions and activities is provided to help engage the reader with the material covered.

The book can form the basis of a semester-long course or module of study at undergraduate or postgraduate level. Alternatively, it can be 'dipped into' on a chapter-by-chapter basis. The following summaries will help the reader access the material quickly.

Chapter 1 gives an introduction to sponsorship and events, analysing the origins and growth of event sponsorship partnerships. Public funding is also examined, particularly in relation to art, culture and community events with a case study from Arts Council England. The chapter concludes with an interview with Andy Macleod, founder and Director of Club Fandango, a music promotions company. Focusing on his experience of delivering live music over two decades Andy offers valuable insights into funding streams available to music promoters.

Chapter 2 argues that sponsorship should be at the centre of the integrated marketing communications mix. The importance of experiential marketing to sponsorship partnerships is highlighted and the range of experiential marketing events considered. Taking a more critical perspective, the chapter examines the concept of authenticity, and a research insight and two sponsorship insights contribute to the discussion.

Chapter 3 focuses on application – the delivery of sponsorship campaigns. In doing so the chapter builds on the conceptual and theoretical material set out in Chapter 2 and includes an analysis of two leading practitioners and writers in the fields of experiential marketing and brand activation, Bernd Schmitt and Shaz Smilansky. The chapter then applies this analysis in an extended case study of Christian Aid's sponsorship of the Greenbelt Music

Festival and in a wide-ranging interview with Nick Adams, founder of the experiential marketing agency Sense London.

Having examined the delivery of sponsorship campaigns, in Chapter 4 the focus turns to how to attract sponsors' and grant makers' support for an event. Alignment of event and sponsor audiences, key concepts such as sponsorship fit and the motivations of sponsors are discussed in relation to wider marketing concepts such as market segmentation. Finally, these orthodox topics are discussed from the alternative perspective of postmodernism.

Chapter 5 focuses on application and develops some of the theories examined in Chapter 4. In the first section sources of funding in Scotland are evaluated as a template for how public funding models are organized. The second section presents an interview with James Pearce, a sports marketing professional with wide-ranging experience of event sponsorship and fundraising.

Chapter 6 concentrates on how to develop a sponsorship proposal that will have the best chance of securing a sponsor's support. The chapter highlights that while the preparation of innovative, individual proposals that speak to a prospective sponsor's needs are very important, even more so is the ability to develop positive, personal relationships, which is the primary goal of a sponsorship manager.

Chapter 7 sets out the key legal and ethical considerations relating to managing a relationship with a sponsor or funding body. The relationship between sponsors and event properties is considered and contract law examined as it relates to sponsorship agreements. Importantly, we argue in this chapter that ethical knowledge and the ability to apply it are core competences of the event manager. A number of ethical issues relating to recent events such as the Olympics that support this argument are examined.

Chapter 8 builds on the material discussed in Chapter 7. In a very detailed and practice-based interview James Tibbetts, Chief Operations Officer of the Female Sports Group, covers a number of important legal, insurance and intellectual property issues and links these to the valuation of sponsorship packages. Other topics are also discussed, including ethics and ambush marketing. The interview concludes with a discussion of the differences between managing a relationship with a grant funding body and a sponsor.

Chapter 9 examines evaluation, one of the most contentious areas of sponsorship and grant funding. The chapter deals with broad approaches – return on investment and return on outcomes – before turning to a range of metrics commonly used, such as media awareness, image and awareness. The chapter concludes with an analysis of social media evaluation.

Chapter 10 concludes the book by drawing together the main issues, themes and topics set out in Chapters 1 to 9. Moreover, the authors identify important influences for continuity and change in the sponsorship and grant-making sectors. Drivers for continuity are the need for authenticity and networking, while drivers for change include the increased spend on brand activations as opposed to sponsorship fees and the growth of online events, in particular e-sports.

Chapter 11 provides support material for the book. A framework for developing a sponsorship campaign is set out along with checklists of information required by commercial sponsors and grant makers.

Finally, in the Afterword, we offer some suggestions and advice for those who are interested in pursuing careers in sponsorship and fundraising.

ACKNOWLEDGEMENTS

The authors would like to thank the following people and organizations for their generous support and contributions to this book: Nick Adams (Sense London), Jim Andrews (IEG), Andy Macleod (Club Fandango), James Pearce, James Tibbetts, Rhodri Thomas, Christian Aid, Rapha, Charlotte Owen and everyone at Kogan Page.

Introduction to event sponsorship, fundraising, partnerships and relationship development

LEARNING OBJECTIVES

Having read this chapter and worked through the questions and activities you should be able:

- to examine the nature, role and application of sponsorship, fundraising and partnerships in the events industry;
- to analyse the growth of sponsorship;
- to demonstrate the relevance of sponsorship to various events sectors, namely live music, sport and arts, and cultural events.

This introductory chapter aims to provide the foundational knowledge necessary to understand sponsorship, first by shedding light on the nature of this type of partnership. The recent growth of sponsorship as a communication method will be highlighted, along with reasons why companies use sponsorship, and particularly why they choose to sponsor specific types of events. An overview of the content and structure of this book is provided at the end of the chapter to facilitate the reader's navigation and use of the book.

Defining sponsorship

Nowadays, there is no doubt of the crucial importance of sponsorship as a marketing communication method, not least because of the critical role it can play in building brands and forming deeper relationships with stakeholders. Sponsorship is a remarkable phenomenon that, in a relatively short period of time, has developed into a major global industry, while also attracting growing interest among scholars and researchers.

Over the years there have been numerous attempts to define the term 'sponsorship', with little agreement on a single, widely accepted and all-encompassing definition. One of the earliest efforts to provide a succinct statement that describes the nature of sponsorship was that from the academic Tony Meenaghan of University College Dublin, who stipulated that 'sponsorship can be regarded as the provision of assistance either financial or in kind to an activity by a commercial organization for the purpose of achieving commercial objectives' (1983: 9). Cornwell and Maignan (1998), in their comprehensive review of sponsorship literature prior to 1996, highlight that, albeit commonly used by researchers, this account fails to clarify what the purpose of sponsorship is, and specifically what types of commercial and non-commercial objectives it can achieve. Subsequent efforts to conceptualize sponsorship have been more systematic in including a clarification of sponsorship goals; for example, Gardner and Shuman (1988) see sponsorship as facilitating the achievement of corporate objectives such as enhancing corporate image, and/or marketing objectives such as increasing brand awareness. Along these lines, the International Chamber of Commerce (2003) provided the following definition of sponsorship when they revised their Code of Sponsorship to read:

> any commercial agreement by which a sponsor, for the mutual benefit of the sponsor and sponsored party contractually provides financing or other support in order to establish an association between the sponsor's image, brands or products and a sponsorship property in return for rights to promote this association and/or for the granting of pertained agreed direct or indirect benefits.

The International Events Group (IEG), the leading global sponsorship insights source based in Chicago, echoes the above by stating that sponsorship is 'a cash and/or in-kind fee paid to a property (typically in sports, arts, entertainment or causes) in return for access to the exploitable commercial potential associated with that property' (IEG, 2017b).

Despite the fact that there exists such an array of definitions, the similarities among them are evident. Sponsorship is to be considered a commercial/business agreement, a specific deal set out contractually that is aimed at delivering a range of commercial outcomes. Hence a non-commercial activity such as charitable giving is not to be deemed sponsorship. Importantly, sponsorship is emphasized as being a two-way process. It is fundamentally a mutual relationship – a partnership – based on an exchange of benefits between the sponsor's organization and the sponsored activity, such as an event. The sponsor provides either money or other non-monetary support (for example, equipment) and the event offers certain rights (for example, on-site signage) and other types of associations that can be utilized by the sponsor for commercial gain, for instance to increase brand awareness or sales. Within the context of events this exchange relationship is illustrated by Crompton (1994), as shown in Figure 1.1. Perhaps unsurprisingly, much of the debate around sponsorship centres on the extent to which the relationship is beneficial to each party involved in the sponsorship deal.

As stressed by authors including McDonnell and Moir (2013), knowledge of the benefits that can accrue to sponsors on the one hand enables the sponsor to maximize the worth of the sponsorship and on the other hand helps the sponsored property to make the sponsorship opportunity more attractive. Sponsorship benefits are classified by Crompton (1996) into four main categories, namely:

- increased awareness;
- image enhancement;
- product trial or sales opportunities; and
- hospitality opportunities.

Figure 1.1 The exchange relationship in event sponsorship

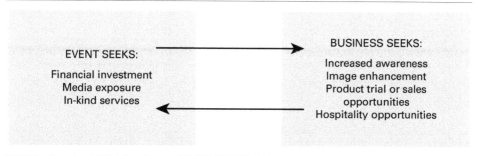

SOURCE Crompton, 1994. https://doi.org/10.3727/106527094792292050

Sponsorship can deliver multiple benefits across these categories (Crompton, 1996). McDonnell and Moir (2013) also stress that the ability to target specific audiences is a key benefit of sponsorship. Moreover, recent research by IEG (2017a) and Key Note (2016) highlights that today's sponsors value greatly the opportunities offered by new technologies, such as access to audience data that enables sponsors to specifically target relevant content at each customer group and at each social media platform in a personal way.

Meenaghan (1991: 8) stresses that the versatility of sponsorship 'enables it to fulfil many of the basic functions performed by other elements of the marketing communication mix' and at a significantly lower cost compared to other tactics, and in particular advertising. However, he suggests that sponsorship works differently from other forms of marketing in that it associates the sponsor's brand in a subtle and indirect way with an activity (eg sport or art) with which the consumer has an intense emotional relationship, in turn generating goodwill, image transfer and other related consumer responses such as brand preference and even purchase (Meenaghan, 2001).

Cornwell and Maignan (1998: 11), drawing from Otker's (1998) argument that sponsorship consists of both *buying* and *exploiting*, posit that sponsorship involves two main activities: the first is the exchange between the sponsor and the sponsored activity already mentioned above; the second is the marketing of the association by the sponsor, which consists of 'all marketing and communication efforts undertaken by the sponsor to leverage their investment in the sponsored activity or event'. Cornwell (1995) refers to these practices as sponsorship-linked marketing. Cornwell and Maignan (1998: 11) go as far as saying that 'the marketing communication value of sponsorship is null unless the sponsor widely promotes the relationship established with the organizer of a special event or activity'.

The growth of sponsorship

Origins

The practice of sponsorship has existed in one form or another for a very long time. Its origins can be traced back to Ancient Greece and the Olympic Games, thought to have begun in 776 BC, as well as the Roman era when wealthy individuals would finance gladiatorial events as well as supporting athletes and artists, mainly to gain political advantage (Kolah, 2015; McDonnell and Moir, 2013; Skinner and Rukavina, 2003).

Gaius Maecenas (c70–8 BC), counsellor to the first Roman Emperor Octavian Augustus, was a patron of literature including poets such as Virgil and Horace and he is believed to have 'sought to use the genius of the poets of the day to glorify the new imperial regime of Augustus' (Encyclopaedia Britannica, 2007). Still today, and in various languages, his name is used as an archetype to signify a protector or benefactor of the arts (Enciclopedia Treccani, no date). In French, the term *mécénat* is used to refer to both sponsorship and philanthropic activities, and worldwide up until the 1980s the concepts of sponsorship and patronage were synonymous (Gregory, 1984 cited in Cornwell and Maignan, 1998; Meenaghan, 1983 cited in Ryan and Fhay, 2012). Patronage was a practice that took place extensively during the Renaissance period, which spanned roughly from the 14th to the 17th century, when many patrons and donors supported painters, musicians and inventors (Sanghak, 2009). Notably, members of the Florentine banking family, the Medici, especially Cosimo the Elder and his grandson Lorenzo the Magnificent, sponsored artists such as Leonardo da Vinci, Donatello and Botticelli. In the same vein as a logo is used today, the *Insigna Florentinorum*, the family emblem, which consisted of five red balls and one blue on a gold shield, was emblazoned on any building to which the Medici had connections or that they had financed, including the world's first art gallery, the Uffizi (Hibbert, 1979; Arts and Business, 2005).

Sanghak (2009) suggests that what characterizes these precursors of sponsorship compared to current sponsorship activities is that:

1 Most patrons were members of the royalty or nobility, not a company.

2 Decisions on who to monetarily support were based on the patron's personal interests or hobbies, not a company's commercial objectives.

3 Because there were no mass media, sponsorships had limited exposure, usually by word of mouth.

4 Sport sponsorships were limited.

Sponsorship is nonetheless clearly seen to emerge from these practices, and indeed scholars divide sponsorship into two main eras: philanthropic sponsorship before the 1970s and commercial sponsorship thereafter. In today's iterations, however, as mentioned earlier, patronage and sponsorship are to be considered distinctive activities, as stressed by the Association for Business Sponsorship of the Arts. As McDonnell and Moir (2013: 6) suggest, the main distinguishing factor is that 'the philanthropist expects no commercial benefit from his/her gift (except perhaps a warm feeling of good being done)'. Thus patronage and charitable donations are not to be considered marketing activities, as opposed to sponsorship, and even the tax position is likely to be different, as is the case in the United Kingdom (UK) (Fishel, 1993). It is true nonetheless that philanthropic giving can lead to public relations (PR) benefits for the company, for instance prestige and improved reputation, and indeed some companies may treat sponsorship and patronage 'as two aspects of the same strategy' (Fishel, 1993: 24).

Recent developments

Instances of activities that can be considered closer to sponsorship as we know it today can be found in the 19th century, which for example sees Coca-Cola's and Kodak's involvement in the first modern Olympics in Athens in 1896, although there is limited research examining sponsorship during this period (Sanghak, 2009). Also, the scale was small and instances were rare (Meenaghan, 2001). Conversely, it was during the 20th century, especially the latter part, that sponsorship grew into the phenomenon we know today. The advent of colour television broadcasting made televised events more popular, creating opportunities for sponsors as it enabled access to larger audiences (Crompton, 1995; Meenaghan, 1991). This was taken advantage of by tobacco and alcohol companies, who made extensive use of sport sponsorship to circumvent bans on television advertising (Crompton, 1993). For example, Marlboro, a Phillip Morris owned brand of cigarettes, began its longstanding involvement with Formula 1 in 1972 with the sponsorship of the BRM team, later of McLaren and from 1997 of Ferrari. This partnership lasts to this day, even though tobacco sponsorship was banned in the European Union by the Tobacco Advertising Decree in 2005. In the same year the World Health Organization Framework Convention on Tobacco Control was instated, which requires member countries to introduce a comprehensive ban of all forms of tobacco advertising, promotion and sponsorship (European Commission, 2017).

Moreover, as suggested by Crompton (1995: 99), 'the success of sponsorships associated with the 1984 Los Angeles Olympics received high visibility and helped legitimize sponsorship to the corporate sector as an effective promotional medium'. For the first time in the history of the modern Olympics, funding for the Games came with limited public subsidy; instead they were heavily financed through revenue from television broadcasting rights and corporate sponsorship. As reported in *Marketing News* in June 1984, 'The LA

Olympic Organising Committee had no trouble finding 30 corporations willing to ante up 130 millions for the privilege to be designated official sponsor'.

These are among the factors that set the foundations for the sponsorship boom of the 1980s and 1990s, which Meenaghan (1991: 5) demonstrates by stating that in the UK, which is an exemplar of how sponsorship has evolved, expenditure on sponsorship had grown 70 times between the 1970s and the 1990s from £4m to £288m. Since then, sponsorship has seen sustained growth and at a pace that at various points has exceeded that of other forms of marketing, including advertising (IEG, 2017b).

The current value of the sponsorship market is evidence of its growing importance. IEG (2017b) estimated global sponsorship spend at US$60.1 billion in 2016, an increase of 4.6 per cent from the previous year and the highest growth to date. It is true, nonetheless, that if we look at global expenditure on marketing communications, which, according to the World Federation of Advertisers (2017), exceeds US$900 billion annually, sponsorship clearly constitutes only a small proportion. Estimated brand spend on advertising in 2016 alone was US$540 billion worldwide across all media including digital, according to the research company eMarketer (2016). There is, however, growing concern over cutbacks and reduced growth. Forecasts of advertising spending in North America for the past two years show a downward trend, while sponsorship continues to increase. In the emerging Asian Pacific market sponsorship growth has exceeded global figures to reach 5.7 per cent in 2016, according to IEG. Meanwhile, the European Sponsorship Association (2016) reports that the sponsorship industry in Europe has followed global trends in its growth rate, with expenditure growing from an estimated €5.6 billion in 2000, to peak at €26.44 billion in 2014 boosted by the Winter Olympic Games in Sochi.

Reasons for the growth of sponsorship

Crompton (1995) reviews the factors that have stimulated the exponential growth in sponsorship and attributes it not only to external environmental factors but also to the growing recognition of the intrinsic qualities of sponsorship as a medium of communication. He suggests that sponsorship has two special strengths: first, it is suited to brand image development because consumers associate the attributes of an event to the sponsor and its products; and second, it can offer the opportunity to establish a more intimate and emotional connection with its target audience than other communication methods. Sponsorship of an event approaches the target audience through their genuine interests and in an environment in which they are relaxed and possibly more receptive to the marketing message (Crompton, 1995). This analysis is relevant to factors that Crompton identifies as external, such as the issue of the proliferation of media outlets causing clutter. IEG (2017b) also highlights the fragmentation of the media and the increasing cost of advertising space as key factors contributing to the growth of sponsorship compared to other methods of communication, while adding the conclusion that nowadays 'consumers are not paying attention to ads'. Digital television recorders (as VHS recorders did in the past) enable viewers to avoid marketing messages by simply fast-forwarding the adverts, while ad-free streaming and video on demand services such as Netflix are growing in popularity. On PCs, according to Deloitte (2016), in 2015 there were an estimated 200 million monthly active users of advertisement blockers around the world, of which 77 million were in Europe and 45 million in the United States.

Sponsorship, on the other hand, is not just about transmitting a message to a passive recipient but is about deepening a relationship by meeting with the consumer in an environment that matches their lifestyle and enables a two-way dialogue to take place, which is what today's consumers expect. Schmitt (1999) suggests that more and more businesses are using experiential marketing to connect brands with customers' lifestyles and offering sensory, emotional, cognitive, behavioural and relational values, not just products and services' functional features and benefits as in traditional marketing.

Indeed, today there is recognition that modern consumers want to be stimulated, entertained, educated and challenged by brands that become part of their lives by providing meaningful experiences (Carú and Cova, 2003). In this context, Smilansky (2009) argues that traditional media channels and one-way communications are losing their effectiveness. Meanwhile, the live brand experience, which usually manifests itself in the form of live events, reaches the target audience on a deeper level, in their preferred environment, aligning the brand directly with people's current perceptions of the event itself. This approach builds loyal relationships and brand advocacy, encourages word of mouth and brings brand personality to life, ultimately differentiating the company from its competitors. In this book, experiential marketing is discussed in depth in Chapters 2 and 3.

Sponsorship by sector

Sport continues to be at the forefront of sponsorship investments worldwide. However, brands are taking advantage of opportunities offered by other types of events, including live music and art and cultural events, and are also engaging in increasingly sophisticated types of partnership arrangements. One of the best examples is the newly renewed deal that will see communication service provider O2 keep the naming right to the London venue formerly known as the Millennium Dome until 2027 (Spanier, 2017). Nearby, the new cable car crossing over the River Thames known as the Emirates Air Line is sponsored by the Dubai-based airline. This 10-year deal worth £36 million covered a significant proportion of the construction cost of the cable car that runs between the two new stations named Emirates Greenwich Peninsula in south London and Emirates Royal Docks in north London, creating a direct link between the O2 Arena in Greenwich and the ExCel exhibition centre in east London (BBC, 2011).

Sporting events

Sport sponsorship is the most developed of all sponsorship sectors as well as the largest, commanding 50–70 per cent of global sponsorship spending, much of which is focused on sports events (Lagae, 2005; Masterman, 2004). One of the main benefits is access to a vast audience both live and through the extensive media coverage that many sports receive. Football's popularity has meant that TV broadcasting rights have reached record levels in recent years, with events such as English Premier League football matches reaching audiences of billions of people across hundreds of territories worldwide (Key Note, 2016). Many well-known brands secure their involvement with international footballing bodies such as FIFA and UEFA and football clubs with extremely lucrative deals, such as the one between Manchester City and Etihad signed in 2014 that was worth as much as £80 million a year for shirt sponsorship and stadium naming rights (Key Note, 2016). While some level of sponsorship exists in most spectator sports, Masterman (2004) expresses the concern that 90 per cent of all money spent on sponsorship is on the top sports, which include football, rugby, cricket, tennis, golf and motorsports. Formula 1's global TV audience, its heritage and long tradition of sponsors' involvement makes it popular with multinational brands signing lucrative sponsorship agreements. Interestingly, in Formula 1 sponsorship accounts for 80–85 per cent of the total income accrued by Formula 1 teams (Key Note, 2016).

So what do they get in return for these vast financial contributions? The benefits sought by sponsors go beyond the traditional sponsorship activities such as in-stadium advertising. Instead they look for ways that enable brands to engage and develop relationships with fans via a variety of channels, such as hospitality and the use of social media. Gaining access to Real Madrid's over 15 million followers on Twitter, for instance, evidently has huge commercial potential (Key Note, 2016).

The biggest and most well-known sporting event in the world is, of course, the Olympic Games. Of the various levels of sponsorship on offer the International Olympic Committee's (IOC) The Olympic Partners (TOP) programme is by far the most prestigious in the world, through which brands such as Coca-Cola, Visa and McDonald's gain worldwide rights and category exclusivity. This event epitomizes one of sport's enduring strengths – its international appeal. In addition to increasing brand awareness due to the visibility that these events offer, sport sponsorship can enhance a brand's image by positively aligning it with successful events, sport organizations and personalities. Indeed, image transfer is one of the key benefits of sport sponsorship that has been investigated by scholars. Gwinner and Eaton (1999: 47) explain that 'the pre-existing associations held in consumers' memories regarding a celebrity or sporting event become linked in memory with the endorsed or sponsoring brand'. Because of this, the technique of 'ambush marketing' is increasingly used whereby an organization that is not engaged in a sponsorship deal with an event attempts to gain association with the event in covert ways. For companies that cannot afford to officially sponsor an event, ambushing offers a possible alternative strategy (Shani and Sandler, 1998). Ambush marketing will be further discussed in Chapter 8.

Live music sponsorship

In light of the exponential growth that the live music sector has experienced worldwide in recent years, and with evidence to suggest the brand sponsorship of concerts and festivals leads to positive associations, it is no surprise that, today, more and more brands are utilizing affiliation with live music as a marketing tool. Its ability to engage with young audiences, who are increasingly more elusive to traditional types of marketing communications, is particularly valuable.

Sponsorship spending on live music has seen a continuous increase over the past several years and at a growth rate that is even higher than that of sport sponsorship, according to IEG (2016). Results of recent research by Repucom (2015) show that in the five major sponsorship markets of the United States (US), the UK, France, Germany and Japan, interest in music among people between the ages of 14 and 34 years is very high and surpasses sport, watching television and film/cinema. The fact that live music audiences are 'ageing' means that nowadays there is a much broader spectrum of consumer segments for potential sponsors to tap into by partnering with specific types of music events.

Without doubt, one of the key marketing benefits that live music events offers is access to specific target markets that come ready-segmented into relatively homogeneous audiences (Rowley and Williams, 2008). Music, through its many genres, can represent particular age groups, lifestyles and values hence providing brands with opportunities for targeted communication. Importantly, music fans are highly passionate, as fandom is based on the degree of psychological attachment to particular icons or styles (Lee, 2014). Transferring that emotional involvement to the sponsoring brand is a clear benefit of music sponsorship.

Furthermore, Rowley and Williams' (2008) research on music festivals suggests that sponsorship of these events can have an impact on brand recall, awareness and attitude to the brand, and that the values that music fans associate with sponsoring brands are largely positive. Besides, who could argue that certain live music events might bring a certain 'coolness' to a brand image? Keller (1993: 3) defines brand image as 'the perceptions about a brand as reflected by the associations held in a consumer's memory'. Reaching people in an environment in which they are entertained can create positive associations, affecting attendees' perception of the sponsoring brand (Hackley and Tiwsakul, 2006). Morgan and Watson (2007) (reflecting the views expressed by Pine and Gilmore in their seminal book *The Experience Economy* and elsewhere) draw attention to the use of event sponsorship as a means of associating brands with extraordinary experiences that involve emotional stimulation and stand out from everyday life. In this respect, the emotional pull of music remains undisputed.

A look at the current state of the live music sector can justify why a growing number of brands are getting involved. In the UK alone, the sector has seen steady growth since the beginning of the last decade and has now overtaken recorded music sales as the main source of revenue for the music industry. In 2016 the live music market was worth in the region of £2.1 billion according to Mintel (2016). Their research also found that as many as 35 per cent of adults have been to a concert in the previous year and 21 per cent to a music festival. PRS for Music estimates that of the 60,000 concerts that take place each year in the UK over 300 are festivals, a considerable increase compared to only 12 in the year 2000 (Mintel, 2016).

Within a sector with such potential for brands to exploit, opportunities for sponsors are many and varied, ranging from major three-day festivals to a small gig in a local pub and an array of options in between, including the sponsorship of music venues. For these events, financing from sponsors is increasingly important. This is because of the escalating cost of producing large-scale festivals and international tours on the one hand and, one the other, for the smaller events, among other factors, because of the limited sources of funding available. However, the 'professional insight' interview with music promoter Andy Macleod later in this chapter highlights why organizers of these events may be deterred from working with sponsors.

Art, culture and community events

Sponsorship is increasingly considered an important revenue stream for organizations and events within the field of art and culture. Mostly not-for-profit in nature, they sustain their work through funding from a variety of sources, which include income earned directly from audiences through the sale of admission tickets, programmes, merchandise, food and drink, membership fees, etc. Art and cultural organizations also raise funds through donations, which are gifts from individuals, businesses, trusts and foundations for which no return is sought (Arts and Business, 2005). One of the most important sources of financial support is public funding in the form of subsidies and grants. Governments have always played a crucial role in providing support to the arts. This is particularly true for the UK, which has a strong tradition of public funding. The Arts Council has been supporting and promoting art and culture in Britain since the end of the Second World War, and since 1994 it has distributed National Lottery funds for good causes – the share apportioned to the arts, sport and heritage now accounts for 60 per cent of income (National Lottery, 2017).

CASE STUDY 1 Grants for the arts – Arts Council England

The Arts Council England is a non-departmental public body and registered charity that serves the function of a national development agency for the arts, museums and libraries in England. Funded by the Government through the Department of Culture, Media and Sport. the Arts Council shares the responsibility for distributing National Lottery money in England with the British Film Institute, the Big Lottery Fund, the Heritage Lottery Fund and Sport England.

It was set up by Royal Charter in 1940 as the Committee for the Encouragement of Music and the Arts and became the Arts Council of Great Britain in 1946 when it first began getting funds from local and national government and distributing them to promote and support arts and culture. In 1994, the same year in which the National Lottery was established, the Arts Council of Great Britain was devolved into separate National Arts Councils and in England became known as the Arts Council of England, renamed Arts Council England in 2002. In 2011 it also assumed new responsibilities for the support and development of museums and libraries.

In March 2018 Arts Council England's open access funding programme Grants for the Arts was rebranded Arts Council National Lottery Project Grants to acknowledge where the funds that it distributes come from. Under this scheme grants are given out to individuals and organizations involved in the provision of arts-related activities such as dance, music, theatre, the visual arts, literature and combined arts including festivals and carnivals, while libraries and museums can also apply for arts projects or projects that help people engage with their collections.

The programme is intended to fulfil the Arts Council's mission of 'Great art and culture for everyone' by supporting projects that help people in England to engage with quality arts and culture. This aim is reflected in the programme's four criteria – quality, public engagement, finance and management – which applicants are expected to demonstrate when completing the application form. The awards typically range from £1,000 to £100,000 but may be more depending on specific circumstances and are for projects up to three years in length. The scheme is always open so applications can be made at any time.

The main change from the previous Grants for the Arts scheme is a streamlined provision of grant options as it absorbed other previously offered grants for the likes of international and national touring projects that were provided under the Strategic Touring and Ambition for Excellence funds. It is also now possible for those working in creative and digital media to apply for funds.

The other major funding schemes under Arts Council England are the National Portfolio Organisations programme, which supports over 800 established and leading arts organizations as well as museums and libraries, and Arts Council Development Funds, which includes two programmes, Creative People and Places to tackle low engagement in arts and culture, and Developing Your Creative Practice to support independent creative practitioners.

Overall, between 2018 and 2022 the Arts Council Strategic Vision includes investing £1.45 billion of public money from the Government and an estimated £860 million from the National Lottery in creating arts and cultural experiences that engage as many people as possible across the country.

SOURCE Arts Council England (no date)

Public sector involvement is justified by a number of social and economic imperatives, from the traditional view of the arts as a 'civilizing influence' to more contemporary policies of utilizing it as an instrument to support urban regeneration. Indeed, as noted by Walmsley and Franks (2011: 6), 'research has clearly established direct links between participation in the arts (both passive and active) and improved health, wellbeing and community or social capital'. Nonetheless, sponsorship has also become an increasingly popular way to fundraise, and yet sponsorship within arts and culture is not without criticism, particularly with regard to its impact on artistic freedom and fear of over commercialization resulting in the prioritizing of more mainstream 'safe' programmes (Bovaird and Bovaird, 1997; Fishel, 1993). On the other hand, greater involvement on the part of businesses is seen as beneficial in terms of supporting audience development programmes and policies of widening participation.

From the point of view of a sponsor, there are attractive benefits to be gained by partnering with a cultural event. For instance, these events can make excellent settings for 'corporate hospitality' whereby stakeholders such as clients, customers, key suppliers and shareholders can be entertained to help foster positive business relationships. At the same time, a sense of commitment and enthusiasm can be engendered in staff, leading to increased efficiency and productivity (Arts and Business, 2005). A certain degree of visibility for a sponsor can be obtained through inclusion in publicity material, although the ability to reach the levels of mass sports television audiences is not a prerogative of arts sponsorship. However, one of its key strengths is 'the degree of accuracy with which specific target segments, ie potential customers to the sponsor, can be targeted', as stressed by Fishel (1993: 37).

Sponsoring art and culture is a way for a brand to differentiate itself from its competitors, and is particularly effective in brand image building and maintenance. It is likely that image enhancement and improving the brand reputation are objectives of British oil and gas company BP's arts partnership programme. This longstanding programme sees the company sponsoring four of the UK's major cultural institutions – the British Museum, the National Portrait Gallery, the Royal Opera House and the Royal Shakespeare Company, as well as its continued involvement with Tate Britain.

Moreover, incorporating cultural events into a company's corporate social responsibility (CSR) strategy allows brands to strengthen their reputation for good corporate citizenship, build trust and improve credibility through improved community links. While the 'high arts' (opera, ballet and classical music concerts) tend to attract mainly white, middle-aged and middle-class audiences with high levels of education, income and cultural competences, other cultural events such as festivals and carnivals have a much broader appeal among the general public and are also often staged and performed by members of the local community (Smith, 2009). Hence they provide that all-important route for business to connect with them in a meaningful and effective way.

Professional insight 1: financing live music – interview with Andy Macleod, founder and director of Club Fandango

Andy McLeod founded independent music promotions company Club Fandango in 2001 with Simon Williams of Fierce Panda Records. Since then Club Fandango has been promoting up-and-coming alternative indie music at venues across London and the UK hosting gigs by the likes of Coldplay, Kaiser Chiefs, the Killers and many more. Nowadays, in addition to live promotion they offer artist development services, which include putting out records, artist management, doing press and radio and helping with publishing. The interview provides a valuable insight into the live music sector and into how income from sponsors and grant funders has changed over a relatively short space of time, as well as highlighting some of the difficulties of producing events with sponsors and the importance of grants from bodies like the Arts Council. Moreover, Andy's insights introduce important themes that are examined in more detail in this book, such as managing relationships, preparing proposals and evaluating sponsorship.

What are the main sources of funding for your organization?

What is growing the most is probably the streaming from the label side. There are two sides to the business now. The more commercial side is doing the records and managing bands, trying to make them successful commercially and critically fantastic and all that. But the grants are there to underwrite the less commercial side, which is effectively the gigs, now. Because gigs can be very profitable once you get up to having Ed Sheeran doing three nights at Wembley, but not in our niche, which is up to 800 people.

From a managerial point of view the bands need to move on to a bigger promoter that can get them on the bigger supports and we don't have that infrastructure. So the sources of funding are streaming, tickets and award, and we get PPL money (Phonographic Performance Ltd is a collection society that licenses recorded music played in public) as well from being played on the radio – not a huge amount – and we get the odd bit of consulting coming in sometimes.

We've always had sponsorship income, but it's been slowly dwindling away. In the past we had up to three monthly partners: INgrooves (digital music distribution and publishing), 7digital (digital music services and platforms), and *Rock Sound* (magazine). We did nights with BMI (Broadcast Music, Inc – US collection society). We just did loads even if they didn't pay cash. I mean, some did. They used to be really quite easy to get. They give you a monthly sum to help with the costs of the shows and they put their banner behind the gig, they deal with some of the promotion and then they give you a rider. I think it is really hard on live gigs now, especially where we are at. We have had to do fewer and fewer shows to make sure that they actually work, because it's so competitive and we don't get huge audiences at the gigs. A 200 capacity for a big sponsor is not a huge audience they are hitting. They want to go to festivals or where they know there is going to be a brand. Or our brand is just not seen as very sexy because we have been going for so long. I think brands like to jump on things that are brand new and have that kind of kids appeal, you know?

Could you tell me more about why you think grassroots promoters are not attractive to brands at the moment?

In the past the live side was really attractive, especially during the indie boom. Now with the big acts, brands see an easy way to connect with large audiences of young people. And it doesn't matter how good the artists may be; they are not after that, they just want the big audiences, don't they?

Why do you think is it getting harder to get audiences to come in to these live events?

It's a combination of reasons, I think. It's society changing, it's saturation of gigs, it may be the cost. You can't sell tickets because music is expected to be free. As well, the last 10 years have seen things like *X Factor*, those TV shows, and a lot of venues in the region are shutting down, which tells its own story, because they can't afford to put on bands. There are many reasons why. And the Arts Council, for all its box-ticking, has been an absolute saviour because it recognizes that there is an issue. It never used to give awards to commercial music companies like us but then it kind of looked around internationally, and other countries that were suddenly breaking artists, like Canada and France with Arcade Fire, Daft Punk. In these countries they subsidized their grassroots and they are starting to see the results. And so I think if it wasn't for the Arts Council and PRS supporting new music, I think it would be just absolutely all over. They put a lot of money in that would have been put in as development money from the major record labels. They are not investing in talent because the Government is doing it or the Lottery. It's the Lottery money that funds us, it's people playing the Lottery who are the ones that are supporting new music; really, really randomly.

How do you go about identifying suitable grants?

I think what happens with those grants is that they had to do a bit of a PR push initially to let people know that they've got money. Then they get absolutely swamped and it goes the other way when they are turning people down. In fact Grants for the Arts is doing a push now to get more people applying because it changed the name of the project. I think it looks good for them politically as well. If they can say, 'look, this amount of people applied and then this is the success from it'. That's why they want their logo on everything, you know.

What is the process of applying for these grants?

The forms take a long time to do because you really have to think about the angle and how you're going to make your argument. A good application is one where you literally articulate what do you need to do and why you need to do it. You have to make your case for the activity, make your case for why their support is important and then how you are going to build the audience, and then you also have to have a bit of a unique take on it. But it takes a while to really work that out. You have got to live with the application for a while and think about it. Is it really doable? Also a good application should be quite an exciting proposal. And then you have to do your budget. Another thing I'd say is that grant-makers want to see that they are going to give money to a commercially successful company and there is a slight paradox there because really the whole point to going for a grant is that you don't have the money to do what you want to do. With the Arts Council you have to provide matched funding, you have to show that you are bringing in money from elsewhere. That's why the ticketing income and the streaming income are really important, because you can't just ask for 100 per cent of the money. A lot of potential grantees can't get that other money, so it's frustrating. They may have a great project but they cannot get that other income.

Once you do get the grants, are the grant-makers involved at all?

That's the weird thing, really – they are not. Other than online activities, interim report, activities reports, they just let you get on with it, which is fantastic in one way. But you really put a lot of work into getting the money. A lot of work is in that form. They really drill you. So I think they must have a certain amount of confidence. Also, over the years we have always delivered. I think they feel we have a decent track record so they are a bit more confident in giving us the money. But the good thing is if they don't like it you can re-submit. They tell you the reasons why they didn't like it so you can amend it. You can be successful the third time around. Basically you can turn the project into what they want to fund, but that's something you don't want to do with your creative project. Besides, they are just as interested in failures as success because then they learn from that as well.

How does Club Fandango work with sponsors and other funders to evaluate sponsorship and funding partnerships?

The evaluation is another area where if you just got money... You need an entire department just to do proper evaluation, so it's really hard. You do have to report back, do activity reports. Basically, they just ask you how it's gone and then you tell them. You tell them to the best of your ability and you can assess it through things like ticket sales, streaming, social media interaction. If an artist you are working with has their Spotify plays going up, their gigs are getting bigger and people join the artist's Facebook group and all of that stuff, you just know it's going well and that's your evaluation. In some ways, the technology has given us some great evaluation tools but working out whether a certain promotion tool has had that effect you want is really hard; that's where you need a department of people to do the evaluation.

In your experience, do sponsors and other funding partners communicate to you their objectives for getting involved with your event at the outset of the relationship?

Not on the grant side. The application should demonstrate how the proposal fits with their directives so effectively they have told you. In the case of the Arts Council it is about getting great art to the greatest number of people. With a sponsor it should also be like that. It should be 'We want you because of this. You are there to fulfil this'. There should be that communication, but sometimes you don't deal with the sponsor directly. You may deal with the consultancy in between and it can get a bit muddled.

What are the main reasons why an organization like Club Fandango would seek the support of a sponsor?

Where we'd do it now would be if you had a certain event, a one-off event where you may look for a sponsor... We have applied for funds to set up Radio Fandango, an internet radio station. I think if that actually went ahead and it grew an audience you could probably get some sort of sponsorship for it because there are various models now that work, where there is an online affiliate... but, again, it is quite a small amount of money at that level. I think ultimately, if you have got a brand that is really strong and it's a big audience then a sponsor would come to you, but if you are going to the sponsor they have the power.

What would you look for in a sponsor to consider partnering with them?

Ideally you'd want a like-minded sponsor, but we are not fussy! I think nowadays if they were offering a lot of money to do stuff it'd be hard to turn it down. Dr Marten's was always the one we thought would fit the most, or Jack Daniels or Rizla.

Arts organizations can sometimes be wary of involving sponsors for fear of loss of creative control. Is this a concern for you when considering partnering with sponsors?

It can look a bit corporate or it can sort of dilute the grassroots nature of it. I think it depends on what your role is. Say we did those Fistful of Fandango things, which were five nights with lots of gigs, and we were looking for sponsors to help underwrite the show costs – that's quite hard to find. They'd say, we'd give £10,000 but in return we want this, and at that point you maybe have to give them naming rights. Once you start doing that what ends up happening is that you can up your costs elsewhere. If you get a brand on board like Ben Sherman the band agents all up their fees. They say, 'Right, it's a branded thing, can we have more money?' So in some ways it can be a false economy to get a sponsor like that. It's better to do it as a one-off service. At our level the little bit of money the sponsor gives can take away the point of it in the first place.

If you do a project because you want to do a project and then the sponsor wants to change the project to something they want to do… It's just having everyone knowing where they are, what their role is, that can get blurred a bit as soon as money comes in. Sponsors can really take over and you kind of go, 'Great, brilliant, we have a sponsor', and then you go, 'Wait a second this is meant to be a Fandango night and now it's basically the sponsor's.'

In your experience of working with sponsors what would you say are the key benefits that brands seek when developing partnerships with live music events/ bands. What can sponsorship of live music do for a sponsoring brand?

It's always a combination of things. They want to show their audiences that they are getting out there with the kids, they are being a bit groovy, or it may be they are perceived a certain way. For us it can be getting to big audiences. I think for them it is making associations. Or it may be that they just have a bit of tax money they need to use and think 'Let's do some gigs for a tax break', or something.

Could you provide some examples of when you have worked with sponsors in the past?

The best is example is probably when we worked with a well-known British clothing brand. They wanted British bands that had played British festivals to tour around the country wearing the brand's clothes as a 'Best of British' at the festivals. So we went on our way with a big budget to try to lure in these bands, and of course as soon as we had a backdrop of a famous brand the agents upped the price. But the whole thing just got really silly because we were never really dealing with the brand, we were dealing with brand consultants who were then dealing with other brand consultants who were then dealing with the sponsor, so it was like Chinese whispers. We got some bands together which were British and had played the festivals and they came back saying no, they are not the right look for us, and it got to the point where they eventually said, what about this band? And we said well we can ask them but they are not British and they didn't do any festivals. And they were like, yeah, it doesn't matter they are the look we want. It just becomes the art of the possible a lot of the time at this level.

Another experience was with one of the most famous international brewing companies. They wanted us to do live shows in certain venues around London and when it came to the day they realized that the venues didn't stock their beer so that was a bit of a farce.

The best ones are when there is a brand partner. The BMI nights were great where they gave us a set amount of budget. The nights with *Rock Sounds*, 6 Music, lots of those ones always great, INgrooves, the ones we do with the Association of Independent Music (AIM). Everyone knows their role. We do the live promotion and production, and they are just interested in having a logo and can supply some artists. It knits together nicely. But I think when a bigger sponsor is involved, it's sort of, who's got the power at that point. If you have a massive audience you can call the shots. But if it's the other way around and you are trying to chase a sponsor to get money to support your business then you've got to jump through hoops with what they want, so I tend to avoid situations like that.

Conclusion

The purpose of this chapter has been to provide the basis upon which an understanding of sponsorship can be built. In its very essence, sponsorship is a partnership, as it is founded on mutual advantage between the parties involved, which seek to gain commercially from the relationship. Events gain by obtaining much-needed financial or in-kind support, while businesses use them for their ability to deliver on important marketing and corporate objectives in a cost-effective manner. Sponsorship is an effective medium for targeting specific customer groups, and especially useful as a means of influencing their perceptions by way of positive association. This is the case for the types of events discussed in this chapter, namely sport, live music, and art and cultural events. The insights provided by the interview with Andy Macleod highlight, however, that for small to medium-size companies, events sponsorship may not always be a viable proposition. Indeed, the phenomenon of sponsorship has changed and adapted over time, and its growth in recent years has been truly remarkable, as this chapter has illustrated.

Discussion questions and activities

1 What are the characteristics of sponsorship that distinguish it from charity/patronage/corporate philanthropy?

2 What are some of the internal and external factors that have set the foundations for sponsorship to develop into the phenomenon that we know today? Identify and discuss current societal/marketing trends that affect sponsorship. Visit the ESP/IEG website http://www.sponsorship.com/ and click on the 'insights' tab to locate useful resources.

3 Explore two case examples of event sponsorship that you have come across in day-to-day life and outline each partner's motivation for working together.

4 Using the internet, research a country of your choice to identify grant-making bodies and the funding that they make available for music, sport and art type events. Do similar bodies to the Arts Council, described in this chapter, exist? Which ones?

Further reading

The following articles, albeit not recent, should prove useful as a foundation for understanding sponsorship and its evolution.

Cornwell, TB and Maignan, I (1998) An international review of sponsorship research, *Journal of Advertising*, **27** (1), pp 1–21

This article, by prominent authors Bettina Cornwell and Isabelle Maignan, has long been the most relied upon review of the literature investigating sponsorship as a marketing communication method. It identifies 80 articles published up to 1996, which are grouped into five research streams: the nature of sponsorship; managerial aspects of sponsorship; measurement of sponsorship effects; strategic use of sponsorship; and legal/ethical considerations. This provides a useful categorization for further exploration of the key aspects of sponsorship.

Walliser, B (2003) An international review of sponsorship research: Extension and update, *International Journal of Advertising*, **22**, pp 5–40

Building on and expanding Cornwell and Maignan's work, Walliser's review of the literature adds a further 153 articles to the analysis. In addition to covering an additional six years of published material, it makes a greater effort to include international research to complement the mostly Anglo-Saxon body of literature included in the 1998 review.

Crompton, J (1995) Factors that have stimulated the growth of sponsorship of major events, *Festivals Management and Event Tourism*, **3** (2), pp 97–105

John L Crompton has written extensively about sponsorship. We have referred to this article earlier in this book when examining reasons that have led to sponsorship's growth in importance.

References

Arts and Business (2005) *Sponsorship Manual*, 5th edn, Arts and Business, London

Arts Council England (nd) [Online] https://www.artscouncil.org.uk/ [Accessed 06/08/18]

BBC (2011) Emirates sponsors Thames cable car [Online] http://www.bbc.co.uk/news/uk-england-london-15217173 [Accessed 27/03/17]

Bovaird, T and Bovaird, N (1997) *Arts Sponsorship: The case for and against*, Birmingham, Aston Business School Research Institute

Carú, A and Cova, B (2003) Revisiting consumption experience: A more humble but complete view of the concept, *Marketing Theory*, **3** (2), pp 267–86

Cornwell, TB (1995) Sponsorship-linked marketing development, *Sport Marketing Quarterly*, **4** (4), pp 13–24

Cornwell, TB and Maignan, I (1998) An international review of sponsorship research, *Journal of Advertising*, **27** (1), pp 1–21

Crompton, J (1993) Sponsorship of sport by tobacco and alcohol companies: A review of the issues, *Journal of Sport & Social Issues*, **17** (3), pp 148–67

Crompton, J (1994) Benefits and risks associated with sponsorship of major events, *Festival Management and Event Tourism*, **2** (2), pp 65–74 [Online] https://doi.org/10.3727/106527094792292050

Crompton, J (1995) Factors that have stimulated the growth of sponsorship of major events, *Festivals Management and Event Tourism*, **3** (2), pp 97–105

Crompton, J (1996) The potential contribution of sports sponsorship in impacting the product adoption model, *Managing Leisure*, **1** (4), pp 199–212

Deloitte (2016) *Technology, Media and Telecommunication Prediction 2016* [Online] www2.deloitte.com/content/dam/Deloitte/global/Documents/Technology-Media-Telecommunications/gx-tmt-prediction-2016-full-report.pdf [Accessed 23/01/17]

eMarketer (2016) Worldwide ad spending growth revised downward [Online] www.emarketer.com/Article/Worldwide-Ad-Spending-Growth-Revised-Downward/1013858 [Accessed 20/01/17]

Enciclopedia Treccani (no date) *Mecenate* [Online] http://www.treccani.it/enciclopedia/mecenate/

Encyclopaedia Britannica (2007) *Gaius Maecenas: Roman Diplomat and Patron* [Online] https://www.britannica.com/biography/Gaius-Maecenas [Accessed 13/02/17]

European Commission (2017) Ban on cross-border tobacco advertising and sponsorship [Online] https://ec.europa.eu/health/tobacco/advertising_en [Accessed 15/02/17]

European Sponsorship Association (2016) *Sponsorship Market Overview 2016*, European Sponsorship Association

Fishel, D (1993) *Arts Sponsorship Handbook,* Directory of Social Change, London

Gardner, MP and Shuman, P (1988) Sponsorship and small businesses, *Journal of Small Business Management*, **26** (4), pp 44–52

Gregory, P (1984) Sponsoring et mécénat: Instruments de communication institutionnelle, *Revue Francaise de Gestion* (September–October), pp 163–75

Gwinner, KP and Eaton, J (1999) Building brand image through event sponsorship: The role of image transfer, *Journal of Advertising*, **18** (4), pp 47–57

Hackley, C and Tiwsakul, R (2006) Entertainment marketing and experiential consumption, *Journal of Marketing Communicatios*, **14** (3), pp 145–58

Hibbert, C (1979) *The Rise and Fall of the House of Medici*, Penguin Books, London

IEG (International Events Group) (2016) *What Sponsors Want and Where Their Dollars Will Go in 2016*, IEG, Chicago, IL

IEG (2017a) *IEG's Guide to Sponsorship* [Online] www.sponsorship.com/IEG/files/59/59ada496-cd2c-4ac2-9382-060d86fcbdc4.pdf [Accessed 25/01/17]

IEG (2017b) *What Sponsors Want and Where Their Dollars Will Go in 2017*, IEG, Chicago, IL

International Chamber of Commerce (2003) *ICC International Code on Sponsorship* [Online] http://www.abfi.ie/Sectors/ABFI/ABFI.nsf/vPagesABFI/Responsibilities~sponsorship/$File/ICC+International+Code+on+Sponsorship.pdf [Accessed 23/01/17]

Keller, KL (1993) Conceptualizing, measuring, managing customer-based brand equity, *Journal Of Marketing*, **57** (1), pp. 1–22

Key Note (2016) Sport sponsorship [Online] www.keynote.co.uk [Accessed 21/01/17]

Kolah, A (2015) *Improving the Performance of Sponsorship*, Routledge, Oxon

Lagae, W (2005) *Sports Sponsorship and Marketing Communication: A European perspective,* Prentice Hall, Harlow

Lee, H-K (2014) Transnational cultural fandom, in *The Ashgate Research Companion to Fan Cultures*, ed L Duits, L Zwaan and K Reijnders, pp 195–208, Ashgate, Surrey

McDonnell, A and Moir, M (2013) *Event Sponsorship,* Routledge, London

Masterman, G (2004) *Strategic Sports Event Management: An international approach*, Elsevier Butterworth-Heinemann, Oxford

Meenaghan, JA (1983) Commercial sponsorship, *European Journal of Marketing,* **17** (7), pp 1–73

Meenaghan, T (1991) Sponsorship: Legitimizing the medium, *European Journal of Marketing,* **25** (11), pp 5–10

Meenaghan, T (2001) Understanding sponsorship effects, *Psychology & Marketing,* **18** (2), pp 95–122

Mintel (2016) *Music Concerts and Festivals – UK – 2016*, Mintel

Morgan, M and Watson, P (2007) *Resource Guide in Extraordinary Experiences: Understanding and managing the consumer experience in hospitality, leisure, events, sports and tourism*, Project Report, Higher Education Academy, York

National Lottery (2017) Life changing [Online] https://www.national-lottery.co.uk/life-changing/where-the-money-goes [Accessed 06/05/18]

Otker, T (1998) Exploitation: The key to sponsorship success, *European Research,* **16** (2), pp 77–85

Repucom (2015) *Live Music Sponsorship* [Online] http://nielsensports.com/wp-content/uploads/2014/09/Repucom-Live-Music-Report-2015.pdf [Accessed 21/01/17]

Rowley, J and Williams, C (2008) The impact of brand sponsorship of music festivals, *Marketing Intelligence and Planning,* **6** (7), pp 781–96

Ryan, A and Fhay, J (2012) Evolving priorities in sponsorship: From media management to network management, *Journal of Marketing Management,* **28** (9–10), pp 1132–58

Sanghak, L (2009) The commencement of modern sport sponsorship in 1850s–1950s, paper given at Sponsorship Marketing Association Conference, 2009

Schmitt, B (1999) *Experiential Marketing: How to get customers to sense, feel, think, act, and relate to your company and brands*, Free Press, New York

Shani, D and Sandler, DM (1998) Ambush marketing: Is confusion to blame for the flickering of the flame? *Psychology and Marketing,* **15** (4), pp 367–82

Skinner, BE and Rukavina, V (2003) *Event Sponsorship*, Wiley, Hoboken, New Jersey

Smilansky, S (2009), *Experiential Marketing: A practical guide to interactive brand experiences*, Kogan Page, London

Smith, MK (2009) *Issues in Cultural Tourism*, Routledge, London

Spanier, G (2017) O2 has renewed the naming rights for The O2, the world's most successful entertainment arena, in a ten-year partnership with the London venue, *Campaign Magazine*, 23/02 [Online] https://www.campaignlive.co.uk/article/o2-renews-naming-rights-o2-greenwich-10-year-deal/1425091 [Accessed 05/05/18]

Walmsley, B and Franks, A (2011) The audience experience: Changing roles and relationships, in *Key Issues in the Arts and Entertainment Industry*, ed B Walmsley, Goodfellow

World Federation of Advertisers (2017) What is WFA? [Online] https://www.wfanet.org/about/who-we-are/ [Accessed 20/01/17]

Event sponsorship 02
at the centre of
the integrated
marketing
communications mix

LEARNING OBJECTIVES

Having read this chapter and worked through the questions and activities you should be able:

- to assess the role of event sponsorship in the integrated marketing communications mix;
- to examine how the principles of experiential marketing apply to sponsorship campaigns;
- to evaluate the authenticity of sponsorship campaigns.

In this chapter we will examine the role event sponsorship plays in an organization's integrated marketing communications mix and the importance of using appropriate experiential marketing techniques highlighted. The role of authenticity and co-creation in event sponsorship is also assessed.

Defining integrated marketing communications

In order to develop an organization's brand resilience and enable it to succeed it is essential for marketing managers to develop their communications techniques from the mass marketing approach of the past to more nuanced and sophisticated strategies. An integrated approach is vital to address the changing nature of the consumer in a digital age, the fragmentation of mass markets and the advent of new communications technologies – in particular social media platforms.

Kotler and Armstrong (2014: 431) define integrated marketing communications (IMC) as the practice of '[c]arefully integrating and coordinating the company's many communications channels to deliver a clear, consistent and compelling message about the organization and its products.' This characterization is close to the first definition of IMC offered by Caywood *et al* (1991: 2):

> a concept of marketing communications planning that recognizes the added value of a comprehensive plan that evaluates the strategic roles of a variety of communications disciplines (for example – advertising, direct response, sales promotion and public relations) and combines these disciplines to provide clarity, consistency and maximum communications impact.

However, Schultz revised the definition he wrote with Caywood *et al* (1991), to 'IMC is a strategic business process used to plan, develop, execute, and evaluate coordinated measurable persuasive brand communication programs over time with consumers, customers, prospects, and other targeted, relevant internal and external audiences' (Schultz and Kitchen, 2000: 65). So IMC has developed as a concept that deals with planning and coordinating marketing communications to incorporate a wider, more comprehensive and holistic approach that takes in both communication of the benefits of products and services to customers but also communication of an organization's brand to internal and external audiences.

IMC is made up of combinations of promotional tools: advertising, personal selling, public relations, direct marketing and sales promotion (Figure 2.1). Keller (2016) suggests that the future of advertising and marketing communications will be marked by an increasingly diverse collection of digital options as well as the traditional approaches already available. In Figure 2.2 the relationship between traditional media and new media channels is contextualized in relation to events and experiential marketing.

IMC aims to ensure that, at every point or situation where the customer encounters an organization and its branding, the impression communicated is positive and persuasive. The term 'look and feel' is often used to refer to the complimentary nature of different promotional tools. So, not only will a TV

Figure 2.1 Integrated marketing communications' relationship to marketing channels

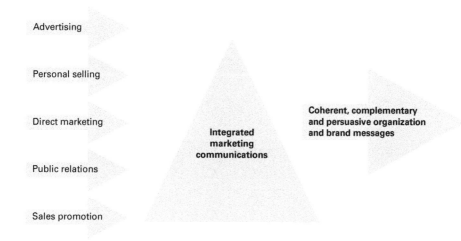

Figure 2.2 The relationship between events/experiential marketing, and traditional and new media marketing disciplines

advert have the same message, there could be an aligning strapline or image/logo for the corresponding newspaper adverts, direct marketing and web pages. In an effective IMC driven campaign different promotional channels will fulfil specific functions, such as gaining attention, delivering information and persuading customers. In sponsorship contexts an important role is to develop participation and a sense of community or tribe among customers. Where successful, brand communities and tribes will create value in many ways, including brand advocacy practices among consumers, who will help to promote a brand to potential customers on the organization's behalf (Schau *et al*, 2009). This links nicely into our next topic, experiential marketing.

Event sponsorship and experiential marketing

There is a tendency for writers to suggest that both experiential marketing and events led marketing are new phenomena. For example, reading Hanlon's article from 2012 one could get the impression that events led marketing had just been discovered. However, it is clear that events led marketing has been established as an important aspect of the integrated marketing mix for some time. For example, almost a decade earlier, Gupta (2003: 87) announced: 'Event marketing is fast emerging as a promotion catalyst vis-à-vis the traditional marketing communication tools'. Moreover, the link between sponsorship and experiential marketing was made six years earlier in relation to Mastercard, the American Financial Services Company (Coulton, 1997). At the time, Mastercard was among the first to use sponsorship as a key part of their experiential marketing campaigns.

In a similar way, experience and experiential marketing have been claimed as a new form of marketing or, as Pine and Gilmore (1998) suggest, a new stage of economic value. But, as Holbrook (2006: 259) points out, the importance of experiential consumption can be traced back to the 1950s and subsequent writers, particularly management gurus, have published on the topic, 'blithely oblivious to the long-established tradition of the experiential perspective in marketing and consumer research'. Nevertheless, Pine and Gilmore do provide a useful link between experiential marketing and event-led marketing with the observation: 'An experience occurs when a company intentionally uses services as the stage, and goods as props, to engage individual customers in a way that creates a memorable event' (Pine and Gilmore, 1998: 98).

Similarly, Wood (2009) suggests that experiential marketing events should be limited to those events that are created first and foremost for marketing purposes. This is so that marketing theory can be usefully developed. This is a useful distinction but it needs to be considered carefully, particularly as it could preclude sponsorship of pre-developed events. Such events would include sporting events and community festivals, which, this book suggests, provide excellent examples of event led marketing and sponsorship as part of the integrated marketing mix. This is because brands often create new events that are embedded within existing events that they sponsor.

Themed parties, seminars and conferences are examples of how a brand's event sponsorship can include the creation and embedding of new events into pre-existing events as part of a wider IMC campaign. Donlan and Crowther (2014) give the example of GE, a worldwide partner of the Olympic Games, which in 2012 combined an innovative moving image campaign on the side of London taxi cabs with business events that aimed to educate audiences about the complex infrastructure issues and solutions for host cities. The target audience were senior executives from the public and private sectors. Importantly, GE didn't just use the sponsorship of the Olympics to embed events that marketed to external audiences. The company also created the Decathlon Challenge, a themed sales incentive programme that involved approximately 40,000 GE salespeople worldwide (GE, 2008). From these examples it is clear that while event-led marketing involves the creation of experiences specifically for marketing purposes, these may be embedded within pre-existing events.

Experiential marketing events occur in a range of contexts. These are some of the main types:

- **Conferences** – These are often focused on educational objectives and organized by professional associations. There are many opportunities for sponsorship at conferences, such as programmes, website and delegate bags. There is also a range of fora for demonstrating products; often sponsors will provide services or products to the event so delegates get to experience them first hand, for example technology services such as delegate voting systems.

- **Brand-driven events** – These events are created specifically by a particular brand as a vehicle to connect with a target audience. For example global fitness brand Les Mills partnered with Reebok to stage an event at ExCel London. It was called 'the world's biggest fitness party', combining rock concert sound and lighting with a mass workout for thousands of fitness lovers.

- **Corporate entertainment and incentive/reward events** – Events are often used by businesses to offer corporate hospitality to clients, for example a 'corporate box' at a football or rugby match with private dining and viewing of the game. These kinds of experiences can also be used as rewards for staff who achieve a particular sales target or complete a project on time.

- **Non-profit/charity events** – Events organized by non-profit or charitable organizations can fulfil three functions. They can raise funds, such as the British Heart Foundation's London to Brighton cycle ride or Oxfam's community festival Oxjam. Alternatively, they can be for publicity purposes, such as to draw attention to a new report or issue relating to the organization's work. For example, many international aid agencies like Christian Aid and Action Aid campaigned on the issue of corporate tax evasion and organized events to persuade local and national government in the UK to change tax laws so that corporations pay more.

- **Product launches/publicity events** – Used by many companies, product launches are used to maximize media exposure for new or improved products. Good examples are Apple iPhone launches and new cars. These launches can be very extravagant – Tesla, the electric car company, sent the Tesla Roadster into orbit round the earth at a cost of £64.8 million.

- **Product sampling** – Linked to product launches, product sampling, which is sometimes called field marketing, allows consumers to try or experience a product or service. These are often used in areas of high footfall such as shopping malls or train stations. They can also target particular audiences by locating in geographic areas.

- **Road shows** – These are events that travel to several different locations to generate brand awareness. Crayola, the children's arts and crafts brand, celebrated its centenary with a branded double decker bus that went to retail sites across the UK and invited families inside to enjoy games and performances.

- **Exhibitions** – These events can range from trade shows to art and craft exhibitions, and can be aimed from business to business or business to consumer. Sometimes called shows, exhibitions are often sponsored by a portfolio of brands, for example the MOVE IT dance show at London's ExCel exhibition centre.

- **Open days** – These are often public relations events where employees, members of the public or other stakeholder groups are invited to a range of activities that are hosted in the organization's workplace. For example, Veolia, the waste disposal company, often holds open days at facilities such as incinerators where the public can be taken on tours to see how waste is processed.

- **Press conferences** – These are aimed at the media and are used by a range of organizations including political parties, corporations and brands to present information that they want to push up the media's agenda. Press conferences can also be used for crisis management to ensure that messages or vital issues are communicated correctly. For example, the police will often use press conferences in major investigations such as murders or missing persons appeals.

- **Visitor attractions** – These events can be developed by brands to be long lasting or permanent, for example Cadbury World. Alternatively, they may be shorter term. Museums often adopt this strategy with temporary exhibitions. For example, Samsung and the British Museum's award winning Digital Discovery Centre opened in 2009 and was originally intended to run for five years. However, it is still running as Samsung renewed its sponsorship in 2014.

- **Leagues, competitions and contests** – Brands have got involved with different kinds of contests. This may involve the brand creating the event or sponsoring an existing one. The most famous brand in this area is the Red Bull drinks brand, which creates events such as music festivals and air races but also sponsors existing events such as Formula 1.

From this list it is clear that experiential marketing events take many forms and can be utilized by a wide range of different industry sectors. What these events have in common is their physicality, interactivity and embodied nature, and it is this that defines them as experiential marketing events. Schmitt (1999) suggests that experiential marketing is made up of four key characteristics, namely:

1 a focus on customer experience;
2 treating consumption as a holistic experience;
3 understanding that customers are driven by rational and emotional factors;
4 recognizing that experiential marketing as a methodology draws on both quantitative and qualitative approaches and is multifaceted in its use of methods.

The first of these characteristics links to the physical, interactive and embodied nature of experiential event marketing, which connects 'the company and the brand to customers' lifestyle and places the individual customer actions and the purchase occasion in the broader social context' (Schmitt,1999: 26).

The broader social context of experiential marketing is closely related to Schmitt's (1999) second point regarding consumption as a holistic experience. Consumption, consumer behaviour and, in particular, consumer decision making have attracted a huge body of literature, part of which draws on the concepts of ritual, the sacred/profane, co-creation and authenticity. These concepts are important and provide a significant critique of writers like Pine and Gilmore (1998). As Sherry *et al* (2007: 11) suggest, consumers have always lived in an experience economy and 'acts of consumer imagination are complex and multifaceted, embodied and erotic, often driven more by needs for authenticity and self-expansion than by the desire for entertainment.' This links the third of Schmitt's (1999) characteristics, namely that consumers are driven by rational and emotional factors, which has been extensively theorized by Holbrook and Hirschman (1982). These topics will be dealt with later in this chapter; suffice to say at this point that it is important to avoid oversimplification when considering experiential events marketing.

Schmitt's final characterization of experiential marketing methods as diverse and multifaceted comes with the advice to be 'explorative and worry about reliability, validity and methodological sophistication later' (Schmitt, 1999: 30). On the face of it, this is the most problematic aspect of his definition, in that clients commissioning experiential events marketing as part of their IMC campaign will demand a robust explanation and justification of the methodology and methods from agencies pitching for business. Methodology and methods are closely tied to evaluation and cannot be considered an afterthought. However, Schmitt's point that experiential marketing may draw on a range of qualitative and quantitative methods depending on the context of a particular brand is valid.

Nick Adams, Managing Director of the experiential marketing agency Sense London, defines experiential marketing as '[c]ommunicating through creating or doing something tangible in the real world' (Sense London, 2015: 23). This definition shows that experiential marketing goes beyond what would be considered events led marketing in a sponsorship context but it is clear that creating or doing something tangible in the real world is a good working definition for the purposes of events led and sponsorship marketing. Moreover, events led experiential marketing can be placed at the centre of an integrated marketing communications strategy, as shown in Figure 2.3.

Figure 2.3   Event-led experiential marketing and integrated marketing communications

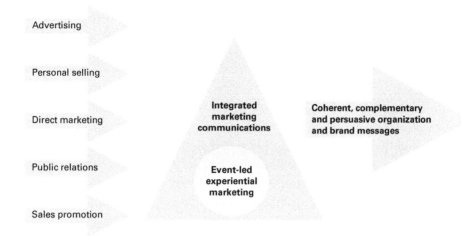

As discussed in Chapter 1, sponsorship can be defined as:

> any commercial agreement by which a sponsor, for the mutual benefit of the sponsor and sponsored party, contractually provides financing or other support in order to establish an association between the sponsor's image, brands or products and a sponsorship property in return for rights to promote this association and/or for the granting of certain agreed direct or indirect benefits.

(ICC, 2003: 2)

This definition, which is part of a comprehensive code of conduct for sponsorship arrangements, makes clear that sponsorship is a business arrangement, not some form of charitable philanthropy. Both sponsor and sponsored parties need to benefit from what is essentially an exchange of rights.

Sponsorship insight 1: don't overlook the local connection...

Early in his career as an event fundraiser for a major UK charity, Tom Lunt was asked to develop new ideas for fundraising events. After a brainstorming session with his manager and other members of the team several ideas were generated. Tom was particularly excited about the idea of a food and drink event that had the working title 'A taste of Spring'. The concept was a ticketed event with cooking demonstrations from local hotel chefs and opportunities to try new cuisine from different restaurants and local delicatessens.

'I can still hear my manager saying, "it's a great idea but you're going to need a sponsor if this is going to work",' Tom recalls. 'I put on my suit and started visiting local businesses that I thought might be interested in the idea. The manager of one local delicatessen showed an interest. I already had some experience of sales but it was nerve-racking when I was asked straight "How much will this cost me?" But the feeling when everything was agreed and the contract signed was unbeatable.

'The sponsorship money went towards some of our promotional costs for the event and the delicatessen did very well on the day, getting significant media exposure, and as the sponsorship agreement set out that it would be the only delicatessen at the event it sold plenty of its products.'

Looking back, Tom suggests that the sponsorship worked on several levels for the delicatessen. From an IMC point of view, the business got its name and logo out in the local community on banners and printed materials. It also got good public relations through local media reporting both in the press and local radio. From an experiential angle, having sole rights to sell certain products at the event allowed potential customers to experience what the business had to offer. Finally, in supporting a local good cause the delicatessen presented itself to the local community as an authentic business with values.

Event sponsorship and authenticity

The importance of achieving authenticity in event sponsorship campaigns is well established. As Fitzgerald (2000: 22) observed, 'grass-roots events have become a staple of automotive marketing, car brand strategists are working to differentiate their events using entertainment and authenticity.' This statement highlights some of the internal tensions in event marketing sponsorship and its pursuit of authenticity. The term 'grass-roots events' implies shared ownership through a bottom-up approach but, as Fitzgerald (2000) shows, the reality is that marketing executives at car brands such as Nissan and GM are not just looking to sponsor pre-existing events but also to take ownership of events they have commissioned for their brands. In this way they can control the event's content and potentially the consumer experience. While sponsorship of pre-existing events is still important, the trend is to tailor-made event experiences that immerse consumers in a brand. These can be either standalone events or events within events where a brand sponsors an event such as a festival or sporting occasion and then creates an event experience on site.

To deliver successful event experiences that facilitate positive interactions between consumers and brands requires a sophisticated understanding of what authenticity means and how it may be delivered in real-life situations. Central to understanding brand authenticity in relation to event sponsorship is the recognition that brands are integral to consumers' sense of identity – consuming certain brands is one way in which an individual consumer presents their self to the world. However, in using brands as a form of self-expression consumers are faced with so many choices of products and services that they may become meaningless and counterfeit. In a similar way to the marketing executive's desire to control grassroots events there is an internal tension between brands as conduits of self-expression and authenticity.

Given the tensions between brand and authenticity, control and identity, it is perhaps unsurprising that both academics and practitioners in the industry agree that it is vital to understand the dynamics and nature of authenticity in relation to products and services. As Gilmore and Pine (2007: 5) suggest, 'authenticity has overtaken quality as the prevailing purchasing criterion, just as quality overtook cost, and as cost overtook availability'. This may be overstating the case somewhat, for quality is an important driver of brand authenticity and there are other drivers that it is important to factor in when framing authenticity of brands, products, services and event experiences in sponsorship contexts.

Underlying all debates regarding authenticity is the suggestion that contemporary life is increasingly inauthentic. This is not a new debate; Boorstin (1964) used the term 'pseudo event' to describe the phenomenon of events created by the media and used to deceive and influence an audience, and suggested that consumers in the West embrace the escapist and constructed reality of pseudo events and are part of a world where 'fantasy is more real than reality, where the image has more dignity than its original. We hardly dare face our bewilderment, because our ambiguous experience is so pleasantly iridescent, and the solace of belief in contrived reality is so thoroughly real' (Boorstin, 1964: 37).

This theme of inauthenticity was extended to social activities of consumers by Baudrillard (1988), who argued that in today's society social and consumption experiences are deficient in depth, originality and sense of place. He used the word *simulacrum* (which he defined as a copy with no original) to describe the nature of consumption as denying the original and blurring the line between fake and real. Baudrillard (1988) called this condition 'hyperreality' and defined it as 'the generation by models of a real without origin or reality'. According to Baudrillard, an example of hyperreality is Disneyland, where a false reality engineers an illusion of fake nature that satisfies visitors' daydreams and fantasies. When people go to Disneyland they form queues for each attraction and follow the instructions of attendants in special uniforms. If visitors follow these rules correctly they will experience the 'real thing'.

Morhart *et al* (2015) suggest that authenticity may be categorized into three perspectives; objectivist, constructivist and existentialist. The objectivist perspective suggests that authenticity is an objectively measurable quality to be evaluated by experts. An authentic product or service, according to the objectivist perspective, is 'the real thing' – authenticity resides in the product or service and the consumer is advised to beware of imitations. Examples of objective authenticity could be Coke sponsoring American football or Barbour sponsoring a county show in England.

The constructivist perspective holds that authenticity is socially or personally constructed. Unlike the objectivist approach the constructivist perspective suggests authenticity does not reside in the product or service but is a projection of an individual's beliefs and expectations. Morhart *et al* (2015) illustrate constructivist authenticity by drawing on MacCannell's (1973) concept of touristic space, which can be 'called a stage set, a tourist setting or simply a set depending on how purposefully worked up for tourists the display is.'

The third perspective is existentialist authenticity, which is about being true to oneself. By consuming a particular brand an individual feels they are upholding values or traditions they see as important to their life. MacCannell (1973) suggested that the search for authenticity of experience that is prevalent in modern society parallels that of primitive peoples for the sacred.

Research insight 1: authenticity – perception is everything...

Today, authenticity is important to brands and the event sponsorships they invest in. Morhart *et al* (2015) developed a framework for the concept of authenticity. Based on this framework the researchers report on the design of a scale (questionnaire) for measuring perceived brand authenticity (PBA). The scale measures PBA according to four dimensions: credibility, integrity, symbolism and continuity. It was tested with over 900 respondents in Europe, Russia and America. The results suggest that PBA depends on the consumer's marketing scepticism. The results also indicate that PBA may increase emotional brand attachment, word-of-mouth and the likelihood of consumers choosing a brand.

Morhart, F, Malär, L, Guèvremont, A, Girardin, F and Grohmann, B (2015) Brand authenticity: An integrative framework and measurement scale, *Journal of Consumer Psychology*, **25** (2), pp 200–18

Unlike Boorstin (1964), who suggested that pseudo events were created by tourists in search of superficial experiences, MacCannell (1973) suggests that tourists are always in search of authentic experience but the level of authenticity is related to their sense of adventure. MacCannell draws on Goffman's (1959) front stage/back stage theory and suggests that in social spaces there is a division between the front stage and back stage. The front stage, in a service context, is where hosts meet guests. The front stage is where the service experience is performed. The back stage is where service providers go to relax or prepare the performance. The back stage may contain props or allow activities to take place that would discredit the service experience, so customers are not normally allowed to enter this space. MacCannell (1973) takes the idea of front stage and back stage and relates it to authenticity, suggesting that tourism is a ritual aspect for society that performs some of the functions of religion in the modern world. This book suggests that, to be seen as authentic, brand experiences also need to have ritual aspects that imbue them with authenticity.

An important aspect of any ritual is the idea of collective effervescence (Durkheim, 1912). For Durkheim, collective effervescence is the state of togetherness of thought and action experienced by a group of individuals in a religious ritual. These states of togetherness could be high energy (singing or dancing) or quiet and reflective (mediation or prayer). In the context of event led experiential marketing it is the time when consumers interact with a brand and with each other utilizing, understanding and enjoying the brand's benefits.

Figure 2.4 Brand experiences as rituals

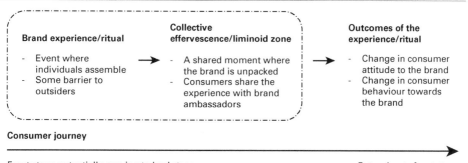

In Figure 2.4 his theory is adapted from the tourism context to that of experiential brand management in the events sponsorship context. In this revised model it's important to understand that the front stage and back stage are conceived differently for a brand. The front stage comprises the normal communication channels available to integrated marketing communications. The back stage for brands is when they attempt to move into and/or appropriate social spaces and experiences that they are not normally a part of. Understanding this continuum from front stage to back stage is really important. Sponsors need to ensure they make an appropriate intervention into a target audience's social space and experience so that a positive outcome in terms of brand perception is achieved. This point cannot be understated, as Gilmore and Pine (2007) suggest authenticity is a more important driver of consumer decision making than availability, cost or quality. While the claim that authenticity trumps all in consumer decision making is debatable, particularly as factors such as quality are closely linked to authenticity, it is undeniably a significant factor. Brands using sponsorship, experiential marketing and events need to consider how to develop authenticity, and to what degree, in an event led, experiential sponsorship campaign.

Sponsorship insight 2: what's in the goody bag?

Many events, such as conferences, product launches and exhibitions, offer 'goody bags'. 'We used to give out goody bags to everyone who took part in the sponsored walks we put on each year,' recalls Tom Lunt. 'The goody bags worked in several ways – they had visual impact as they were brightly coloured, so having hundreds of people walking the streets with these bags really announced the event and pushed our brand.

'The goody bags also gave our sponsors an opportunity to be experienced by our supporters, who were their target audience. We included a bottle of water, a bar of chocolate, some information about the sponsors, reports on our charity's work as well as ribbons and balloons. We always ensured that there was something for the participants to do, for example complete a pledge or write a postcard to their MP. In this way there was a multi-level experience in the goody bag – delicious chocolate to taste, thirst-quenching water, but also something to think about and act on.

'It's so important that the goody bag contains worthwhile things because if the contents of the bag are just cheap throw-away items of no relevance to the event then participants will feel disappointed. And that's a feeling that needs to be avoided at all costs. Water and chocolate are very important if you're walking any distance, especially on a hot, sunny day in London. I think our supporters appreciated our sponsors' gifts, which contributed to the event in a good way. Because the gifts were relevant to the event they were seen as authentic and that helped to develop positive perceptions of the goods and services they offered. Furthermore, by including different messages and requests for our supporters we were, in a way, cross-selling different aspects of the charity's work. Some of these our supporters might not have known about before. I hope that they would be more open to new ideas and requests for help when they were having fun and enjoying a day out with their friends and family.'

Conclusion

This chapter has demonstrated the importance of placing event led experiential marketing at the centre of integrated marketing communications planning. This is because rather than being seen as a channel, event led experiential marketing contributes to a range of channels in an integrated marketing mix.

Moreover, this chapter highlights the need for tangible, real and embodied experiences as the cornerstone of effective event sponsorship marketing. Therefore, it is very important to ensure that sponsorships of events are not merely clumsy, inappropriate 'bolt-ons' to an event but closely fit and complement the values and aspirations of the event and those that go to it. Ensuring a close fit between sponsor and event is closely related to discussions of authenticity. In exploring the nature of authenticity from a range of perspectives, this chapter argues that for an event sponsorship to have authenticity it must fit with the target audience but also be designed with elements of ritual in mind. In this way consumers can experience collective effervescence – feelings of togetherness with the brand and, if appropriate, with each other.

This chapter has briefly examined the work of Schmitt's (1999) important work on experiential marketing and strategic experiential modules. In Chapter 3 we'll examine Schmitt's work in greater detail in relation to the BETTER model (Smilansky, 2009) as we consider how experiential marketing relates to sponsorship. Both writers offer important guidance on experiential marketing, in particular that consumer responses to experiences can be rational and/or emotional so it is important to design experiences holistically. These aspects are explored in detail in Chapter 3.

Discussion questions and activities

1 Read the article by Morhart *et al* (2015) and visit some sponsorship agencies' websites (eg Slingshot Sponsorship, Synergy Sponsorship and BDS Sponsorship). Look for their work, case studies and blog pages to find examples of sponsorship campaigns, and decide which of the four dimensions of perceived brand authenticity their clients are drawing on (credibility, integrity, symbolism and continuity).

2 Check out the websites for the soft drink company Mountain Dew and the Dew Tour.

   – Discuss the ways in which Mountain Dew's brand identity is integrated across the digital and physical channels.

   – In what ways is the Dew Tour a 'real' or authentic experience?

   – Why might these events be seen as inauthentic?

3 Consider the Mountain Dew and Dew Tour websites and the campaigns on the sponsorship agencies' websites. Discuss what appeals they are making to the consumer. How do these fit with the information processing and experiential marketing views of consumer decision making set out in Holbrook and Hirschman's (1982) article?

Further reading

Donlan, L and Crowther, P (2014) Leveraging sponsorship to achieve consumer relationship objectives through the creation of 'marketing spaces': An exploratory study, *Journal of Marketing Communications*, **20** (4), pp 291–306

This is an insightful research paper that examines how sponsorship managers are starting to set relational objectives for their campaigns. The authors then consider how relational objectives can be achieved and, importantly, evaluated.

Grohs, R (2016) Drivers of brand image improvement in sports-event sponsorship, *International Journal of Advertising*, **35** (3), pp 391–420

This is a wide-ranging research paper that examines the last 20 years of research on what influences brand image improvement in sports event sponsorship. The author suggests a way to measure image change in sponsorships.

Holbrook, MB and Hirschman, EC (1982) The experiential aspects of consumption: Consumer fantasies, feelings, and fun, *Journal of Consumer Research*, **9** (2), pp 132–40

This is a tough article to read, *but* it is one of the most important and authoritative articles on experience as a driver of consumer decision making. The authors identify the prevalent mode of analysing consumer decision making, which sees the individual as rational and making decisions based on information. In contrast, the experiential view put forward in this paper suggests that consumption is primarily subjective and is driven by 'fantasies, feelings and fun'.

Keller, KL (2016) Unlocking the power of integrated marketing communications: How integrated is your IMC program? *Journal of Advertising*, **45** (3), pp 286–301

This article examines integrated marketing communications in the light of the widening range of digital platforms available to marketers. The author sets out seven criteria that marketers should use to inform the design of their IMC programmes.

References

Baudrillard, J (1988) *Selected Writings*, Polity, Cambridge

Boorstin, DJ (1964) *The Image: A guide to pseudo-events in America*, Harper & Row, New York

Caywood, C, Schultz, DE and Wang, P (1991) Integrated marketing communications, Northwestern University Medill School of Journalism, Evanston, Illinois

Coulton, A (1997) With sports alliances, cards make big play for fans, *American Banker* [Online] https://www.highbeam.com/doc/1G1-19834689.html [Accessed 24/11/16]

Donlan, L and Crowther, P (2014) Leveraging sponsorship to achieve consumer relationship objectives through the creation of 'marketing spaces': An exploratory study, *Journal of Marketing Communications*, 20 (4), pp 291–306

Durkheim, É (1912) *The Elementary Forms of Religious Life*, Allen and Unwin, London

Fitzgerald, K (2000) Events offer new level of brand immersion, *Advertising Age*, **71** (17) [Online] http://adage.com/article/news/events-offer-level-brand-immersion/58677/ [Accessed 25/06/18]

GE (2008) GE launches marketing initiatives for London 2012 Olympic Games, GE Newsroom [Online] http://www.genewsroom.com/Press-Releases/

GE-Launches-Marketing-Initiatives-For-London-2012-Olympic-Games-235162 [Accessed 12/11/16]

Gilmore, J and Pine, BJ (2007) *Authenticity: What consumers really want*, Harvard Business Review Press, Cambridge, MA

Goffman, E (1959) *The Presentation of Self in Everyday Life*, Penguin Books, Harmondsworth

Gupta, S (2003) Event marketing: Issues and challenges, *IIMB Management Review* (Indian Institute of Management Bangalore), **15** (2), pp 87–96

Hanlon, P (2012) Face slams: Event marketing takes off, *Forbes* [Online] http://www.forbes.com/sites/patrickhanlon/2012/05/09/face-slams-event-marketing-takes-off/ [Accessed 05/11/16]

Holbrook, MB (2006) The consumption experience – something new, something old, something borrowed, something sold: Part 1, *Journal of Macromarketing*, **26** (2), pp 259–66

Holbrook, MB and Hirschman, EC (1982) The experiential aspects of consumption: Consumer fantasies, feelings, and fun, *Journal of Consumer Research*, **9** (2), pp 132–40

International Chamber of Commerce (2003) ICC International Code on Sponsorship [Online] http://www.abfi.ie/Sectors/ABFI/ABFI.nsf/vPagesABFI/Responsibilities~sponsorship/$File/ICC+International+Code+on+Sponsorship.pdf [Accessed 23/01/17]

Keller, KL (2016) Unlocking the power of integrated marketing communications: How integrated is your IMC program? *Journal of Advertising*, **45** (3), pp 286–301

Kotler, P and Armstrong, G (2014) *Principles of Marketing*, 15th edn, Global Editions, Boston, MA; Pearson, London

MacCannell, D (1973) Staged authenticity: Arrangements of social space in tourist settings, *American Journal of Sociology*, **79** (3), pp 589–603

Morhart, F, Malär, L, Guèvremont, A, Girardin, F and Grohmann, B (2015) Brand authenticity: An integrative framework and measurement scale, *Journal of Consumer Psychology*, **25** (2), pp 200–18

Pine, BJ and Gilmore, JH (1998) Welcome to the experience economy, *Harvard Business Review*, **76** (4), pp 97–105

Schau, HJ, Muñiz, AM and Arnould, EJ (2009) How brand community practices create value, *Journal of Marketing*, **73** (5), pp 30–51

Schmitt, B (1999) *Experiential Marketing: How to get customers to sense, feel, think, act, relate to your company and brands*, The Free Press, New York

Schultz, DE and Kitchen, PJ (2000) *Communicating Globally: An integrated marketing approach*, Palgrave, Basingstoke

Sense London (2015) *Real World Ideas: A guide to modern experiential marketing*, Sense Marketing Services Ltd, London

Sherry, J, Kozinets, RV and Borghini, S (2007) Agents in paradise: Experiential co-creation through emplacement, ritualization and community, in *Consuming Experience*, ed A Carú and B Cova, Routledge, London/New York

Smilansky, S (2009), *Experiential Marketing: A practical guide to interactive brand experiences*, Kogan Page, London

Wood, EH (2009) Evaluating event marketing: Experience or outcome? *Journal of Promotion Management*, **15** (1–2), pp 247–68

Delivering event sponsorship campaigns 03

LEARNING OBJECTIVES

Having read this chapter and worked through the questions and activities you should be able:

- to examine how the principles of experiential marketing apply to sponsorship campaigns;
- to develop brand activations for sponsorship campaigns;
- to evaluate the issues arising when sponsorship campaigns are operationalized in event contexts.

In this chapter we will examine two important contributions to experiential marketing – Schmitt (1999) and Smilansky (2009) – and how their approaches contribute practically to designing and delivering event sponsorship campaigns. In the case study of Christian Aid's sponsorship at the Greenbelt Festival we will examine some of the practicalities and potential difficulties relating to activation of sponsorship campaigns. We will then turn to the insights of Nick Adams, Managing Director of the experiential marketing agency Sense London, who in a wide-ranging interview gives unique insights into how his agency works with major brands on sponsorship campaigns.

Schmitt (1999) suggests the importance of moving 'from Brand=ID to Brand=Ex'. He means that branding moves from being a static identifier of a product or service to being a provider of experience. This involves a combination of names, logos and slogans that generate awareness and image with sensory, affective, creative relations and lifestyles with the brand. To achieve this, Schmitt puts forward a model of experience types based on what he calls strategic experiential modules (SEMs), namely: sense, feel, think, act and relate (Schmitt,1999: 64). This model is very useful for designing and evaluating event sponsorship programmes and the experiences designed into them.

- **Sense** – When designing an experience, Schmitt suggests that sense marketing is about engaging consumers through sight, sound, touch, taste and smell.
- **Feel** – Feel marketing makes an emotional appeal to the consumer, focusing on an individual's positive feelings of pride in an achievement.
- **Think** – Think marketing looks to engage with consumer intellect and encourage creative approaches to finding solutions to issues.
- **Act** – Act marketing is about consumer lifestyles, their bodies and activities. Schmitt (1999) suggests that consumers are driven by a range of factors that lead to changes in behaviour. Rational approaches are one factor, but equally important are emotional, spontaneous and inspirational factors.
- **Relate** – Relate marketing is linked to an important point noted earlier in Chapter 2, namely that consumption experiences are closely linked to self-expression (Aaker, 1999; Hogg *et al*, 2000). Schmitt (1999) sees relate marketing as a combination of sense, feel, think and act marketing, which appeals to a consumer's need to self-improve and to be seen by others in a positive way. Relate is of particular interest to event sponsorship, because of the social dimension it encompasses, which links it to the concepts of brand communities and tribes.

Schmitt (1999: 72) also offers a useful model that sets out how the SEMs are implemented or 'instantiated'. SEMs are delivered through experience providers (ExPros), namely:

- communications;
- visual, verbal identity and signage;
- product presence;
- co-branding;
- spatial environments;
- websites and electronic media;
- people.

The key point to take away here is Schmitt's (1999) guidance that SEMs and ExPros need to be used together as a strategic planning tool. ExPros should be used to create a particular SEM that will communicate brand messages effectively. The ExPro model locates event marketing and sponsorship as part of co-branding and identifies their ability to generate emotional, memorable connections with consumers as key to their success. Schmitt (1999: 85) observes that 'Event marketing requires a qualitative understanding of the appropriateness of a particular event as well as quantitative research to demonstrate its effectiveness in reach'. This chapter will examine the qualitative side, while Chapter 9 will focus on evaluation techniques.

Schmitt's (1999) ExPro model is a good starting point in any consideration of an event marketing and sponsorship campaign. It sets the context well and highlights the fundamental importance of ensuring the match or fit between a brand and a particular event or experience. However, for the purposes of this book it is necessary to develop a model that places event led marketing and sponsorship at the centre and then sets out the components that will create the experience. To do this it is important to construct the model in the form of a journey or narrative. This has been considered in some detail by a number of writers, such as Getz (2007). Before setting out a specific approach to experience creation for event led sponsorship, it is necessary to examine a second experiential marketing model and method developed by Smilansky (2009) in relation to Schmitt's (1999) approach.

Smilansky's (2009) model uses the acronym BETTER to set out a systematic brainstorming approach to developing experiential marketing campaigns. This is shown in Figure 3.1. The BETTER model is an excellent way to develop a qualitative understanding of how appropriate an event marketing approach is in a sponsorship context (Schmitt, 1999). The model can be divided into four stages.

Stage 1: consider the brand's personality

When considering a brand's personality Smilansky advises a form of anthropomorphism – giving human characteristics to the brand. So is the sponsor's product service serious, playful, smart or shy? Smilansky suggests that brand values can be identified by building up a picture of the brand's personality.

Figure 3.1   Top-line concept using the BETTER model

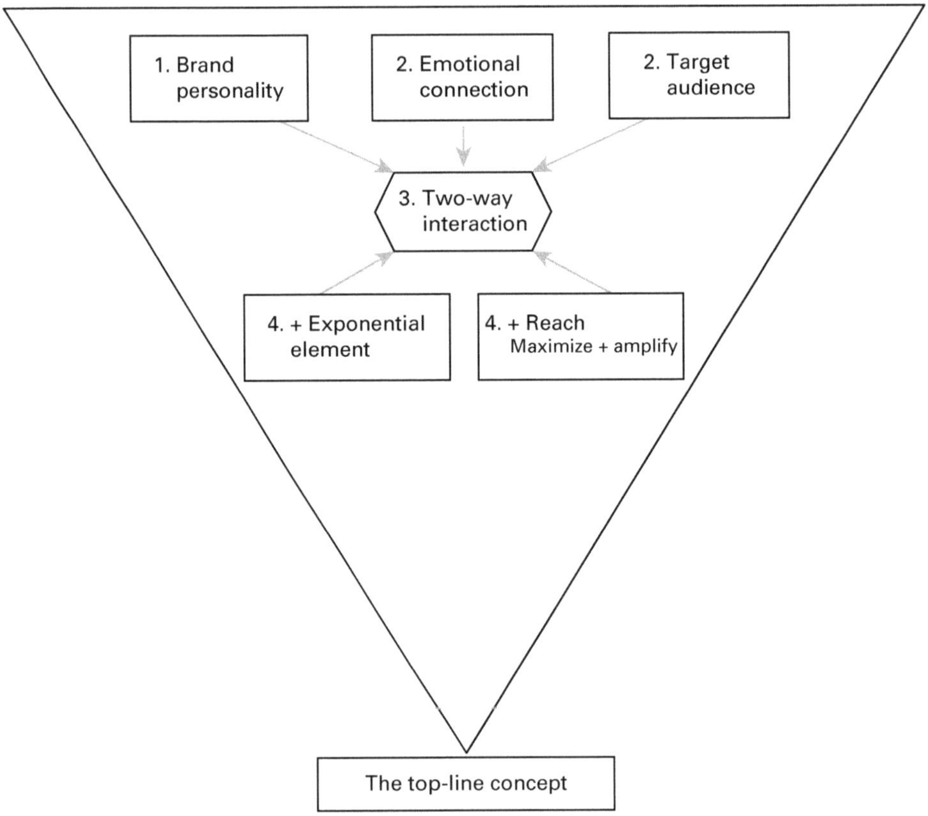

SOURCE Smilansky, 2009: 53
NOTE The numbers in this figure have been added and refer to the stages set out in this chapter.

Stage 2: developing an emotional connection between a brand and its target audience

The nature of the connection is central, and Smilansky agrees with Schmitt (1999) that '[e]xperiential marketing should always make a deep emotional connection with the target audience through their feelings... three key elements should be thought about at this stage: authentic, positively connected and personally meaningful' (Smilansky, 2009: 56).

These three elements are in keeping with Pine and Gilmore (1998) who emphasize the importance of maximizing positive cues and minimizing negative cues in an experience. The key to achieving this is excellent service. Poulsson and Kale (2004: 272) also support Smilansky's key elements; they include personal relevance as part of their experiential scorecard and describe it as 'the individual's internal state of arousal, activation and preparedness to engage in a specific experience.'

The individual consumer's readiness to engage in an experience is fundamentally important. When the experience matches with a consumer's needs and expectations sponsors can communicate their brand clearly and positively to an interested audience. Failure to secure a good match will result in communications at best being ignored and at worst creating negative impressions. Smilansky (2009) focuses on the importance of brands having a precise and deep understanding of their target audience's likes and dislikes.

Stage 3: two-way interaction

The outcomes of stages 1 and 2 – brand personality, emotional connection and target audience – are used to develop the two-way interaction. For brand sponsorship it is this element that is of crucial importance and what differentiates an event led sponsorship campaign from other one-way marketing channels and, specifically, basic adverts displayed at events. As Nick Adams, Sense London's Managing Director, makes clear, 'experiential marketing isn't a channel, it's a technique' (Sense London, 2015). Marketing is often said to be about building relationships with consumers, but in an event led experience the brand and consumer are in a live, face-to-face moment. A conversation, physical contact and unspoken communications between the brand and the consumer are all possible. Both brand and consumer need to achieve something positive from the interaction.

Stage 4: exponential element and reach

This relates to how the experience that a consumer encounters with a brand is communicated beyond the interaction itself. It is often referred to as 'word of mouth' and can happen unprompted. A consumer who has a positive experience is likely to tell friends and family about it. The significant game changer for experiential marketing has been the spread of internet based social media. This has enabled experiential marketers to meet the challenge of sceptics who argue that event led experiences are not able to broadcast effectively to large audiences – they don't achieve adequate reach – the final component of Smilansky's (2009) model.

Smilansky (2009) suggests that above the line marketers will question the cost per view of an experiential marketing campaign compared with that of above the line marketing such as TV, where the opportunities to see are millions of times greater. However, there are several points to make here. The nature of the interactions found in a live brand experience should, if they are perceived as genuine, authentic and make emotional connections with consumers, have far more impact, than one-way communications like TV adverts. Moreover, as Smilansky (2009: 65) suggests, on average a person who has taken part in a live brand experience is likely to tell 17 others, so 5,000 becomes 5,000 x 17 = 85,000. While not comparable to TV advertising, it is significant. In a similar way, American Express (2011) found that Americans are likely to tell nine people about a good customer experience but, even more important, they will tell 16 people about a poor experience. So for sponsors it is vital that they develop experiential campaigns that deliver positive experiences for event attendees, as more people will find out about a poor experiential campaign than a good one.

Maximizing reach through experiential marketing is about combining a number of elements, such as physical location, with other channels. When selecting a location it's not just about choosing a busy shopping mall or town centre. Site selection should be based on footfall but also on the right kind of feet – meaning that the location should fit with the target audience's demographic profile. For sponsors, identifying the correct event whose audience has the right profile is key to the experience being accepted by those at the event and the brand messages being heard and acted on. A good example of this is Christian Aid's sponsorship of the Greenbelt Festival in England (see Case Study 2).

CASE STUDY 2 Christian Aid and the Greenbelt Arts and Music Festival – making the ask

In the early 2000s Christian Aid reviewed its sponsorship arrangement with the Greenbelt Festival. As a major international development agency Christian Aid has a responsibility to ensure that the money spent on its objectives is achieving as much as possible. In the past, the sponsorship arrangement with Greenbelt festival had been seen as an education and awareness raising opportunity. A large tent with a café, performance space and area with information and opportunities to discuss and interact with Christian Aid volunteers and staff were available.

Figure 3.2   Inside the Christian Aid tent at Greenbelt Festival, themed activities for children and adults that communicate key messages (in this case global warming) to festival goers are central to maximizing sponsorship benefits

SOURCE Christian Aid/Stuart Keegan

A significant change was to introduce a fundraising outcome into the sponsorship objectives. A team of specially trained volunteers and staff were given the task of asking visitors to the tent if they had considered giving to Christian Aid on a regular basis. This approach was similar to the street fundraising approach that had become popular with charities. However, one main difference was that Christian Aid made an agreement with the festival that the team could only work in the tent and at Christian Aid events, such as talks, in other parts of the festival. Another significant difference was that the team were volunteers, which gave them an authenticity that those who are paid to do the job do not have. Furthermore, because the volunteers were not on commission they were less likely to be pushy in inappropriate situations. Nevertheless, there were occasions when volunteers had to be asked to confine their activities to the designated areas because they were enthusiastic to go into other parts of the festival.

There had been a significant amount of concern regarding the change in sponsorship objectives. In particular, three issues were identified:

- The appropriateness of one of the main sponsors approaching people who are enjoying themselves at the festival to ask for financial support was questioned.
- Christian Aid would be asking people who already supported the organization financially and this duplication could lead to a loss of support.

- Changing the dynamic between volunteers, staff and supporters at the festival was also identified as a potential problem.

The initiative did go ahead and was a success. The number of people who signed up to give a regular monthly donation exceeded expectations and was significantly higher than that achieved over a similar period of time by a commercial face-to-face street fundraising campaign. In addition, the size of the regular donations and length of time that the donations were given for also outperformed commercial street campaigns. There were no significant issues or complaints related to the activity. This activity was run for several years, then paused as it became clear that saturation point had been reached when numbers signing up to give regularly decreased. The festival had a significant number of loyal supporters who came each year and it was recognized that they could not be approached every year. After a few years the initiative was re-commenced. Christian Aid remains one the main sponsors of the festival.

This case study demonstrates that in sponsoring the Greenbelt Festival, Christian Aid had successfully identified an event that attracted a large number of people who fitted its target audience. Moreover, it is a good example of carefully conceived, designed and executed brand activation tactics, which were perceived as authentic by attendees in the context of the event. These tactics allowed Christian Aid to maximize the benefits of the sponsorship.

There are several types of reach – direct, indirect, social and PR. Sense London (2015: 31) define valuable reach as 'any kind of contact your campaign has with someone – direct or indirect – which communicates your message.' Direct experiences fall into primary and secondary experiences. Primary experiences relate to the optimum consumer experience where an individual interacts with all the touch points with the brand that have been developed by the experience designer. However, in any context there will be consumers who will attend, but don't want to engage in the primary experience because they don't have the time, or for some other reason. For this audience the secondary experience is a less involved set of activities that happen around the periphery of the primary, optimum experience.

To expand on this in relation to the Christian Aid case study, the primary experience would be those who visited the tent, took part in the activities and spoke to one of the team, and made a decision at that time to give on a regular basis. Meanwhile, someone who visited the tent, had a cup of tea in the café area, listened to a talk on work of the organization and received a leaflet on their way out can be said to have had a secondary experience – that is, they had direct but limited contact with the experience itself. Indirect reach is about individuals who were never physically at the event but hear the message via word-of-mouth – someone who is told about an experience by another who has direct experience. Alternatively it can be opportunity to see, for example via social media or advertising.

Reach is not just about traditional word of mouth and physical location. Maximizing reach is often about how an event experience can be amplified through other marketing channels, such as TV and social media. There are many examples of field marketing featuring in TV advertising. A good example is the Pepsi Challenge where members of the public were shown tasting Pepsi and another type of cola without knowing which was which. They were then asked to say which one they preferred. The amazed reaction of the participants when they find out they preferred Pepsi was the climax of the advert.

Professional insight 2: interview with Nick Adams, founder of Sense London

Nick Adams has worked in live and integrated marketing for over 18 years. He founded Sense London in 2004. Since then Sense London has grown into an agency that specializes in helping brands do exciting things in the real world, creating authentic communications across the marketing spectrum. Sense London manage campaigns from strategy to evaluation, and have offices in London and New York. In this interview Nick gives valuable insights into IMC, experiential marketing and events that are important to those planning sponsorship campaigns and in particular brand activations at events.

How does experiential marketing fit in an IMC campaign?

As an agency we are all about real-world ideas; that's the common thread that runs though our work. The marketing activities that we specialize in manifest themselves in real action in the real world, in activities that have meaning and purpose for consumers. IMC is topical at the moment for us because we are currently refining our proposition to recognize that consumers have a real desire for brands to have meaningful involvement in their lives. This is well documented but it's more important than ever for brands to back up and complement their advertising and more traditional media with activities that are action based, put their money where their mouth is and produce something in the real world. And that's where we see experiential marketing fitting into an integrated communications plan.

Over the last three to five years the requirement and need for brands to bring to life what they're doing and not just talk about it in more traditional advertising has exponentially grown. For a lot of our clients it's now the cornerstone of their marketing activities. That's where it fits into the integrated mix. It's still about integration; brands, of course, still need traditional media to create that broadcast awareness, but brands that are not backing up and following through with activities that really bring it to life are falling behind somewhat.

What are the main ingredients of a successful sponsorship campaign from an experiential marketing viewpoint?

Before we get to the point of translating a sponsorship relationship into experiential marketing, it is very important to move up upstream and ask, 'What is that sponsorship partnership, how has it come about and what's the relevance behind that?' It was quite usual a number of years ago for brands to not really think that hard about the relationship between their brand and the sponsorship asset. It was really about tagging your logo onto something that was in the public eye on TV, or wherever. Sponsorship was a blunt tool, if you like. Now, what has a big impact for Sense London in terms of how we bring a relationship to life is the relevance of the partnership, and there has to be real meaning and reason as to why the brand has chosen the partnership. This has a big bearing for us, because our job is to bring that partnership to life to explain to consumers and make it contextually relevant why brand X has linked with property Y. Our job is incredibly difficult if there's not a real, true relevance as to why the two partners have got together. It's very hard to make sense of that sponsorship relationship in a way that consumers are going to understand and see as a natural fit.

The key ingredients start with making sure that there's real meaning behind why the brand is sponsoring that property first and foremost. Then, the key ingredient for us is thinking, what is the role of experiential in exploiting that sponsorship? Our role is then to unpack the brand in the context of that sponsorship environment. We need to be doing a job for that brand, which is explaining their product, the rationale, the benefits of that product in the context of that sponsorship in a relevant way.

Two contrasting examples are Glaceau Vitamin Water and Powerade, which is a really good example. Coca-Cola has a longstanding relationship with the Olympics. For the Olympics in the UK in 2012 they went about their sponsorship exploitation in a very well thought through, strategic way. They pulled three brands from their portfolio and really thought about the role of those three brands as hero Coca-Cola brands in the context of the Olympics. Glaceau Vitamin Water had a very specific role within the Olympics that goes back to the proposition of Glaceau and what the brand is all about, and that it was the brand for fans of the Olympics.

Coca-Cola broke down three brands for three audiences. Coca-Cola's main brand was all about the live action, for the people who go to the stadium and watch the live action. Glaceau was a little bit more irreverent and fun. It was about acknowledging that the vast majority of the population would not go to the Olympics because it was too expensive or they couldn't get a ticket. It was about bringing the fun of the Olympics in a very Glaceau way to them in their street, in their homes, gardens, barbecues, watching television, etc. Going back to what I said, our role was made a lot easier because we had a brief from the client that said, we've sponsored the Olympics, we've broken that down into three hero brands, and this is the specific role that Glaceau is going to be playing. So it was defined for us, and the activity almost wrote itself in some respects because it was, we've got to bring the fun of the stadium to life in public places, so we did activities in city centres. We went to some of the fan parks. We did some fun things like recreating the games and introducing some interactive experiences for consumers in a very fun way. We also went into offices and encouraged people to sit down in long lines and do rowing races for prizes. So it was all very tongue in cheek, just bringing that sponsorship to life in a completely different way to how Coca-Cola was doing it in the stadiums. The final brand was Powerade. Coca-Cola was for fans in the stadium, Powerade was for the competitors. All of the exploitation there was about partnerships with the individual competitors, a product for them driving that association – a drink that would help them perform at their best – and Glaceau was for the fun.

What process do you go through with a sponsorship client when you develop an experiential marketing campaign?

The process follows a path similar to any brand that we work with, not just sponsorships. Our insight team will first and foremost analyse the brief and get under the skin of the brand to find the 'sweet spot' in terms of what is the brand insight and what is the consumer insight? And finding the bit in the middle where the two marry up is the solution to the brief. What are the key messages about the brand that need to be communicated through the activity to that audience? The second part is, what change do we want to stimulate? Is it a change of attitude towards the brand or, more often than not, is there a behavioural change in their purchase or brand selection?

The key step that is different for a sponsorship activity, which can be hard to navigate, is the delicate relationship between the brand and the sponsor. This can be a real point of compromise between two brands; each brand in a partnership has to accept some compromises and brands can sometimes be very, very headstrong about what they want their activities to be and how they will work. With a sponsorship activity there is always the sponsor's interests and brand to protect and represent as well. Some of the most successful ways are where clients approach the sponsorship that starts with their brand but they have a specific strategy for how they are going to satisfy, protect and do the right job for the sponsor as well.

A very good, tactical example is some of the work we've done for Mars with some of its outline brands like Maltesers, who sponsored *Britain's Got Talent*. Obviously this is a huge media asset that is very carefully protected by the producers of the show with pages and pages of brand guidelines, and on the other side is the might of Mars. Often it's the agencies that are positioned as the mediators in the relationship; it's our job to find a path through the middle and make sure both parties are happy.

In that situation we had a competition that ran nationally through traditional media. There were 150 VIP winners who were invited to a house party at a very grand Victorian house in London, and they had a VIP evening watching the final of *Britain's Got Talent*. And there were a whole range of activities in and around that evening to make the event special. There were various other stakeholders involved in the event, so some were their retail customers – members of the general public. The other 20 per cent were key trade customers and some internal stakeholders.

The emphasis for that activity was the earlier part in terms of the competition, so it was on millions of packs of chocolate and on displays brought to life in stores. So, really, the house party element was a little bit of the means to an end, the cherry that attracted consumers.

Another good example of our work is with Cadbury's and its sponsorship of the National Trust (NT) Easter egg trails. Cadbury's wanted to celebrate Easter in a way that would engage families in a fun and active way. So, it needed an innovative solution, which is why a partnership with NT made complete sense. The NT organize about 350 Easter egg trails across their properties, which was a perfect way to get families out and about at Easter and being active in the grounds of the NT properties.

The other important thing to note was the successful ingredient, where the sponsor's brand and client brand both share the same values. Looking at what the NT is about, it's a million miles away from chocolate, but very similar in other regards in that it's a British brand with strong ethical values.

How do Sense London design brand activation for sponsorship clients?

Another activity we worked on, which was a big challenge but was hugely successful, was with Kingsmill when it sponsored an initiative called The Big Lunch. This was an initiative that was put together in close association with the Eden Project, and the Big Lunch pulled in about 12 brands that sponsored the initiative. It was about getting communities back together to share lunch and go back to traditional values of sitting round the lunch table, talking to your neighbours and having street parties in the summer. Our brief was to make sense of this from a Kingsmill perspective. How do we underpin all the media they were doing, which was getting some great awareness, with some activities that make the brand relevant to consumers? We ended up doing a nationwide tour, taking a big mobile rig that went to the hearts of communities up and down the country. We were organizing lunch for communities and designing activities that would get families engaged with both Kingsmill and the meaning of the Big Lunch initiative. The activity had a large scale. We identified areas of the country that were most relevant from a demographic and lifestyle perspective. We targeted those communities and then if there were tactical ways to drive a deeper relationship we pursued those, but to all intents and purposes the activity was designed as a blueprint or template that could be dropped into multiple locations.

Could you give some examples of amplification created for sponsorship clients?

It's about approaching the brief in a multi-level way, so the starting point often for a brand is about going straight to the heart of the activity in terms of what we can do at the sponsor's event. In the case of the Easter egg trails and NT properties, what can we do on the site? That will always produce the lowest level of reach but the richest level of experience because you're right in the heart of where that sponsorship relationship is coming to life in the environment where it's at. That's always going to be a much smaller reach of the experience. Our job, then, and this goes back to the design of these activities, is about laddering it out, looking at the different tiers of the activity.

In the context of Cadbury's and the NT Easter egg trails activity it had a pretty small reach across those 350 sites and the families who were there. We then looked at the PR layer, so there was a Blue Peter presenter who made a personal appearance at some of the sites, which was communicated via social media. There was a competition that happened in loads of Tesco and Sainsbury's stores across the country, again relating back to the sponsorship activity. And then there's another layer again that is more about how we communicate the partnership and the activities as they happen.

To switch examples, in the case of Glaceau Vitamin Water, it's simply a matter of communicating the partnership, and the activities we're doing are to get past the consumer scepticism. The fact that Glaceau Vitamin Water had set up the studio and were actually doing it really won a lot of battles with consumers. We start by designing the core of the experience, but often that's not really the most important part; the most important part is the bit that is going to get to the critical mass of the general public. The work we did for My Little Pony was similar; we created a My Little Pony Friendship Bus that toured the country and interacted with several thousand people, but the social media work reached millions

I think at the heart, the experience design is a consideration of the consumer journey. That is where we break down the experience from a creative perspective. How do we walk them though the experience? When they arrive, what's their mindset? What's their experience? The commonality through all of these activities is getting to the point where you do the job of bringing the brand to life in terms of its features and benefits, emotional benefits. That's the key thing we can't miss in any sponsorship activities and that's done in many different ways. If you're at a music festival now, if you're Vodafone, Sky, Orange or whoever, there is a moment in the consumer journey where the brand is unpacked, where consumers understand through that sponsorship how that brand is going to fit into their life. Why it's relevant to their lifestyle. That's the common thread. Like Coca-Cola at the Olympics, when consumers are at the Olympic Park. There was a brand moment where it was brought to life for consumers as to how the brand fits into their life.

The brand moment can be a surprise to consumers in terms of a specific creative execution. It may be designed that way to maximize memorability and impact. I think, even if it's a surprise, it can't be forced and should be natural. We've seen sponsorship exploitation develop over the years, making sure that there's that permissibility for consumers. Consumers have become sceptical about brands

Figure 3.3 Designing live experiences that incorporate social media effectively is vital to the success of brand activations for sponsors

SOURCE Sense London

just slapping their logos onto the Formula 1 car because it's going to get loads of eyeballs on TV. I think consumers are the first people to spot if a brand doesn't have any part in being associated. You still do see it sometimes and think why is brand X sponsoring event Y? What's the connection? And, on top of that, what if the brand isn't doing anything to exploit that connection? In the past, the majority of the brand's investment went into the sponsorship, and often the problem then was that there was no money left to exploit it. Now brands have changed their investment strategy and the most successful sponsors keep back a large part of the investment because they realize that the more you exploit it the more the benefits are maximized.

The best sponsorship activities touch all of the marketing mix specialisms. So advertising creates awareness, experiential brings it to life in an interactive way, social and digital are involved with amplification and we also work closely with PR agencies. So it's really brands using all the ammunition they've got.

What do you look for in brand ambassadors?

Brand ambassadors are very interesting. We believe that this is developing quite quickly in the industry. We have recently rolled out our 'Real People' proposition, which is recognizing that the promotional staffing or brand ambassadors community, historically, have been all about resting actors and actresses. The brand ambassador job was acting the brand, putting on the t-shirt and drawing on those acting skills to do Pot Noodle one day, because you need to be funny and irreverent and loud and energetic; then the next day it's *The Times* so one needs to be more discerning. That's been the way historically and why it's attracted lots of actors and actresses. We think that will become a dated approach.

What we try to achieve now in our brand ambassador service is a proposition around real people that has authenticity. We look for people, yes they have the skills sets for whatever job you're asking them to do, but more importantly they share the same sort of DNA profile as the brand. A lot of brands break down their DNA, whether it's a brand onion or a brand wheel. The same thing can be done with behaviour or personality traits. So we're doing a lot of interesting work at the present. It's a very simple proposition looking at what the brand stands for, right at the heart of the brand, and finding authentic people who share those same skillsets and qualities. They may never have done brand ambassador work before. To give you an example, we work with a pasta brand called Giovanni Rana, Italy's leading pasta brand, which launched in the UK only a few years ago. We need that real, authentic Italian passion and understanding of pasta at more than a superficial level. Asking actors and actresses to put on an Italian accent would have been utterly wrong, so we recruited real Italians waiters and waitresses, people who were between jobs in this country, and some came over from Italy. The end experience for consumers was so much more effective and authentic because they shared a lot in common. I think the time will come when the brand ambassador community is a lot less populated by actors and actresses and more by real people.

It all goes back to making the experience believable for consumers. A few years ago we worked on a Pampers campaign at the Baby Show and lots of events targeting young mothers and expectant mums. We quickly realized that, however good a brand ambassador you are, unless you've had a child yourself or you're an aunt or uncle actually trying to drive a connection with mums, it's incredibly hard and you'll be seen though unless you've got that genuine authentic experience.

Research insight 2: brand experiences and the two roads to happiness

Schmitt *et al* (2014) suggest that attending sponsored events can positively affect brand experience, and consequently brand equity. In a wide-ranging discussion of experiential literature the authors suggest that future research should focus on how different types of brand experience lead to two different types of happiness – subjective pleasure, and the achievement of meaningful goals. The paper concludes by suggesting that brand experiences will become essential to making customers happy.

Schmitt, BH, Brakus, J and Zarantonello, L (2014) The current state and future of brand experience, *Journal of Brand Management*, **21** (S9), pp 727–33

Conclusion

In this chapter we have examined Schmitt's (1999) argument that brands need to move from static methods of identification such as logos to being providers of experience. Smilansky's (2009) BETTER model provides an excellent guide to how brands can deliver experiences. However, this is not a straightforward process and requires considerable planning and sensitivity to stakeholder concerns. Both the case study and practitioner insight reinforce these points and also give examples of how to develop two-way interaction and reach between brands and consumers.

Discussion questions and activities

1 In terms of authenticity, discuss the similarities between the not-for-profit sector case study of Christian Aid and the practitioner insight offered by Nick Adams from the commercial for-profit sector.

2 Locate three examples of event led sponsorship campaigns that have generated direct and indirect reach. Are the brand values of the sponsors communicated effectively?

3 Prepare a plan and presentation for a brand activation activity as part of a sponsorship. You will need to:
   – select an event and clearly identify the target audience;
   – identify a product or service that fits the target audience of the event;

- prepare two or three objectives that the product or service should achieve through the sponsorship;
- using the experiential marketing principles set out in this chapter, develop a brand activation activity that will engage the event participants with the brand;
- set out methods for maximizing reach around the brand activation;
- outline how the sponsorship of the event will be evaluated.

It's good to include diagrams, maps, floor plans, YouTube videos and photos to augment your presentation.

Further reading

Novais, MA and Arcodia, C (2013) Measuring the effects of event sponsorship: Theoretical frameworks and image transfer models, *Journal of Travel & Tourism Marketing*, **30** (4), pp 308–34

This article is very useful in that it summarizes the main research areas relating to events and sponsorship, including leveraging sponsorship at events. This is an important article that reviews a significant amount of up-to-date research on events and sponsorship. The authors also make suggestions for future research in this area.

Schmitt, B (1999) *Experiential Marketing: How to get customers to sense, feel, think, act, relate to your company and brands,* The Free Press, New York

This book was written nearly 20 years ago and so some of the examples are a bit dated. However, the ideas and concepts are very useful for sponsors and event managers who are looking to activate brands. In particular Chapters 4–8 set out the Sense, Feel, Think, Act and Relate experiences and how to create them.

Smilansky, S (2009), *Experiential Marketing: A practical guide to interactive brand experiences,* Kogan Page, London

This book gives practical, how-to advice on putting together interactive experiences that will enable brands to engage with their target audiences. There are useful chapters on setting experiential marketing objectives, recruiting brand ambassadors and insights from leading experiential marketers in the form of Q&A interviews.

References

Aaker, JL (1999) The malleable self: The role of self-expression in persuasion, *Journal of Marketing Research*, **36** (1), pp 45–57

American Express (2011) American Express global customer service barometer [Online] http://about.americanexpress.com/news/pr/2011/csbar.aspx [Accessed 03/01/17]

Getz, D (2007) *Event Studies: Theory, research and policy for planned events*, Events Management Series, Elsevier Butterworth-Heinemann, Amsterdam and London

Hogg, MK, Cox, AJ and Keeling, K (2000) The impact of self-monitoring on image congruence and product/brand evaluation, *European Journal of Marketing*, **34** (5/6), pp 641–67

Pine, BJ and Gilmore, JH (1998) Welcome to the experience economy, *Harvard Business Review*, **76** (4), pp 97–105

Poulsson, SHG and Kale, SH (2004) The experience economy and commercial experiences, *The Marketing Review*, **4** (3), pp 267–77

Schmitt, B (1999) *Experiential Marketing: How to get customers to sense, feel, think, act, relate to your company and brands*, The Free Press, New York

Schmitt, BH, Brakus, J and Zarantonello, L (2014) The current state and future of brand experience, *Journal of Brand Management*, **21** (S9), pp 727–33

Sense London (2015) *Real World Ideas: A guide to modern experiential marketing*, Sense Marketing Services Ltd, London

Smilansky, S (2009), *Experiential Marketing: A practical guide to interactive brand experiences*, Kogan Page, London

Identifying and securing sponsors and funding opportunities

04

LEARNING OBJECTIVES

Having read this chapter and worked through the questions and activities you should be able:

- to assess the importance of aligning event audiences with sponsors' audiences;
- to examine how events can be developed to 'fit' or be 'sponsor ready';
- to identify the motivations of sponsors and other funding bodies for sponsoring events;
- to examine how sponsors and other funding opportunities can be generated;
- to consider the impact of postmodernism in relation to sponsorship.

In this chapter we will examine what event managers need to consider when looking to source sponsorship and grant funding for an event. The process of understanding how to 'fit' a sponsor to an event property will be explored and in particular the importance of having a detailed understanding of the audiences that come to an event. Having discussed orthodox approaches to acquiring sponsors we will highlight key issues relating to brand tribes and communities from a postmodern perspective.

Developing the correct 'fit' between sponsors and events

The importance of developing a good fit between a sponsor and the property has been highlighted by McDonnell and Moir (2013), who discuss the related concept of congruency. So what do these terms mean? Both fit and congruency are closely related to that of 'match up' in celebrity endorsement. Olson and Thjømøe (2011) see the terms fit, match up, congruence, similarity, relevance and relatedness as more or less interchangeable. So we can take it that 'fit' is essentially the similarity or the logic of association between a sponsor and an event. In their comprehensive study Olson and Thjømøe (2011) found that a sense of fit is based on a variety of factors, including whether and to what degree a sponsor's products are used by event participants, the match between the sponsors and the event's target audiences, attitudes and geographic location.

In a similar vein, studies such as Escalas and Bettman (2017) on celebrity endorsement of products and services have identified how consumers link their own self-image to that of celebrity endorsed brands and the importance of matching celebrity image with that of a brand. This is supported by Close et al (2009) in a retail context, who suggest that event attendees focus on how the sponsoring retailer fits with their image and sense of self. McDonnell and Moir (2013) highlight Fleck and Quester's (2007) observation that people attend an event for its content, for example sport or music, and the sponsorship aspect of the event is peripheral. While this may be true in many instances, we argue that it is not necessarily the case where brands with strong fit and well thought-out activations can become far more than a peripheral aspect of an event, contributing to a memorable experience (see Chapter 8 – for example the Hendrick's Gin example in the interview with James Tibbetts). That said, being peripheral is often a desirable place to be in the attendees' perception of the event.

The benefits of congruence and fit have been examined by McDonnell and Moir (2013), and these are summarized in Figure 4.1.

Given the potential benefits to events it is vital for an event manager to establish an effective fit between the sponsor and event property. The terms expectancy and relevancy have been highlighted as the most important criteria for establishing a good sponsor/event property fit.

Figure 4.1   The potential benefits of congruence/fit between sponsor and event property

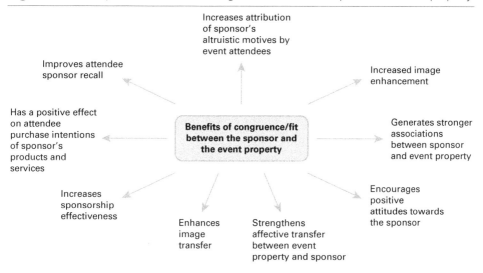

SOURCE Adapted from McDonnell and Moir, 2013: 53

Expectancy is the extent to which the consumer could have predicted a particular brand would be a sponsor of a particular event. This could be due to the theme, programme, audience and location of the event. In a way, expectancy is like a well-chosen piece of clothing that complements a particular fashion style, or a new picture that, when hung on the wall, looks like it's been made to hang in that room.

Relevancy is about the consumer's reaction to, and understanding of, a brand's involvement and message through the event sponsorship. This relates to the logic of association mentioned earlier in this chapter. We could easily conclude from this discussion that the stronger the logic of association between a brand sponsorship and an event, the more positive the impact with the consumer will be. They will be more interested in the sponsor's product or service and more likely to try it and continue to purchase it in the long term. This is true in some cases but there is also a certain illogicality of association too. Where a sponsor's logic of association in the consumer's mind (congruence) is moderate it is more likely to have a positive outcome than a high or low level. This makes sense; we know that a sponsor will need to move from the periphery to the centre of a consumer's consciousness, if only for a short period of time, this can be done through surprise or the unexpected. Why, for example, would a big pharmaceutical company that produces cough sweets sponsor the Sydney Opera House? It's not immediately obvious, but every classical concert-goer fears an outbreak of coughing during a performance (Fleck and Quester, 2007)!

Alongside relevancy and expectancy, McDonnell and Moir (2013) also cite Pentecost and Spence's (2004) criteria of target market, image, geography, typicality, complementarity and clash.

Aligning audiences with sponsors

Skinner and Rukavina (2003) emphasize how important it is for you as the event manager to develop an understanding of the marketing objectives of a potential sponsor and use this understanding to look at your event through the potential sponsor's eyes. To do this successfully the first step is to develop an intimate understanding of the audiences that attend your event. So often, opportunities for audience development through more sophisticated market segmentation are missed. This can result in a failure to grow audiences effectively or, worse, lead to the decline of audience figures and the failure of an event. Anything less than an intimate understanding of an event's audiences will hold back the identification and engagement of sponsors and grant makers.

For both established and start up events, Bowdin *et al* (2011) recommends the event manager and event marketer must to be able to clearly identify and articulate:

- **Audience measurability** – The attributes of an audience segment(s), for example gender, age, socio-economic status, must be accessible by the event marketer from the point of view that they can be measured.

- **Audience size** – The audience segment(s) must be large enough to be worth engaging with.

- **Audience accessibility** – The audience segment must be accessible via integrated marketing communication campaigns.

- **Audience actionability** – Can the audience segment(s) be marketed to given the budget and other resources available to the event marketer?

This is because the process of securing sponsorship and grants is premised on how well event managers are able to match their audiences with potential sponsors and grant makers. Where there is a good match it is likely that the aims and objectives of the potential sponsor will be fulfilled through the event.

Established events and start up events face different challenges when sourcing sponsorship and grant income, but in both situations it is necessary to be clear about the event's audience or potential audience profiles. Kotler and Andreason (2003: 144) suggest a more rigorous approach to the analysis of audience segmentation that features six criteria:

- **Mutual exclusivity** – Is each segment conceptually separate from the others? For example, breaking attendees into past and present might be confusing to an individual who has attended and continues to attend an event.

- **Exhaustiveness** – Is every potential audience member included in a segment? If an audience is to be segmented by household status there will need to be categories to cover relationships like unmarried couples.

- **Measurability** – As with Bowdin *et al* (2011), can the size, motivation, ability to act, etc of the audience segments be measured? Certain audience segments, such as elite, high-income business people, can be hard to measure.

- **Reachability** – Can the audience segments be reached and served? It would be difficult to develop an effective event marketing campaign to transient groups such as international students studying for six months or a year in a different country, especially if the event itself occurs when the students are not being taught on campus.

- **Substantiality** – Again similar to Bowdin *et al* (2011), is the size of the audience segment worth pursuing? It's important to note that size is a combination of number of individuals and their consumption capacity (spend).

- **Differential responsiveness** – While a set of audience segments may meet the above criteria, several or all of them may respond in exactly the same way to marketing campaigns. In such a situation, while conceptually it makes sense to segment the audiences it is not useful to do so from a marketing manager's perspective. Therefore, differential responsiveness may be the most important criterion for audience segmentation.

(Adapted from Kotler and Andreason, 2003)

You should keep in mind that it's often very difficult to answer all of the questions posed by the six criteria above. Data on responsiveness and reachability are hard to collect. One way to address this might be to collect surrogate data, for example segmenting potential customers for a dance exhibition by age and gender, then exhibitors by business type, based on the general assumption that young females are interested in dance; hence businesses that offer dance lessons and apparel will be responsive. Social media channels such as Instagram could be used to reach younger audiences while adverts on dance industry websites and telemarketing campaigns would reach businesses interested in taking exhibition stand space.

At the outset of a new campaign, reachability and responsiveness are always going to be an estimation. However, as a marketing campaign for an event develops, it is vital to experiment and test which segmentation approaches get the best response rates. In this way, over time an event's marketing team can develop a clear picture of the reachability and responsiveness of key segments. Being able to quantify this information will be of considerable value when approaching potential sponsors and grant makers. To be able to say, for example, 'We have a database of 50,000 individuals with the following attributes (eg females aged 18–25, living in South East England) who on average respond to 75 per cent of our email communications by clicking through to our website and purchasing tickets' will be very helpful in persuading a potential sponsor that your event has the right audience profile for them to invest in.

A useful vehicle for segmentation has been developed by Frank *et al* (1972). While this model is nearly 50 years old it remains important as it sets out the two key ways in which segmentation variables have been, and continue to be, categorized: general/behaviour specific variables and objective/inferred measures.

- General variables:
    - Objective measures are those that may be independently observed, such as gender, income and age.
    - Inferred measures are mental states unique to each respondent that need to be deduced from what the respondent says, for example perceptions, beliefs and benefits sought. Well-known methods include PRIZM life stage groups and VALS-2 psychographic segmentation.
- Behaviour specific variables:
    - Objective measures include purchase quantity, brand preference and loyalty.
    - Inferred measures are beliefs, perceptions, benefits/costs/others/self-efficacy (BCOS), and stage in decision.

It is often the case that objective measures are preferred by marketers because it's easy to identify customers by variables like sex and geographic location.

Furthermore, objective measures are not affected by respondents answering in a way that intentionally or unintentionally renders the response inaccurate. Likewise, the composition of a question will not lead to an inaccurate response. Objective measures are widely available census data, etc, and can be applied in different contexts.

At the same time, it's really important not to ignore inferred measures. For inferred general measures these include consumer personality, values and lifestyles (Andreason and Belk, 1980). Inferred behaviour specific measures include: stages of change (Bowen, 1998), benefit segmentation (Li *et al*, 2009) and sacrifice/barrier segmentation (Bagozzi, 1974). Inferred measures can be very useful for event marketers at the start up stage of an event as they can offer a rich picture and narrative of particular audience segments. As Cowan (2012) advises in relation to technology start ups, it is vital to build up a very clear story of an audience type's day – what do they see and do, and at what time of day? What are they feeling at those times as they go about their daily business? By building up vivid characters that clearly communicate audience type lifestyles, personalities and values, then actually going out into the field and seeing if these people exist by talking to them, event marketers can build up a powerful case that a potential sponsor can identify with their own marketing objectives and target markets.

Identifying sponsor motivations

Why do companies and other organizations sponsor events? The obvious answer is to sell more of products or services to a particular target audience. However, there is a range of reasons. The pioneering sponsorship agency IEG (2017) suggest the following motivations:

- **Increase brand loyalty** – There is a considerable amount of research that shows that events and live entertainment have an emotional link with consumers (Martensen *et al*, 2007; Wang and Kaplanidou, 2013; Mida and Zaiem, 2015). Existing customers are a company's most valuable asset; by sponsoring particular events, companies can make an emotional connection with this vital audience that will help to contribute to the longevity of the relationship.

- **Create awareness and visibility** – Events often have significant exposure via both traditional and digital media that would be too expensive to purchase directly via TV and print channels.

- **Change/reinforce image** – Sponsorship can help to build, change or reinforce a brand's image. Sponsorship can be more authentic than advertising or other paid media. As discussed in Chapter 2, consumer experiences in today's (post) modern society can take on the role of sacred rituals that by their nature are imbued with a high level of authenticity.

- **Drive retail traffic** – Sponsors can design very effective promotions that encourage potential consumers to visit either physical stores or websites. For example, tickets to an event can have the sponsor's logo printed on them. After the event ticket holders can then take their ticket stub to the sponsor's retail outlets and get a discount or other reward.

- **Showcase community responsibility** – Well-focused sponsorships that deliver tangible benefits to communities can have significant impact. Sponsors who are able to demonstrate integrity through corporate social responsibility will have a very positive impact on consumer impressions of their brand.

- **Drive sales** – Brands sponsoring an event should encourage retailers of the brand's products/services to give them greater prominence. This could be through increasing the number of product displays in stores and/or participation in cooperative advertising (where distributors and manufacturers share the cost of advertising).

- **Sample/display brand attributes** – Unlike traditional communication channels, sponsorship allows potential customers the chance to actually try out a product for themselves. Well-designed brand activations can make a very significant contribution to maximizing the overall success of a sponsorship campaign.

- **Entertain clients** – This can be a very important part of an event sponsorship package. Both existing and potential clients can be invited to enjoy corporate hospitality at an event such as a rugby match or classical music festival. The needs of existing clients can be understood better and stronger relationships generated, which may lead to increased business or longer client relationships. At the same time, prospective clients can be entertained and introduced to satisfied customers – what better way to convince a potential client that they should sign a contract with your company than by hearing how satisfied some of your existing customers are?

- **Narrowcasting** – Sponsorship allows companies and organizations to focus on specific niche markets.

- **Recruit/retain employees** – Companies can use sponsorships of events to offer their staff free access to art exhibitions and other prestigious events.

- **Merchandising opportunities** – Linking an event sponsorship to a point of purchase promotion can generate excitement about in-store displays and longevity merchandising programmes. These opportunities can be promoted in the weeks running up to the event.

- **Incentivizing retailers, dealers and distributors** – Often, event sponsors aren't just reaching out to consumers. Competition for shelf space in retail outlets is fierce. Sponsorships can be used to encourage retailers and distributors to give more prominence to particular brands. By offering the opportunity for the winner of a sporting event to appear at their flagship store, sponsors can incentivize retailers to give their products greater prominence. Similarly, offering tickets for in-store displays can be a useful incentive.

- **Differentiating from competitors** – Some services, such as banking, can take the properties of their sponsorship arrangement and use them as a foundation for differentiation from competitors offering similar services.

- **Combating larger advertising budgets of competitors** – Sponsorship of events can be highly cost effective and allow smaller companies to compete with larger competitors.

It's important to realize that a sponsor may be looking to meet several of these objectives in one event.

Getting an event 'sponsor ready': layers of sponsorship

Before attempting to source sponsors for an event it's important to ensure that the portfolio of sponsorship opportunities are clearly identified and valued. To do this, an event manager needs to set out the levels of sponsorship that are available. O'Toole (2011: 181) suggests five categories: naming sponsor, programme sponsor, co-sponsor, media sponsor and in-kind sponsor. Some examples of each of these sponsorship categories are set out below.

Naming sponsor

A naming sponsorship entitles the sponsor to incorporate their name and/or logo in the title of the event. The variety of naming sponsors in, for example, events in the World Surf League (WSL) include the Drug Aware Margaret River Pro, where the naming sponsor Drug Aware is an agency funded by the state of Western Australia that develops educational strategies designed to address illicit drug use among young people in the state. Another example from the WSL is the Outerknown Fiji Pro; Outerknown is a sustainable surf clothing brand that produces great looking menswear in a sustainable way.

Programme sponsor and co-sponsors

Programme sponsors and co-sponsors are entitled to invest in part of the event programme, for example the corporate hospitality or an area of the venue. At the Royal Horticultural Society's Chelsea Flower Show in London some of the show gardens are sponsored by major banks and other organizations. For example, in 2017 Visit Yorkshire sponsored a garden called 'The Welcome to Yorkshire Garden'.

Media sponsor

Media sponsorship takes place where an event needs help with promotion, especially when the objective is high-profile promotion in major newspapers, or on television and radio networks with large local and regional audiences. A media sponsor should provide a combination of free promotions, and free/discounted advertising space. In return, the event will provide the media sponsor with visibility (eg a banner or booth at the event, logo recognition in print materials and on websites) and priority access to celebrity interviews, backstage passes, or other benefits that will not be offered to other media organizations.

In-kind sponsor

In-kind sponsorship is sometimes called contra sponsorship and involves an organization providing products or services to an event. So media sponsorship can be seen as a form of in-kind sponsorship. Another example would be the provision at a conference of touch screens to display social media.

Applying sponsorship layers

While it may seem more straightforward to secure a single naming sponsorship, the creation of layers of sponsorship has the important benefit of mitigating the risk of sponsors pulling out. If there's only one sponsor and they pull out it may have a disastrous effect on the event's future. So in most cases it's better to aim for several sponsors at differing levels that have rights to discrete parts of the event. To this end the event manager should compile a list of the event's assets, which could include merchandising rights, hospitality and signage along with many others.

In their examination of preparing an event to be sponsor ready, Bowdin *et al* (2011) discuss two approaches to sponsorship portfolios: tiered and tailor-made approaches. Tiered portfolios offer a hierarchy or pyramid of benefits. At the top is the most expensive level, sometimes called a gold or platinum package, that offers the premium benefits. Less expensive silver and bronze packages are also offered that confer fewer benefits. The alternative is to offer tailored packages that are grouped under broad headings such as naming rights or team sponsor. Further attributes can then be purchased according to a particular sponsor's preference.

Bowdin *et al* (2011) recommend the use of bespoke or tailored sponsorship packages and cite Welsh (2003) who recommends individualized sponsorship solutions for the following reasons:

- Tiered sponsorship portfolios with predetermined benefits are unlikely to meet a sponsor's exact needs.

- Sponsors want more control over how they leverage their sponsorships.

- Poor sponsorship portfolio management by event managers may lead to ambush marketing where brands that haven't paid to sponsor the event are able to pass themselves off as sponsors.

- Multiple layers of sponsorship can be contradictory and confusing to event audiences (see Research insight 3 below).

A flexible approach to sponsorship is certainly the best course of action. However, it is important to have a clear framework in place that defines what is available to be sponsored and its cost.

In fundraising it's important to give sponsors, grant makers and other philanthropists a range of opportunities to support an event to a greater or lesser degree. By providing a 'shopping list' of different opportunities – naming rights, website advertising, stage sponsorship, etc – that cost different amounts, the prospective funder is given a choice, which makes it more likely that they will respond positively.

Research insight 3: be careful which portfolio you get into...

Many events have a portfolio of sponsors. Cobbs *et al* (2015) ask, 'What effect, if any, do the other sponsors of this event have on your sponsoring brand?' The authors advise marketing managers who are considering sponsoring a property to look carefully at the other sponsors in the portfolio and assess the number of sponsors and their congruency to the event property. The advice is to ensure brand clarity and distinctiveness; potential sponsors should avoid small portfolios with congruent sponsors and look for events with either a small portfolio of incongruent sponsors or a large portfolio of congruent sponsors.

Cobbs, J, Groza, M and Rich, G (2015) Brand spillover effects within a sponsor portfolio: The interaction of image congruence and portfolio size, *Marketing Management Journal*, **25** (2), pp 107–22

Identifying a sponsor or grant-maker 'universe'

There are several approaches to identifying a 'universe' of organizations that will potentially be interested in sponsoring or funding an event. When prospecting for sponsors, event managers will do well to be familiar with the event's stakeholders. Suppliers in particular may be receptive to sponsoring part of the event through in-kind sponsorship, which is less risky for an organization. Once in-kind sponsors have been sourced they can then be asked to provide endorsements to support approaches to other potential sponsors.

Sometimes an organization will create an event that aims to achieve a particular objective, such as building a brand or energizing employees. There are different approaches here. Typically event managers working for an experiential agency or in house will be asked to develop an event concept and then deliver the event itself. In other situations they might be required to use entrepreneurial skills to identify particular groups with a particular problem or need that a new event can help to meet. On these occasions, using tools and methods from business start up planners, such as Osterwalder and Pigneur's (2010) business model canvas, is a sound approach. Understanding different patterns of business models is important. In particular, multi-sided platforms can be defined as bringing together:

> two or more distinct but interdependent groups of customers. Such platforms are of value to one group of customers only if the other groups of customers are also present. The platform creates value by facilitating interactions between

the different groups. A multi-sided platform grows in value to the extent that it attracts more users, a phenomenon known as the network effect.

(Osterwalder and Pigneur, 2010: 77)

A good example of a multi-sided platform is exhibitions (shows). The exhibition industry covers both business to business and business to consumer shows and includes food festivals, home improvement, dance, cycling and many more. Exhibition managers identify groups of businesses through trade directories in a particular sector. They also estimate the number of consumers that will be attracted to visit the exhibition (show). If the numbers of potential exhibitors and visitors suggest the show is viable then a venue is provisionally booked and the sales teams will start to contact businesses with a view to selling space at the show. The shows themselves, if successful, can become attractive sponsorship opportunities.

It is difficult for new events to attract sponsors unless the sponsor has commissioned the event. So event managers should not rely on sponsorship to deliver the financial viability of an event in the start up stages. If possible, multiple income streams should be developed so that if a sponsorship deal doesn't come through or is not renewed the event's existence is not jeopardized.

For new, start up events O'Toole (2011) identifies the problem that sponsors won't commit to an event until they see other sponsors have done so. To break through this cycle of who will sponsor first, O'Toole (2011: 182) suggests that endorsement from celebrities or political leaders can help to develop a sense of stability and confidence around a new event that will facilitate sponsorship. However, event managers should not rely on such endorsements to deliver sponsors. A strong business plan and an event that has been running successfully for two or three years is a much more attractive proposition for both grant makers and commercial sponsors.

Fragmentation of audiences and the rise of postmodern marketing

So far this chapter has set out a relatively conventional approach to the acquisition of sponsors through such methods as market segmentation, understanding sponsors' motivations and the multi-sided business platform. You may have noticed that several sources were drawn on, some of which are several decades old. This section deals with more recent developments in consumer behaviour that may have significant implications for how events marketers approach audiences, and consequently how sponsors engage with target audiences.

We have already touched on some of these issues in Chapter 2 in relation authenticity and in particular 'hyperreality' (Baudrillard, 1994). Hyperreality is, according to Firat and Shultz (1997), one aspect of the postmodern condition that is summarized as follows:

- **Openness/tolerance** – Acceptance of difference (different styles, ways of being and living) without prejudice or evaluations of superiority and inferiority.

- **Hyperreality** – Constitution of social reality through hype or simulation that is powerfully signified and represented.

- **Perpetual present** – Cultural propensity to experience everything (including the past and future) in the present, 'here and now'.

- **Paradoxical juxtapositions** – Cultural propensity to juxtapose anything with anything else, including oppositional, contradictory and essentially unrelated elements.

- **Fragmentation** – Omnipresence of disjointed and disconnected moments and experiences in life and sense of self – and the growing acceptance of the dynamism that leads to fragmentation in markets.

- **Loss of commitment** – Growing cultural unwillingness to commit to any single idea, project or grand design.

- **Decentring of the subject** – Removal of the human being from the central importance she or he held in modern culture – and the increasing acceptance of the potentials of his/her objectification.

- **Reversal of consumption and production** – Cultural acknowledgement that value is created not in production (as posited by modern thought) but in consumption – and the subsequent growth of attention and importance given to consumption.

- **Emphasis on form/style** – Growing influence of form and style (as opposed to content) in determining meaning and life.

- **Acceptance of disorder/chaos** – Cultural acknowledgement that rather than order, crises and disequilibria are the common states of existence – and the subsequent acceptance and appreciation of this condition.

(Firat and Shultz, 1997: 186)

A postmodern reading of marketing raises several factors that are important for event marketers and sponsors. Of central importance is the role of
narratives or stories created by groups to create meaning and reality. The
philosopher Lyotard (1984) defines postmodernism as incredulity at meta-
narratives. By this he meant that today people are no longer prepared to believe
or sign up to ideas, doctrines or faiths that claim to have all the answers.
There are several implications of this for marketing and consumer behaviour:

- Consumers are increasingly fickle, making it almost impossible to predict
  or categorize behaviour over a significant period of time (Gabriel and
  Lang, 2008).

- Advances in technology, in particular Web 2.0, have led consumers to form
  communities that are significantly empowered in their relationships with
  brands. This has led not only to collaboration with brands but also to
  unexpected and unwanted outcomes from the brand manager's perspective
  (Cova and White, 2010).

Events can act as an important medium for brands to positively engage with
what Gabriel and Lang (2008) have called 'The Unmanageable Consumer',
who has become increasingly hardened to conventional marketing channels,
which are increasingly saturated. Sponsorship of an event has been researched
from the perspective of image transfer from event to brand (Gwinner, 1997)
and cognitive and affective perceptions from the sponsored entity to the
sponsor (Ganassali and Didellon, 1996). More recently, Vila-López and
Rodríguez-Molina (2013) have shown the importance of attendee immersion
in an event through participation in a brand experience, which can then lead
to a positive impact on brand personality and brand reputation.

It is important to sponsors that consumers are willing to get involved in
events that are associated with a particular community (McAlexander *et al*,
2003). Using a postmodern marketing framework, Simmons (2008) identifies
the complex relationship between individual and communal brand experiences, and demonstrates that the postmodern consumer is searching for social
bonds and community through what he calls 'neo-tribalism'. The internet is
identified as the main driver for the creation of neo-tribes – communities
that will enable marketers to deal with the increasingly fragmented nature of
society. However, the enduring popularity of sporting events, music festivals,
conferences and exhibitions suggests that real, embodied events and experiences are equally, if not more, important to the sustenance of both individuals

and communities. The importance of the virtual/real nexus is highlighted by Hakala *et al* (2017), who observed how the craft beer maker Brewdog's online community contributed to the choice of location for a new public house. The Brewdog example shows how tangible offline outcomes such as events can come from online communities that give agency to consumers and legitimacy to brands.

The factors outlined above are fundamental to the rationale that underpins event sponsorship. However, we suggest that rather than constructing consumers as isolated individuals who self-consciously consume products for utilitarian outcomes sponsors will find it more productive to recognize the nature of social relationships formed by consumers as emotional and hedonistic. The social relationships result in marketplace cultures – groups of consumers that interact with brands, often at the events they attend. In this way we suggest that sponsorship campaigns that are sensitive to the dynamics of social relationships will be more successful in building brand loyalty.

Consumption communities, brand communities and brand tribes – powerful, double-edged phenomena for sponsors

In their ethnographic and quantitative research McAlexander *et al* (2002) examined how the brands Jeep and Harley Davidson use events to develop relationships with consumers in brand communities. A key finding is that brands using these methods are redefining the terms of competitive advantage by focusing on the experience of ownership and consumption. The value of such events to consumers is that they can experience both anticipated and unanticipated benefits of the products they own. This can be done either by interactions with other more experienced consumers of the brand or from marketers. At Camp Jeep, McAlexander *et al* (2002) observed how experienced off-road drivers met up with those who'd never taken their Jeep off the road before. There were barbecues and round table discussions, and marketers helped to create a sense of community by facilitating a sense of belonging. Interaction with brand ambassadors allows consumers to experience first hand how the company operates, how much its employees care about the brand and its authenticity and wish to share it in their 'community'. For consumer/marketer relationships to flourish, it's vital that marketers don't see consumer relationships as one way. For the relationship at an event to become valuable there must be reciprocity that ultimately leads to consumers recognizing that far from being just sold to, they are getting more from the event in terms of education, experiences and entertainment than the costs involved in attending.

Discussion of the facilitation of consumer tribes has evolved from a focus on how they can be used to leverage brands to how they form and are used strategically (McAlexander *et al*, 2002, Goulding *et al*, 2013). Importantly, Goulding *et al* (2013) differentiate between brand communities – groups that focus activities and relationships around a particular brand, and consumer tribes where members identify with one another, share experiences and emotions and socialize together using a range of brands, products, activities and services (Cova and Cova, 2002).

Goulding *et al* (2013) suggest that insights from communities of practice (CoP) theory (Lave and Wenger, 1997; Wenger, 2000) can be applied in brand tribe contexts. For example, they use Wenger's (2000) dimensions of engagement, alignment and imagination, suggesting they are central to the creation and sustaining of consumer tribes. Using this approach to brand tribes allows for their unmanageable and playful characteristics by placing a brand as part of the process of learning to be part of the tribe. This may be through the provision of physical spaces, virtual platforms, social learning and fashion trends.

At the same time, social marketing in consumer tribes is not necessarily a straightforward, risk-free endeavour. Cova and White (2010) highlight the ascendance of brand community management over other tribal marketing approaches and attribute this in no small part to the advent of Web 2.0. A particularly good example of successful brand community marketing strategy is the motorcycle brand Ducati:

> On the one hand, staff members consume brand products; on the other, consumers can be transformed into producers of events, ideas, and even brand accessories. Thus Ducati and the Ducatists represent a classic example of how brand communities provide a favourable context for the emergence of consumer-producers who can become true partners of the company.
>
> (Cova and White, 2010: 258)

Chapter 2 introduced the concept of co-creation. This is an important factor to consider when securing sponsors and identifying other funding opportunities and the nature of the relationships that will be engendered. There are several reasons for this, and in particular the potential for counter- and alter-brand communities to emerge. Cova and White (2010) suggest that where consumers feel exploited a counter-brand will emerge, and where a brand does not meet all their needs an alter-brand can result.

In this way, when looking to secure a sponsor or other funding for an event, it is an important part of the pitch to alert sponsors to these potential outcomes and offer sponsorship packages that avoid dominating the event. As Kjeldgaard and Bode (2017) observe, it is better for sponsors to engage with playfulness and uncertainty as an opportunity rather than as something to be overcome. This can mean that a sponsoring brand can be either a central focus or a supporting facilitator of a consumer ritual.

Research insight 4: festivals – where does the money come from?

In this research project Andersson et al (2013) surveyed 260 festival managers from Norway, Australia, Sweden and the UK. In all four countries corporate sponsorship and grant funding were a significant source of income, ranging from approximately 30 per cent to 60 per cent, and on average 45 per cent. The researchers then correlated festival income against a range of variables such as fit, which was identified by: the kind of festival (eg music, arts); festival size (attendance); ownership; and professionalism (the number of staff employed by the festival).

The results showed that art festivals are more likely to receive state/national government grants than other festival types, while corporate sponsors prefer sporting festivals and market festivals. Perhaps the most important finding was that title sponsors are more valuable than having several small sponsors. However, the authors recognize that this may only be relevant to larger festivals. Ownership and festival size also seem to have an important influence, with publicly owned and non-profit festivals doing much better at securing government grants than privately owned festivals. On the other hand, privately owned festivals do better at securing corporate sponsorship. As far as festival size is concerned, there seemed to be little impact, for while large events gain more sponsorship and grants as a proportion of income there is no difference between large and small festivals.

The researchers conclude by making suggestions for future research, including:

- more extensive analysis of the fit between external revenue and festival type;
- the professionalism of staff and the levels of sponsorship received.

Finally, the researchers also made an interesting observation regarding the suggestion that many festivals apply a deliberate strategy of dependence on local government to ensure continued financial support in return for sacrificing some of their independence.

Andersson, T, Getz, D, Mykletun, J, Jæeger, K and Dolles, H (2013) Factors influencing grant and sponsorship revenue for festivals, *Events Management*, **17** (3), pp 195–212

Conclusion

In this chapter we have examined the way in which consumers identify with brands to build their own self-image. For event sponsors, this identity-building process is based on two factors: the degree to which the consumer could have predicted the sponsor would be at the event, and how well the consumer understands the sponsor's presence at the event. Sponsors that understand this delicate balance will sometimes go for a more subtle, tangential approach that involves humour or quirkiness.

To develop successful partnerships that really connect with consumers, event managers and sponsors must have a clear understanding of the consumer that comes to the event. This is achieved through a robust process of market segmentation. Moreover, event managers need to take the sponsor's perspective into account and understand the objectives that the brand is trying to achieve.

While it is important to follow the marketing orthodoxies of segmentation, targeting and positioning, it is also vital to be aware that in an advanced, postmodern consumer society consumers are becoming increasingly fickle and market segments may be fragmenting in a particular sector or industry. One way to push back against these phenomena is for sponsors and event managers to work together on building activities, interactive features and content that build communities around their events and brands. In Chapter 5 we will examine how this is done in relation to cycling events.

Discussion questions and activities

1 Take a look at the websites for The Cycle Show (www.cycleshow.co.uk) and The Knitting and Stitching Show (www.theknittingandstitchingshow.com). Looking under the 'exhibitor' tab, bring up the 'exhibitor information' and 'sponsor information' pages and download the exhibitor/sponsor sales pack. List the

different segment types according to general variables (objective/inferred) or behaviour specific variables (objective/inferred).

2   One way to convince new exhibitors to pay to exhibit would be to give the return on investment per square metre. Why might this information be difficult to collect?

3   Sponsorship can be a paid for in cash, but often a significant amount of value delivered by sponsors is through the gifts in-kind and features they contribute to a show. Develop a feature (brand activation) for The Cycle Show and The Knitting and Stitching Show.

Further reading

Cova, B and White, T (2010) Counter-brand and alter-brand communities: The impact of Web 2.0 on tribal marketing approaches, *Journal of Marketing Management*, **26** (3–4), pp 256–70

This research paper does not focus specifically on sponsorship but it does cover important developments in theory relating to brand tribes and communities. In particular, it is important for event managers and sponsors to understand the identification of groups of consumers that oppose and contest how their favourite brands are managed, in relation to their own practices.

Gwinner, K (1997) A model of image creation and image transfer in event sponsorship, *International Marketing Review*, **14** (3), pp 145–58

While this research paper is over 20 years old it is important as it sets out the similarities between the process of celebrity endorsement of products and event image associations transferring to sponsoring brands.

International Events Group (IEG) (2017) *IEG's Guide to Sponsorship* [Online] www.sponsorship.com/IEG/files/59/59ada496-cd2c-4ac2-9382-060d86fcbdc4.pdf

This comprehensive guide covers a wide range of important topics, including why companies sponsor, deal making and leveraging sponsorship, best practice and why sponsorships fail.

Wang, RT and Kaplanidou, K (2013) I want to buy more because I feel good: The effect of sport-induced emotion on sponsorship, *International Journal of Sports Marketing and Sponsorship*, **15** (1), pp 52–66

This important research paper examines how spectators' emotions relate to their attitudes towards sponsors. This is particularly important considering that in sport there is always a winning and a losing side, so sponsors need to be able to appeal to spectators who are experiencing both positive and negative emotions.

References

Andersson, T, Getz, D, Mykletun, J, Jæeger, K and Dolles, H (2013) Factors influencing grant and sponsorship revenue for festivals, *Events Management*, **17** (3), pp 195–212

Andreason, A and Belk, R (1980) Predictors of attendance at the performing arts, *Journal of Consumer Research*, 7 (2), pp 112–20

Bagozzi, RP (1974) Marketing as an organized behavioral system of exchange, *Journal of Marketing*, **38** (4), pp 77–81

Baudrillard, J (1994) *Simulacra and Simulation*, University of Michigan Press, Ann Arbor

Bowen, JT (1998) Market segmentation in hospitality research: No longer a sequential process, *International Journal of Contemporary Hospitality Management*, **10** (7), pp 289–96

Bowdin, G, Allen, J and Harris, R (2011) *Events Management*, 3rd edn, Butterworth-Heinemann, Oxford

Close, A, Krishen, A and Latour, M (2009) This event is me! How consumer event self-congruity leverages sponsorship, *Journal of Advertising Research*, **49** (3), pp 271–84

Cobbs, J, Groza, M and Rich, G (2015) Brand spillover effects within a sponsor portfolio: The interaction of image congruence and portfolio size, *Marketing Management Journal*, **25** (2), pp 107–22

Cova, B and Cova, V (2002) Tribal marketing: The tribalisation of society and its impact on the conduct of marketing, *European Journal of Marketing*, **36** (5/6), pp 595–620

Cova, B and White, T (2010) Counter-brand and alter-brand communities: The impact of Web 2.0 on tribal marketing approaches, *Journal of Marketing Management*, **26** (3–4), pp 256–70

Cowan, A (2012) *Starting a Tech Business: A practical guide for anyone creating or designing applications or software*, Wiley, Hoboken, New Jersey

Escalas, JE and Bettman, JR (2017) Connecting with celebrities: How consumers appropriate celebrity meanings for a sense of belonging, *Journal of Advertising*, **46** (2), pp 297–308

Firat, F and Shultz II, C (1997) From segmentation to fragmentation: Markets and marketing strategy in the postmodern era, *European Journal of Marketing*, **31** (3/4), pp 183–207

Fleck, ND and Quester, P (2007) Birds of a feather flock together... definition, role and measure of congruence: An application to sponsorship, *Psychology and Marketing*, **24** (11), pp 975–1000

Frank, R, Massey, W and Wind, Y (1972) *Market Segmentation*, Prentice Hall, Upper Saddle River, NJ

Gabriel, Y and Lang, T (2008) New faces and new masks of today's consumer, *Journal of Consumer Culture*, **8** (3), pp 321–40

Ganassali, S and Didellon, L (1996) Le transfert comme principe central du parrainage, *Recherche et Applications en Marketing*, **11** (1), pp 37–48

Goulding, C, Canniford, R and Shankar, A (2013) Learning to be tribal: Facilitating the formation of consumer tribes, *European Journal of Marketing*, **47** (5/6), pp 813–32

Gwinner, K (1997) A model of image creation and image transfer in event sponsorship, *International Marketing Review*, **14** (3), pp 145–58

Hakala, H, Nummelin, L and Kohtamäki, M (2017) Online brand community practices and the construction of brand legitimacy, *Marketing Theory*, **17** (4), pp 537–58

International Events Group (IEG) (2017) *IEG's Guide to Sponsorship* [Online] www.sponsorship.com/IEG/files/59/59ada496-cd2c-4ac2-9382-060d86fcbdc4.pdf [Accessed 25/01/17]

Kjeldgaard, D and Bode, M (2017) Broadening the brandfest: Play and ludic agency, *European Journal of Marketing*, **51** (1), pp 23–43

Kotler, P and Andreason, A (2003) *Strategic Marketing for Nonprofit Organizations*, 6th edn, Prentice Hall, Upper Saddle River, NJ

Lave, J and Wenger, E (1997) *Situated Learning: Legitimate peripheral participation*, Cambridge University Press, Cambridge

Li, M, Huang, Z and Cai, LA (2009) Benefit segmentation of visitors to a rural community-based festival, *Journal of Travel & Tourism Marketing*, **26** (5–6), pp 585–98

Lyotard, J-F (1984) *The Postmodern Condition: A report on knowledge*, trans G Bennington and B Massumi, Manchester University Press, Manchester

McAlexander, JH, Schouten, JW and Koenig, HF (2002) Building brand community, *Journal of Marketing*, **66** (1), pp 38–54

McAlexander, JH, Kim, SK and Roberts, SD (2003) Loyalty: The influences of satisfaction and brand community integration, *Journal of Marketing Theory and Practice*, **11** (4), pp 1–11

McDonnell, A and Moir, M (2013) *Event Sponsorship,* Routledge, London

Martensen, A, Grønholdt, L, Bendtsen, L and Juul Jensen, M (2007) Application of a model for the effectiveness of event marketing, *Journal of Advertising Research*, **47** (3), pp 283–301

Mida, F and Zaiem, I (2015) Emotion and sponsorship: Case of television sponsorship, *International Journal of Management, Accounting & Economics*, **2** (4), pp 325–38

Olson, E and Thjømøe, H (2011) Explaining and articulating the fit construct in sponsorship, *Journal of Advertising*, **40** (1), pp 57–70

Osterwalder, A and Pigneur, Y (2010) *Business Model Generation: A handbook for visionaries, game changers, and challengers*, Wiley, Hoboken, NJ

O'Toole, W (2011) *Events Feasibility and Development: From strategy to operations*, Butterworth-Heinemann, London

Pentecost, R and Spence, M (2004) Exploring the dimensions of fit within sports sponsorship, *ANZMAC 2004 Marketing Accountabilities and Responsibilities*, ANZMAC

Simmons, G (2008) Marketing to postmodern consumers: Introducing the internet chameleon, *European Journal of Marketing*, **42** (3/4), pp 299–310

Skinner, BE and Rukavina, V (2003) *Event Sponsorship*, Wiley, Hoboken, NJ

Vila-López, N and Rodríguez-Molina, M (2013) Event–brand transfer in an entertainment service: Experiential marketing, *Industrial Management & Data Systems*, **113** (5), pp 712–31

Wang, RT and Kaplanidou, K (2013) I want to buy more because I feel good: The effect of sport-induced emotion on sponsorship, *International Journal of Sports Marketing and Sponsorship*, **15** (1), pp 52–66

Welsh, J (2003) Reinventing sponsorship [Online] https://jcwelsh.wordpress.com/2010/03/11/reinventing-sponsorship/ [Accessed 24/05/17]

Wenger, E (2000) Communities of practice and social learning systems, *Organization*, 7 (2), pp 225–246. doi: 10.1177/135050840072002

Prospecting for grant funding and sponsorship

Case studies from Scottish cycling events

05

LEARNING OBJECTIVES

Having read this chapter and worked through the questions and activities you should be able:

- to examine how sponsorship and other funding opportunities can be generated;
- to analyse the statutory funding organizations for a particular region or country;
- to evaluate an event from a commercial perspective, with a view to creating sponsorship activations and other opportunities;
- to determine the dynamics between sponsors in a portfolio arrangement.

Introduction

In Chapter 4 we examined how event managers can identify funding and sponsorship opportunities. Chapter 5 builds on the theoretical perspectives and develops a case study on how statutory (government) event funding works in Scotland. The Scottish funding model is based on a national event strategy that is one of the most well thought out in the world.

Following the case study we turn to the commercial sports sponsorship sector, and cycling in particular. James Pearce offers us his insights into how to commercialize an event through sponsorship and other forms of funding.

CASE STUDY 3 Identifying sources of funding in Scotland

EventScotland is part of VisitScotland, the national tourist body for Scotland. EventScotland works to make Scotland 'the perfect stage for events' (EventScotland, no date a). This is achieved through funding a portfolio of sporting and cultural events that raise the country's international profile and generate income to the economy by attracting increased numbers of visitors. EventScotland was established in 2003 and in its first 10 years supported over 1,000 events. Some of the highlights include the Wickerman Festival, and the Open Championship.

The Wickerman Festival in Dundrennan, Dumfries and Galloway started as a local festival. EventScotland began funding support in 2004, and since then it has grown into a major event attracting over 18,000 people and selling out in 2013. Over that period £240,000 was invested in the event, which is now part of the International Events Programme in Scotland.

The Open Championship is Scotland's premier golfing championship. In 2005 EventScotland became a partner with the Royal and Ancient Golf Club of St Andrews (R&A). Over the next eight years EventScotland invested on average £193,000 per annum in the Open Championship tournament. This investment has seen significant returns, with the 2010 tournament generating £47.4 million in economic benefit. EventScotland has worked closely with a variety of organizations including Scottish Enterprise and Fife, South Ayrshire, Angus and East Lothian councils to ensure that the benefits of the Open Championship were maximized in the communities hosting the event.

In 2017 EventScotland invested £5.4 million and generated £113 million from events in Scotland. There were many highlights, including the celebrations around Edinburgh's 70th anniversary as a Festival City. Since 1947 it has played host to the Edinburgh International Festival, the Edinburgh Festival Fringe and the Edinburgh International Film Festival (EventScotland, 2017).

Sources of funding in Scotland

There are three levels of event funding available in Scotland.

Level 1: EventScotland funded programmes

The National Events Programme supports events that take place outside Glasgow and Edinburgh. The programme supports the delivery of the national events strategy, Scotland the Perfect Stage, and is designed to support public facing sporting and cultural events. The objectives of the programme are: to generate economic benefits for specific regions of Scotland and for Scotland as a whole; to attract visitors to specific regions of Scotland; to enhance the profile and appeal of the host region; and to inspire and involve local communities. There are three opportunities to bid for funding each year. The programme does not support core funding (eg salaries, offices/equipment and other direct expenses of day-to-day work) and is designed to support additional elements of an existing event, or new activities with a view to growing events. A maximum of three awards may be granted to any event.

The International Events Programme supports events that generate substantial economic benefits and significant international media coverage, and enhance Scotland's potential to host other major events in the future. Applications can be made at any time of the year. Applicants to the International Events Programme are advised to ask themselves the following:

1 Does your event have potential to contribute to the delivery of Scotland's national events strategy, Scotland The Perfect Stage?

2 Will your event bring a significant number of spectators/participants to Scotland?

3 Will your event provide significant international media coverage of Scotland?

4 Will your event provide an economic return on investment through additional visitor spending?

5 Will your event leave a sustainable legacy for Scotland?

(EventScotland, no date b)

The Beacon Events Programme funds events that have previously received support through the National or International Events Programmes and is for events that are unique to Scotland, generate tourism benefits and act as examples of best practice.

Launched in 2014, the Scottish Clan Fund provides support for legally recognized Clans and Clan Societies wishing to start new or develop existing activities that will grow Clan events and involve local communities. The rationale behind this fund is the market in ancestral tourism in Scotland. Each year hundreds of thousands of people from around the world visit Scotland to explore where they came from. The Fund supported 16 events in 2017, Scotland's Year of History, Heritage and Archaeology, and 11 events in 2018.

Scotland's Winter Festivals is an event programme that contributes to the celebration of Scotland's three national days: St Andrew's Day, Hogmanay and Burns Night. In 2016–17 the programme supported 24 events in 15 local authority areas, which were attended by over 300,000 people. Events included: Glasgow's St Andrew's Day Torchlight Festival; Red, Red Rose Street; and Irvine Harbour's Festival of Light.

Themed years were started in 2009. In 2018, for example, the theme was Year of Young People. EventScotland launched an Open Event Fund and invited the events and festivals sector in Scotland to put in proposals for both new and existing evens that would celebrate the talent and achievements of young people in Scotland. As part of the funding available, Create18 gave young people aged 8–26 the opportunity to develop and put on innovative events in their community. Applications could be made for between £250–£1,000 per event.

Themed years have already been set out for 2020 (The Year of Scotland's Coasts and Waters) and 2022 (The Year of Scotland's Stories).

Level 2: local authorities

Local authorities can provide financial and in-kind support for a range of events. At the time of writing there are 32 local authorities in Scotland. EventScotland advises fundraisers to identify the council's event, sport or culture officer in the first instance to discuss what opportunities are available.

Level 3: other sources of funding, including general, sport and cultural areas

There is a range of organizations and funding bodies that could offer either financial or in-kind assistance. These include:

- The Voluntary Action Fund supports a wide range of local and national voluntary organizations that aim to build safe communities and reduce social disadvantage and inequality.
- The Big Lottery Fund makes grants to support projects that help improve people's lives in their local communities.
- Highlands and Islands Enterprise provides funds for events that support businesses, social enterprises and communities.
- Historic Environment Scotland provides support to non-recurring heritage-related events.
- Sport Scotland has three branches: SportsMatch, which matches commercial sponsorships on a pound for pound basis; Awards For All is a Lottery programme for small community groups looking for small sums of money; and the Sports Facilities Fund offers funding of up to £500,000.
- Creative Scotland allocates funds on behalf of the National Lottery for a range of activities in the arts, screen or creative industries. Over the years it has provided significant funding for events. For example, in 2014–15 it awarded Edinburgh Art Festival £80,000, the Glasgow International Festival £75,000 and Luminate £175,000.

Case study questions

1 Consider Northern Ireland, Wales and England or another country of your choice. Can you find a similar event body to EventScotland that is working to deliver a country-wide event strategy?

2 Pick a local authority in the UK (use this list: https://www.gov.uk/government/uploads/ system/uploads/attachment_data/file/491463/List_of_councils_in_England.pdf). Research that local authority's website for funding opportunities.

3 Go to the Supported Events page on the EventScotland website (http://www. eventscotland.org/events/). Categorize the events (eg sport, music) and consider the target audience each event is aimed at. Discuss how well balanced the event portfolio EventScotland supports is.

Professional insight 3: the Nocturne cycle event and the Rapha cycling brand – interview with James Pearce, Head of Commercial at the Face Partnership

James Pearce has worked in sports marketing and sponsorship for many years, first at the Sports Marketing Agency in the commercial rights division where he secured sponsorship for England Cricket, the Lawn Tennis Association, British Music, Tough Mudder and other sports' governing bodies. Currently he is at the Face Partnership, which specializes in sports cycling events.

Tell me about the events the Face Partnership organizes

Face has two flagship events that we own, run and commercialize. The Revolution Series is Face's first event and has been going for about 15 years. Sir David Brailsford (formerly Performance Director of British Cycling and currently General Manager of Team Sky) challenged our founders to come up with a platform to develop British track cycling talent, and Revolution was born out of that. Over the years it's grown into an elite cycling league, the only elite cycling league in the world. The Future Stars programme is integral to the event and when you look though our Future Stars alumni we're lucky to be able to boast multiple Olympic Gold medallists, the likes of Laura Kenny, Jason Kenny, Owain Doull, Ed Clancy and Pete Kennaugh, and luckily enough they come back and ride as elite riders now and are able to mentor the Future Stars of tomorrow. We are gradually expanding that event. Currently there are three events coming up in the UK – one in London, one in Glasgow and one in Manchester. We've also got enquiries from velodromes in Australia and the Tissot velodrome in Geneva about potentially expanding the events internationally and them taking control of one of our champions league rounds.

You talked about commercializing – how does that work with an event like Revolution?

It's not the easiest job in the world to commercialize track cycling. A lot of people probably see track cycling as something that comes around every four years at the

Olympics. People get very excited about it in that context, but for us to make it an attractive proposition we have to innovate in terms of the format. We have to make sure there's a packed race schedule, so when you come to one of our events an evening session will typically have between 15 and 18 races across a two-and-a-half hour period, which isn't the easiest to run but it keeps the crowd on their feet. We constantly try to bring in and talk to the riders about what races they found exciting to ride in and what they think the crowd will find exciting to watch, to see if there are different spins we can add. That isn't necessarily what they'd do in a Union Cycliste Internationale sanctioned race or a British Cycling race. Then we try to take them on board. Other things we've done in the past to try to innovate is put microphones on some of the riders and on-board cameras. The on-board microphones are very interesting because a lot of people don't realize that the riders are extremely vocal during the race, and not all of it is family friendly sometimes! It's really interesting to hear how they are talking to each other constantly about who's going to attack, who's going to pick what line. Stuff like that's really interesting to the crowd.

So in terms of commercializing it we take a step back and identify what we think are the key areas that are attractive to sponsors. The obvious area is the branding side of things so we have the trackside perimeter boards, which are picked up in the TV coverage, and it's also very obvious for the people who are in house as well. The other big branding pieces are the track safety zone, which allows us to create a vinyl 3–5 metres high, so in terms of visual impact it's huge and that gets a lot of

Figure 5.1   The start of the Brompton race at the Nocturne – Rapha trackside branding is clearly visible

SOURCE The FACE Partnership

TV coverage and is the biggest piece of inventory we have available to us, and then there's also the big screens where the sponsors can either just put their logo up, or if they have a 30 second video clip they are able to show that there too.

We also commercialize the event by splitting it up into hospitality and tickets. The digital side of things is extremely important to brands at the moment. Again, we look to innovate. Last year we started working with a company called Grabyo, where you effectively plug the live feed into this piece of software and it gives you the ability to clip certain parts of the footage, so if there's been an exciting part of the race you can clip, top and tail that piece of footage and then put sponsorship messaging at the top of it and a sponsor logo at the end. We used it very effectively last year with Brother as they were our official results partner. So when it was a particularly close finish to a race we top-and-tailed 30 seconds to a minute of the last bits of the race and it was powered by Brother.

So the three main income streams are sponsorship, corporate hospitality and tickets for these kinds of event. With grants from local government it varies with the event. For Revolution in London and Manchester we don't get paid by the venue or by the city to help put on the event. However, in Glasgow because it's the newest velodrome in the country – it was built for the Commonwealth Games – there's obviously a big legacy piece behind that and Glasgow City Council encourages events to come to their velodrome so that it's being utilized properly. The fact that they are hosting two of our events this year for Revolution, it's a big economic impact on the area and showcases the velodrome facility as well. So we are getting a fee out of Glasgow City to host the two events this year. Last year was the first time we introduced the championship concept to bring the event to the next level by attracting the world's best road tour teams, like Team Sky, Cannondale Drapac and Orica Scott. All these guys flew in from different parts of the world and the leading teams from the road take on the leading teams from the track. So that was a new concept and last year we effectively had UK championship rounds followed by the international Champions League where the World Tour teams compete. Last year Glasgow had a UK qualifying round. This year the city was very keen to have a Champions League round, so they've given us some cash to secure a qualifying round and a Champions League round.

In terms of going out and getting sponsorship and grants, is it the same process for going after a Rapha or Glasgow City Council?

In terms of the event, we have a target to hit for commercial sponsorship. I always identify key sectors that we want to target. So, it's usually a couple of key cycling-specific brands that we want to get on board. Generally it's wheels or bike maintenance, which resonates well with the crowd. We always need a nutrition partner because the guys who are going to be there all day need to be fuelled properly to be able to perform at the top of their game. Then there are other sectors like automotive, where it's attractive to have a car because there are a couple of auto brands that are involved in cycling and we also need a team of vans to move equipment around behind the scenes. With the car brands, if it's a well-established brand we'll try to get them to sponsor both cash and in-kind. Cash is king, as they say! It takes a lot of money to run the events so we'd prefer to have a financial investment. But if we can offset some of our costs with value in-kind we're always open to that as well.

With the grants from Glasgow City Council, was it more of a serendipitous thing or did you always have in your mind that Glasgow would have a legacy programme that Face could tap into?

That very much came about because we wanted an event in Glasgow and it's worked well for them over the past couple of years. They've seen the benefit of Revolution at the venue. So in terms of negotiating the deal, it was very much them proactively coming to us on that occasion to ensure they are getting the highest quality event from the Face Partnership. It's not always the case that brands or local authorities want to come and spend money with you. With the brands and sponsorship it's very much us doing our research into the key sectors and then doing research on the specific brands, as they will have a particular agenda and key objectives they want to hit. So we need to do research to make sure we're not going in completely cold and saying 'We've got this great event.' We need to ensure the pitch effectively marries up with what they're trying to achieve. It makes the conversation a lot easier. Brands are a lot more willing to talk to you if they realize that you have researched their brand.

When doing research we use a combination of methods. Google is a great tool for finding out information. With established brands it's about looking at what they've done in the past. Going through their website and doing a SWOT analysis of their company. We also use a research agency and platform called Pearl Finders, who contact hundreds of brands and then produce reports on what the brands are looking to do in relation to sport. Occasionally this will be specific to cycling. Also, it's very much about picking up the phone to have an initial conversation – putting your hook in there so that they open up to you and talk about what they're hoping to achieve with their brand, and then showing how what they're aiming for is very similar to our own objectives. If this can be done successfully then the next stage is to meet up and have a more detailed conversation, which leads to the creation of a beneficial package that addresses the brand's key drivers.

Thinking about the history of the Nocturne, how has sponsorship developed over time?

When Nocturne first came out a few years ago, there were a few smaller brands involved. Rapha were a founding partner of the event back then, so obviously a key partner at the time. As were Condor Cycles, so they've always had a small involvement. Then Rapha went off and took on the world and became this global superpower in terms of cycle clothing, focusing on their sponsorship of Team Sky and Team Wiggins. However, they felt that made them a little bit too elite. Therefore they've pulled away from the sponsorships with the elite teams so that they can appeal to a wider audience. This is why they've come back to the Nocturne. They can see how much the event has grown over the past 10 years and how our audience has grown and the reach that we get through the event. By becoming a title sponsor they are involved at the highest level, therefore it's opening up their channels to a much wider audience, which is what they want to achieve as a brand. So, as a younger brand partnering with the likes of Team Sky they gained a huge amount of credibility. Off the back of that partnership you can start to engage with people who have heard your name because you're involved with such a successful team. Therefore you've got that name in the industry. Then it's about working on the other sides of the brand that you don't necessarily get with an elite team, which is when you can start to move into events that appeal to a wider audience, like the Nocturne. In doing so, Rapha can demonstrate that they're not this elite brand and over two or three years they can build and educate about what they have on sale, and develop brand affinity and loyalty in a much wider audience.

Do you find it easier to get sponsorship for more well-established events? Is it easier to get sponsorship for the Nocturne or Revolution?

In all honesty it's easier to get sponsorship for Nocturne than Revolution, even though it's a younger event. I am still struggling to put my finger on why that is! With

Figure 5.2   Alongside the elite cycling races at the Nocturne, different features such as the penny-farthing and Brompton races broaden the event's appeal

SOURCE The FACE Partnership

Revolution the events are across two to four months, and having come from a big sports marketing agency you always sell properties on the basis that the brand can extend its conversation with the audience across a number of months. Whereas with Nocturne, although we're building towards prolonged engagement because we're expanding internationally, so far it has always been one day in London. So therefore you can engage with people in the run up to the event as much as you want but then there's only so much you can do after the event. It is ultimately a one-day thing. I think it is also because it's such an exclusive event. It's very hard for brands to engage in a central London location and there are 15–20,000 people round the course and there's live TV coverage in the heart of the city. These factors make it easier for brands to want to engage with it. Other cycling and running events, apart from the major running events like the London Marathon and maybe Ride London, tend to be on the periphery of London, never in the City of London.

Also, the criterium races have a major benefit of being circuit races. Speaking to key sponsors like JLT or Ford about how they engage key stakeholders with their business, like key clients or suppliers, they want to bring them along and entertain them so that they can see the work they are doing in that sport. If they invite them to the Tour de Yorkshire or the Tour of Britain, the cyclists flash past in an instant and that's it. Whereas with a criterium race it's a 1.2 km enclosed circuit the competitors are going round 30–40 times, so you see them every couple of minutes.

Have the demands of sponsors and the sophistication of their needs changed over time?

We have to prove a lot more these days. The benefit of sponsorship to brands. Years ago it was very much a badging exercise, but now it's so much more about engaging with the audience, clients and other key stakeholders. Branding is very much a part of it, because it delivers a media value, but ultimately it's the engagement they can have. And we have to be able to measure that and prove to the brand that it is worthwhile sponsoring the event.

Face do an online survey that we encourage people to fill in for the chance to win prizes, and we have a three or four page survey based not only on the event but also what they noticed in terms of sponsors. And if the sponsors have key questions they want to ask we put those in as well. We also do onsite questionnaires and we work with our media agency, which evaluates the media value, where pick up has come from – online or print. We also get the figures through from Eurosport for the live TV coverage. Because digital is so important for brands now, we've started doing a lot more with Facebook live streaming. The benefit of Facebook Live over traditional TV is you can see the views but also the additional reach of people who are seeing people watching, which is encouraging others to watch. Then because it's aligned with Facebook we are able to gather the demographic data on who is watching, which you don't have with traditional TV channels. So TV broadcasters can see X amount of people watched, whereas Facebook can give the number watching and also their geographic locations, income and so on.

Do sponsorship deals tend to be year by year, or for longer?

Sponsorship deals are more and more about multi-year agreements. It's always a little bit tougher with cycling events. In the past with the Nocturne we've had sign off from the City of London three or four months prior to the event. Whereas now we have a three-year agreement with the City to have it at Cheapside. So that allows us to engage sponsors with multi-year partnerships. The other issue is that British Cycling govern our schedule. So last year we had six events, whereas this year we have four because of the track World Cup at Manchester. So it can be tough to say to a potential sponsor, 'We want to do a three-year deal but we don't know when the events will be in years two and three.'

Have you experienced issues with ambush marketing at your events?

We had a small brand at Nocturne, a clothing brand, that had asked us beforehand whether they could do some minor activities because their team were riding. However, we couldn't allow it because the brand is a competitor to Rapha. We found one of their banners up somewhere, which was swiftly taken down. Aside from that we've not seen it, not a huge amount anyway. More so with Revolution, because the Six Day Series, our nearest competitor, has its event six weeks before our London event. Although it's track cycling, it's very different to Revolution. Theirs is more of a party, whereas ours is more credible in terms of the racing. So there's always playing off against each other a little bit.

Is part of the conversation you have with sponsors about audience fit or brand tribes and communities?

Absolutely, the cycling audience is very much ABC1. It is a highly affluent audience. So there's no point me approaching brands that are targeting CDE. Therefore, it is one of the key hooks that I go in with when I am talking to brands. Brand tribes and communities are not something we talk about so much; they may become more important as we grow the events further.

The question about brand tribes and communities comes from Rapha having the Rapha Cycling Club. As an outsider looking in, they look like a cohesive group of people who are attracted to this brand and this activity.

With Rapha Cycling Club, I totally agree with you. They are a very cliquey group of people. I think they see themselves as an exclusive part of Rapha. However, Rapha need to attend to those groups of people still, but as I said earlier that's why they are engaging in Nocturne because they want to engage with a wider group of people and they don't want to make it so exclusive. Because actually when you look at it, it is around £135 to become a member for a year, which isn't astronomical for a year's club membership. I think a lot of people think that it's a lot more expensive, a lot more exclusive.

What are the main factors that need to be considered when managing a successful sponsorship relationship?

Once it's all signed and over the line, that's when the account management starts. In the run up to a major event like Nocturne it's about making sure that every single detail that's been agreed in the contract is delivered. Whether that's branding, hospitality, tickets. On the surface you can think, 'Oh the hospitality, that's just making sure they've got their tickets', but actually it's getting those 10 names, have any of those 10 people got dietary requirements? Getting out the right information so that their experience of the day is completely seamless. So that it's not affecting us as a brand or the sponsors who have invested financially in the event. In terms of the branding, with a lot of the bigger brands they have their own brand guidelines so it's working with them to make sure the branding is fitting both their guidelines and ours. So it's getting all our ducks in a row. There are so many different elements of branding; with some of the sponsors it's not just the trackside boards, it's the gantry branding, the media backdrops, the logo in the programme, the logo on the website, and therefore there's so many different sign offs we have to go through with any particular brand. We can't just go to print with it if that brand isn't happy with it. So in the lead up it's very much looking after those particular elements and just making sure they're happy with everything. Constantly touching base with them all the way to event day really.

So, when you go out there, do you have in mind that you're going to sell this sponsorship item for this price, or do you offer them a range of things they might buy? Is it hierarchical with a main sponsor, co-sponsor, etc, or is it more bespoke?

There are various ways to do it. You can go in and try to sell the highest possible package. Which I think is absolutely fine with the bigger brands, especially those who've engaged with sponsorship in the past. However, these days especially you have to have the flexibility and I am always reticent to go in and try to sell the be-all-and-end-all, all-singing package because it varies for each brand and each event. They may come back and say 'We don't care about the branding, we just want to use this event for hospitality, as more of an engagement tool. Therefore we're going to cut out the branding because there's X amount of media value attached to the branding, which reduces the cost of the sponsorship package.' But then again if a potential sponsor says they want to go heavy on branding then it's a different conversation. It's weighing up the cost implications to the Face Partnership. So although a brand might not want branding but does want hospitality there is a cost implication so we need to make sure we're still making money out of that. We're very flexible in terms of what we offer, that's why we have the initial conversation and meet up with brands to establish which elements of a package could work well for them. Then we'll go away, think about it and then produce a more bespoke package based on the conversations we've had. Send that over, wait for feedback and then refine it further as the process goes through.

Have you come across issues of corporate social responsibility, or ethical issues, in relation to sponsors?

No, not yet. Each brand has its own corporate social responsibility (CSR) agenda, and generally a brand won't engage with an event unless it matches up with what the event's trying to achieve.

In terms of relationships between sponsors, for the Nocturne there's Mr Porter and Rapha – how do you manage them?

There's definitely a job to be done. With Nocturne this year we had around 15 different sponsors. The likes of Mavic, which is a specialist in wheels, shoes and helmets. We could only accommodate Mavic as the wheel sponsor this year. Mavic wanted to promote their helmets and shoes, but because Rapha has a range of shoes and helmets we have to manage Mavic's expectations from the off. So you have to be upfront to start with. Mavic was extremely happy with how the event went and we were able to include the wheels as prizes for several of the races. So the brand got the association of being one of the leading wheel brands in the world. Likewise, Mr Porter and Rapha. Mr Porter was our title sponsor last year. Rapha came on and offered a higher investment for a longer term, hence why we went with Rapha. Plus it's a cycling brand, so there's a better fit. And initially the conversation with Mr Porter was totally off the table because Rapha has a big online presence. They sell their products exclusively through their portal. Whereas Mr Porter sells other cycling brands through its website so we couldn't continue the conversation there. However, Rapha decided to explore selling some of its kit on Mr Porter, so that opened up the conversation again. There was a bit of a balancing act as to what Mr Porter could promote at the event.

So were the stakes quite high, then, in that it was potentially going to be either Rapha or Mr Porter sponsoring the Nocturne?

Initially it was as title sponsors. Mr Porter withdrew from all conversations with us but Mr Porter came on as an official partner in the end. It was a really strong position for the Face Partnership to be in, having two major sponsors like that competing for the highest level of sponsorship. But also, the other sponsors such as Ford engaged with the NED hotel and took 10 rooms for their hospitality programme. Plus a private room where they had a lunch. Mavic also sells its kit through Mr

Porter. VonCrank is doing work with Rapha on some of its rides because it provides mechanical support. So, lots of different conversations that are bubbling away under the surface between the members of our sponsoring family or portfolio.

Apart from doing research, are there any other aspects you'd say are key to securing sponsors?

You've got to be super-organized when doing your research into potential sponsors. What's so important is to be creative when developing that hook for a brand to engage with you, especially if you don't already have a relationship with them. Some of these brands get approached hundreds of times a day and you've got to stand out. If you've done your research and you're hitting the right notes when sending stuff over or speaking to them directly they're going to engage with you a lot more quickly and effectively. But then, past that initial process, it's important to be super-organized in following up. I could have a conversation with Ford today and they'd be really engaged, but if I then leave it for three or four weeks the opportunity is often gone. So it's about following up. From my experience of working in sponsorship, people are sometimes scared to follow up because they're worried about harassing, but actually you're just doing your job. And more often than not the brands don't mind you doing your job, and if they feel you're harassing them they will say so. And I've had that before and you can back off a little.

Please could you give an example of what you mean by a hook?

An example of a hook for me is Ford. It has a big range of cars, from the Mustang that they were promoting at Nocturne to family cars. With Nocturne, the audience is very ABC1, but it's also got a strong family ethos so the hook we went in with there was that we're hitting the same demographics as you're trying to hit. You're engaged with cycling already through team sponsorship of Sky and Ford Eco-Boost. Your teams can come and ride in the event so you've automatically got the association with the event, not only by being an event sponsor but by the other teams riding in the event. And we've got the opportunity for you to be able to bring along a number of your guests and demonstrate what you're doing in the world of cycling and the events you're engaged with as well. And we can give you XYZ in terms of TV coverage and digital engagement.

Is it always about demographics, or do you talk about lifestyle?

Yes we do talk about lifestyle, and also the CSR angle. With Revolution we have the Future Stars programme, which is integral to the entire event, and we're looking for a Future Stars sponsor at the moment, which is a CSR angle. I've done my research on brands that are looking to engage in youth development. There are some brands out there that have their own 'stars of the future' programme so automatically it's a good conversation starter. They can come in and engage with the future of British cycling and it ties in nicely with what they're trying to achieve as a brand as well.

What's the most satisfying sponsorship deal you have arranged in your career?

I think it would be for British Tennis. There is an Indian information technology (IT) company called Wipro. The chief executive and chief marketing officer were big tennis fans and they used to buy a lot of hospitality from Wimbledon. As we started working more closely with British Tennis and digging down into the workings of the organization we realized they had a big requirement to overhaul their IT systems. So we started chatting with the guys at Wipro and said, you obviously love tennis so there's a natural affinity with British Tennis, but also the opportunity for you to overhaul their IT systems which would give Wipro the opportunity to create a fantastic case study with which to go out into the marketplace and start talking about. It was the first time I've dealt with a purely Indian based company. The negotiations were pretty tough but we got there in the end. And it was a great deal for them, but also for British Tennis. Five years on they are still sponsors, which is two years longer than the deal I negotiated.

Also, it was being invited down to Queens with them and watching it on TV and seeing the WIPro brand up in lights. It was quite a special feeling. And the more you do it the more you say, 'Yeah, that's my work!'

Conclusion

This chapter has examined a range of issues relating to the identification of sponsors and other funding opportunities. In particular, when looking for organizations that may be interested in providing funds for an event it's vital to establish solid, logical links between the event property and the potential sponsor. For example, where the event and the potential sponsor share a geographic location and target audience there is a logic of association between them. When this is done properly, a convincing 'hook' may be developed, as James Pearce sets out clearly in his interview. Following on from this, the sponsorship fit or congruency can be developed effectively in terms of the event audience's expectancy – the sponsor's predetermined connection with the event theme and relevancy (how the sponsor complements the events theme).

The motivations of sponsors must be clearly understood. These will vary from sponsor to sponsor and other agencies such as public bodies. Moreover, in a brand's lifetime motivations will change and so will its sponsorship strategies. Some sponsors will be looking to widen the appeal of their brand, as in the Rapha example, while others will be looking to attract visitors to their city or region. Often a combination of motivations will be applicable. Being able to articulate clearly how an event meets the motivations of a particular funder is vital to establishing a case for support. Furthermore, while it's fine to go out with a predetermined package of sponsorship benefits to sell to potential sponsors, being flexible and developing packages that are individual to a particular sponsor are increasingly the way to go.

A conventional approach to establishing the attractiveness of an event property to a potential sponsor is to demonstrate how the event and the potential sponsor have the same target audience. Identifying industry or product sectors with appropriate target audiences is the first step to a successful potential sponsor/funder prospecting campaign. At the same time, we have argued that while this is important it is also increasingly necessary to understand how the nature of the audience has changed in a postmodern context. An understanding of audience playfulness and lack of commitment, juxtaposed with a need to belong to a brand community or tribe and the importance of narratives (stories) in sponsorship campaigns, will be central to their success.

Discussion questions and activities

1 Identify an event that you are interested in that has one or more sponsors.
   – In what ways do these sponsors fit the event, and what relationship do they have to each other? Consider the sponsor/event property fit as someone who has been or is thinking about going. Use the discussion on target audience, expectancy and relevancy set out in Chapter 4.
   – What other criteria can be used to evaluate sponsorship 'fit'? Apply them to the example you've identified.
   – Describe the target audience both in terms of objective/inferred and general/behaviour specific data.

2 In a group, list brands that you feel really loyal to.
   – Discuss your list with others and see if you have any brands in common.
   – If you do have brands in common, does this mean you're members of a brand community, and what does this actually mean?

3 Think about the brands you've discussed, and identify the main motivations that the sponsors have. What kinds of events would be able to satisfy the brands you have been discussing?

4 Using some of the events your group have discussed in question 1, work out what kind of approach to sponsorship the event has taken:

- Is it hierarchical or bespoke?
- What opportunities for sponsorship have not been exploited?

Further reading

Close, A, Krishen, A and Latour, M (2009) This event is me! How consumer event self-congruity leverages sponsorship, *Journal of Advertising Research*, **49** (3), pp 271–84

This research paper examines sponsored promotional events in shopping centres. The theory of self-congruity is examined and defined as when consumers, in their search for self-esteem, compare themselves to products to determine the products' consistency with their self-image. The paper offers both theoretical and practical insights that are helpful to both students and professionals.

Kwon, E, Ratneshwar, S and Kim, E (2016) Brand image congruence through sponsorship of sporting events: A reinquiry of Gwinner and Eaton (1999), *Journal of Advertising*, **45** (1), pp 130–38

As the title suggests, this article tests the findings of Gwinner and Eaton's (1999) research paper from both a methodological and findings perspective. This is particularly useful as it allows the reader to examine a robust academic critique of an influential piece of research. It will be interesting to see whether Gwinner and Eaton respond!

Olson, E and Thjømøe, H (2011) Explaining and articulating the fit construct in sponsorship, *Journal of Advertising*, **40** (1), pp 57–70

This article offers a comprehensive review of literature relating to sponsorship fit before moving on to present three pieces of novel research in this area that draw on three different research methods: cognitive mapping, survey-based experiment and conjoint analysis. The three pieces of research are linked in that the constructs generated in the first qualitative study are then tested in the following two quantitative studies.

IEG's website (www.sponsorship.com) has a wealth of resources and up-to-date information on the sponsorship industry.

References

EventScotland (no date a) About Scotland The Perfect Stage, EventScotland [Online] http://www.eventscotland.org/about/ [Accessed 27/02/18]

EventScotland (no date b) International events programme, EventScotland [Online] http://www.eventscotland.org/funding/international-programmes/ [Accessed 27/02/18]

EventScotland (2017) A spotlight on Scotland The Perfect Stage 2017, EventScotland [Online] http://www.eventscotland.org/assets/show/5689 [Accessed 27/02/18]

Preparing and delivering a sponsorship pitch

06

LEARNING OBJECTIVES

Having read this chapter and worked through the questions and activities you should be able:

- to recognize the role that the sponsorship proposal plays in the sponsorship selling process;
- to outline the sequential stages involved in developing event sponsorship;
- to share best practice methods for approaching sponsors and communicating the opportunities available;
- to highlight the growing importance of bespoke arrangements between events and sponsors.

Introduction

Event managers and marketers who intend to utilize sponsorship as a means to support their events will have to engage in the task of preparing sponsorship proposals. The previous chapters focused on what constitutes 'fit' between sponsor and event and emphasized the importance of identifying the event audiences and matching these with the sponsors' own. They also discussed how to assess whether the event is 'sponsor ready' by identifying the range of opportunities that an event can offer to sponsors. Indeed one of the keys to winning event sponsorship is the ability to effectively demonstrate how sponsoring the event will create value for a partner organization. The sponsorship proposal is the principal means by which this is communicated to a potential sponsor.

The purpose of this chapter is to provide practical advice on how to prepare and deliver a winning sponsorship proposal. To this end a range of useful techniques are proposed. Furthermore, the chapter discusses how to develop attractive sponsorship opportunities that secure sponsorship deals by highlighting the growing importance of bespoke arrangements between event and sponsors.

The sponsorship proposal

Sponsorship is a business agreement developed for the mutual benefits of the parties involved, hence should not be seen as an easy way to raise finance for an event (McDonnell and Moir, 2013). It is a complex task and indeed much more difficult than selling other forms of marketing communications (Skinner and Rukavina, 2003). Nevertheless, as discussed in Chapter 1, for many events sponsorship constitutes a lifeline – it can provide events with much needed funds and other essential resources, while serving to enhance the event image and create exposure to a wider market. This chapter aims to address the all-important question: how do you go about obtaining such potentially viable support for your event?

A formal proposal is commonly the means by which sponsorship opportunities are presented, forming the basis for negotiation with potential partners. Companies, however, are provided with varying amounts of unsolicited offers of this kind on a regular basis, meaning competition among sponsorship seekers is fierce. According to IEG (2017), leading brands receive over 100 sponsorship proposals a week. Therefore, for a proposal to make an impression and to achieve the desired results, it is important that it has been well developed, that it is focused on the sponsors' perspective and that it addresses all of the required elements of the offer that would enable the potential sponsor to make a decision that is favourable for the event.

Proposal development requires careful consideration because, as McDonnell and Moir (2013) highlight, proposals are a direct reflection of the event that they are representing. They also remind us that since companies invest in sponsorship to achieve certain corporate and marketing objectives and with a focus on achieving return on investment (ROI), the sponsorship proposal must demonstrate how the sponsorship will help the sponsor accomplish its goals. Indeed, one of the keys to winning sponsorship contracts is presenting a proposal that specifically identifies sponsors' benefits and needs and promotes these, not merely the features of the event and of the sponsorship package that is being sold (Stotlar, 2005). Ukman (2012) stresses that you should not expect a potential sponsor 'to wade through your data dump and figure out what they want'. It is very important to remember this, as it would be a mistake on the part of the event manager/marketer to centre the proposal only on why the event is in need of a sponsor and on what will be done with the money and/or resources. It would also be of limited use if the proposal was rich in details about the event and its credentials but did not address what the partnership can potentially achieve for the sponsor. Stotlar (2005) concurs, and draws attention to the fact that since organizations are looking for promotional platforms that can deliver quantifiable advantages, the proposal should focus on the sponsors' needs, not the event.

Indeed, Skinner and Rukavina (2003: 54) suggest that 'if you have looked at sponsorship thorough the sponsors' eye' the proposal will effectively serve as a straightforward letter of agreement. That is because it will clearly articulate the way in which the sponsorship satisfies the sponsor's specific requirements and/or provides solutions. This in turn facilitates decision making on the part of the sponsor while also streamlining the whole deal-reaching process, as any agreement would require only the finer details to be finalized while drafting the sponsorship contract.

Nevertheless, it is still common practice to send generic, standardized sponsorship proposals to a number of different companies at the same time. Masterman (2007: 206), however, explains that an 'off-the-shelf' approach that uses predetermined packages only supplies a set of rights that has been designed with no specific sponsors in mind, and as a result is unlikely to meet any individual requirements. Stotlar (2005) concurs and stresses that a sponsorship seeking strategy founded on a careful examination of the potential sponsor to discover their specific requisites and needs is to be preferred. In line with this view, Skinner and Rukavina (2003: 68) suggest that a proposal must:

1   Be filled with added value and benefits, meeting the company's marketing goals.

2   Contain pertinent demographic information about your event that matches the potential sponsor's target audience.

3 Be highly customized for the business category and for the sponsor within that category.

4 Provide opportunities to be exclusive, thus separating the sponsor from its competitors.

5 Provide plenty of exposure, not just signage and brochure mentions, but substantial media exposure.

Masterman (2007) insists that a tailored and bespoke approach that is strongly grounded on research and knowledge of the prospective partner demonstrates commitment to develop a relationship and makes a positive impression. It follows that researching information about potential sponsors is the essential prerequisite of successful sponsorship sales. Skildum-Reid (2016) provides a useful list of the type of information needed about potential sponsoring organizations before embarking on the task of creating a customized sponsorship offering, namely 'one that will grab their imagination and showcase how they can use this investment to get closer to their customers and achieve their specific objectives':

1 Name and title of the brand manager.

2 Specific brand(s) that are best matched to the sponsorship opportunity.

3 Target markets for the brand(s) you are targeting.

4 Overall marketing objectives for the brand(s) you are targeting.

5 How they use sponsorship to achieve their objectives.

6 Whether they have any sponsorship exclusions (eg they don't sponsor motorsports).

7 How much lead time they need before the sponsorship opportunity starts.

(Skildum-Reid, 2016)

With regard to lead time, generally a sponsorship proposal should reach the targeted organization between 6 and 18 months prior to the event. Sending an application late shows a lack of organization and will not make a good impression on the potential partner.

It is also important to recognize that, understandably, time constraints and the need to maximize the chance that a sponsor will come on board mean that events will have to target more than one sponsor at once, which contrasts with the best practice mentioned above. Ukman (2012) suggests that it is acceptable to send proposals to companies in the same category at the same time and justifies this advice by stressing that 'once you understand the category and if there's a fit for one company in the category, [it is] likely you can apply it to the others'.

Types of proposals

Masterman (2007: 165) categorically states that 'there is no way around it, a proposal is needed', and goes on to explain the important role that the proposal plays in the sponsorship selling process by providing a record that can be referred to and which would not be achieved by a verbal proposition alone. Event managers/marketers should also be aware that the process of selling sponsorship may require the development of a number of proposals, which Masterman (2007) refers to as the *initial proposal* and the *ultimate proposal*, while McDonnell and Moir (2013) call the former a *sponsorship prospectus* and only the latter the *sponsorship proposal*. Regardless of the terminology utilized, two main types can be distinguished, which in this book we refer to as the *preliminary* proposal and the *actual* proposal.

The preliminary proposal

In order to create customized sponsorship offerings, academics and practitioners concur that event representative/s should aim to ensure that they meet with potential sponsors to discuss their requirements prior to submitting a proposal. It is common, however, for organizations to expect to see something in writing first. Hence this document should be designed to enthuse interest in order to instigate that all-important meeting where it will form the basis of the initial discussions. This preliminary version of the proposal should contain a presentation of the event that is to be sponsored and of sponsorship parameters in broad terms (Masterman, 2007).

More specifically, IEG (2017) recommends that this document should:

- identify the property's key selling points;
- emphasize the benefits to the sponsor, not the features of the property;
- include leverage and activation ideas;
- provide specific numbers in audience composition, loyalty, etc;
- share testimonials from current sponsors;
- address accountability for return on investment;
- be tailored to the prospect's business category.

McDonnell and Moir (2013: 74) believe that this prospectus should serve as an event brochure that includes 'facts about the activity, background of the organization, key figures and other facts that add credibility'. To this end, Masterman (2007: 166) suggests that the information it should provide about the event is as follows:

- its history;
- background;
- successes;
- programme;
- people;
- locations;
- venues;
- existing sponsors involved.

McDonnell and Moir (2013) stress the purpose of a pre-proposal meeting is to seek information that will assist in the development of the actual sponsorship proposal by providing insights concerning aspects such as whether sponsorship of an event of this kind fits with the company's plans, whether there is a target audience match and any other activities that the sponsor is involved with that may interfere with or complement what the sponsorship offers.

The actual proposal

This document articulates the details of the proposed partnership with a specific organization, hence it should be tailored to their particular needs.

This means that it is essential that the proposal is informed by research and an understanding of the prospect brand and its motivations for considering investing in sponsorship, and how these fit with the event and the sponsorship opportunity that it presents. It is important that the proposal is detailed and includes all the necessary information and supporting evidence to enable the prospective sponsor to value the sponsorship (Masterman, 2007). A description of the opportunity or opportunities available and rights on offer as well as a valuation of these are necessary, along with suggestions of how the sponsor can maximize the use of the benefits on offer to achieve set sponsorship objectives. According to Masterman (2007: 166), the level of detail required is 'as finite as is needed to place a monetary value on the rights on offer' so that the sponsor can determine if it's good value or not and consequently work out the potential return on investment.

An outline of the sections that the proposal should include will be provided later in the chapter. Importantly, however, before the event manager/marketer is ready to begin the practical task of writing and presenting the proposal a number of key activities must have taken place. These can be broken down into a series of sequential stages, which are discussed in the following section.

The sponsorship development process

Evidently, the necessary premise to embark on the development of a sponsorship proposal is the decision that sponsorship is required for the event and the objectives that sponsorship will help to achieve for the event. Reasons for seeking sponsorship may be many and varied. It is often the case that events require a cash sponsor to provide finances to cover expenses. Increasingly, however, events may be looking for sponsors to provide value in-kind and/or marketing in-kind. For example, an event may be in need of a media partner to elevate the event exposure to the target audience or may require a company to supply specific products and materials that are needed for the event. Collett and Fenton (2011) exemplify this by highlighting Nestlé's sponsorship of the Virgin Money London Marathon as official water supplier, thanks to which the event saved on an item that would otherwise have been purchased from the event budget. This sponsorship sits alongside the long-standing involvement of the event with Lucozade Sport, now in its 18th year. Virgin Money London Marathon Race Director, Hugh Brasher, said of the renewal of the partnership in 2016: 'the event's official sports drink has become an integral part of the race and the Lucozade Mile 23 drink station is a highlight of the day for runners' (Virgin Money London Marathon, 2016).

Indubitably, the provision of products and services, for example donating prizes and other giveaways, means that sponsorship can be seen as useful way to enhance the attendees' experience, which can also be achieved through the experiential activities that the sponsor carries out as part of the activation programmes. Mobile apps, WiFi, charging stations, networking experiences, lounges, samples, entertainment activities are some of the means by which sponsors can deliver better experiences for attendees. IBM has been supporting the All England Lawn Tennis Club and the Wimbledon Championships as official information technology supplier since 1990. The sponsorship enriches attendees' and viewers' experience of the tournament by measuring and presenting real-time analysis and match statistics, and providing media and commentators with mobile and digital solutions to augment coverage around the world (Frericks, 2016; Wimbledon, 2017).

Once the decision to seek sponsorship is made, a number of sequential stages have to be undertaken before and after the sponsorship proposal is written and presented. Identification of assets, prospecting potential sponsors and deciding on the appropriate way to approach suitable companies are preparatory stages that require significant attention. Collett and Fenton (2011: 152) warn: 'failure to prepare adequately is one of the principal reasons for a proposal to be rejected'.

Asset identification

Compiling an inventory of the event's 'sponsorable' assets is the first step in the process of developing sponsorship. This audit is essential in order to fully understand what an event can offer to a potential sponsor. The assets are the rights that may be available for sponsorship packaging, which have been identified but not yet arranged in any desired combination. During this exercise it is also important to identify the resulting benefits to potential sponsors. IEG (2017) lists typical assets as:

- marks and logos;
- audience;
- publications and collateral materials;
- signage;

- website;
- venues/sites;
- guaranteed media;
- hospitality opportunities;
- database;
- events and programmes;
- talent;
- merchandise;
- broadcast package;
- non-owned and borrowed assets.

In addition to these tangibles, Collett and Fenton (2011: 73) specify that intangible assets would include 'the value of category exclusivity, the importance of being associated with a particular set of brand attributes as espoused by the property or the networking opportunities presented by the property in terms of the other sponsors and stakeholders it attracts'.

For small events the process of creating an inventory or assets register would be relatively easy, while it would be more complex for events of greater size and scope. For smaller events with fewer existing assets, a creative approach to developing an inventory should be utilized (Bowdin *et al*, 2011). Collett and Fenton (2011) suggest that appealing assets may be, for example, opportunities for employee engagement, mentoring or offering a direct route to a local community. Joe Waters from Selfish Giving, cited by Eventbrite (2017), recommends looking at the competition to 'see if they are making money from something you are not'. Meanwhile, corporate sponsorship and cause marketing expert Chris Baylis (2016) argues in the Sponsorship Collective blog that:

> speaking opportunities, co-branding, product endorsement, cause marketing, thought leadership, category exclusivity, meeting celebrities or industry influencers, conversion rates and the power of your brand to influence your audience are far more valuable than even a million logo placement opportunities (unless those logo placements convey any of the above intangibles, of course).

Taking advantage of tailor-made assets is undoubtedly beneficial for most sponsoring organizations. In offering to customize a sponsorship package the rights holder gains a competitive advantage over other events targeting the same company. This is because the event is offering a unique and exclusive set of rights that are not available elsewhere.

It would also be advisable to group assets into categories, especially if many have been identified. A simple categorization into marketing, promotion and advertising-related assets may be relatively effective. Alternatively, Collett and Fenton (2011) advise grouping assets according to the benefits that they will deliver to sponsors, namely:

- connection with a target group;
- exposure;
- image transfer.

In a similar vein, Eventbrite (2017) suggest that assets should be categorized by activation type, for example branding, on site, samples, experiential, which would help sponsors quickly understand the potential value of each asset. A valuation of the assets is, in fact, the next step in the assets identification stage of proposal development. Quantity and availability of the assets should be recorded and the sale value and cost of sale should be built into the pricing of the marketable assets. Bowdin *et al* (2011) note that the value of tangible assets such as media exposure, signage and hospitality opportunities can be quantified in monetary terms in a reasonably straightforward manner. However, deciding on the value of intangible assets is a more complex task.

At this stage there would have been no discussion with potential sponsors. Later in the sponsorship selling process, however, the aim should be to combine the benefits into packages that maximize revenue for the event and deliver expected benefits to the sponsor (Masterman, 2007). Importantly, a comprehensive audit of available assets will help to inform decisions about the most suitable framework to be utilized when developing opportunities or a portfolio of sponsorship opportunities, as discussed in Chapter 4. Bowdin *et al* (2006: 241), citing Gerald and Sinclair (2003), indicate the following as possible strategies:

> sole sponsorship, hierarchical packaging (for example tiers of gold, silver, bronze), a pyramid structure (whereby each sponsor level below the principal sponsor jointly spends the amount invested by the top sponsor with proportional benefits), a level playing field (all sponsors negotiate and leverage their own benefits) and an ad hoc approach.

If a tiered structure is employed, IEG (2017) suggest that '[an] important packaging strategy is reserving key benefits for the highest-level sponsors, thus offering an incentive for prospects to opt for the most-inclusive packages and ensuring that there is parity between fee paid and benefits received.'

Prospecting sponsors

The next stage is identifying the sponsors that are to be targeted, which raises the question: how do we decide which companies to aim for? The answer lies in the identification of those companies that are 'a good fit'. According to IEG (2017), to determine the categories and companies that are most likely to sponsor, properties typically use the following criteria:

- active sponsors in the property's market;
- companies based in the market;
- sponsors of familiar properties in other markets;
- companies that target the same audience as the property;
- companies that have a match with the property's brand image;
- companies in active and emerging sponsor categories.

Earlier in this book we have already discussed the importance of identifying organizations that want access to the same target audience, as it constitutes a key criterion for establishing fit. Equally as important, research shows that sponsors are looking to properties to provide audience information as they also use this to ascertain whether there is a match worth pursuing (IEG, 2017; Masterman, 2007). To this end, the techniques identified and discussed in Chapter 4 should be utilized. As a general rule the event target audience profile should include demographic, psychographic and behavioural characteristics, while information on buying behaviour will be useful as well, hence a mixture of both objective/inferred and general/behaviour specific characteristics is necessary. With regard to the size of the audience, it is important that this figure includes not just those that actually attend the event but also those that will be reached by the communications campaign. Audience information may include a mixture of quantitative and qualitative data from external sources such as:

- government statistics;
- industry surveys;
- market research reports;
- Trade Organizations or Associations database;
- published financial data/annual reports;
- news reports/press articles;
- press releases;
- trade journals or directories;
- competitors' sales literature;
- websites.

(IEG, 2017)

Primary methods of data gathering are more time consuming and expensive but, as Masterman (2007: 137) emphasizes, 'the event would be providing a richer and more accurate profile of its audience and in doing so present a more comprehensive and detailed picture to potential sponsors'. Observation, surveys and interviews are among the research methods available to marketers. If the event is not new it would be valuable to reveal information from post-event feedback from the previous year (McDonnell and Moir, 2013).

Today it has never been easier to access an audience's information, and especially to communicate with audiences directly before and after an event. Web analytics, which in this book are covered in Chapter 9, provide the event manager/marketer with an array of useful insights on the target audience and what they like and dislike, and about their opinions and views on a variety of matters, while also affording the ability to find out precisely where and when audiences are active online and when they may be more responsive to marketing messages. This knowledge is invaluable and the capability of the event organizer to share it with sponsors is an appealing benefit of sponsorship that is valued highly by organizations, as research by IEG has confirmed repeatedly in recent years (see Figure 6.1).

As explained in Chapter 4, other essential criteria must be applied if a best fit between sponsor and the sponsorship proposal is to be established. Indeed, as articulated by More (2008: 73), 'an effective prospect research process will involve researching appropriate industry sectors and then identifying companies within each sector based on business priorities, current and/

Figure 6.1   Benefits valued by sponsors

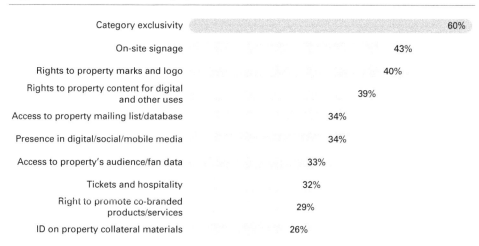

Category exclusivity	60%
On-site signage	43%
Rights to property marks and logo	40%
Rights to property content for digital and other uses	39%
Access to property mailing list/database	34%
Presence in digital/social/mobile media	34%
Access to property's audience/fan data	33%
Tickets and hospitality	32%
Right to promote co-branded products/services	29%
ID on property collateral materials	26%

SOURCE IEG/ESP Properties, LLC (2017). https://www.sponsorship.com/IEG/files/59/59ada496-cd2c-4ac2-9382-060d86fcbdc4.pdf

or historic sponsorship and marketing activities, brand values' as well as the target audiences match already emphasized.

Company information available on the internet, such as press and company reports and industry sources, should suffice at this stage of the research process, which will result in concentrating efforts on companies that have seemingly probable reasons to want to sponsor the event (see Professional insight 3). committee members and board members, as well as event managers and other executives through their personal and professional relationships, may have links with suitable contacts, while existing sponsors can also be a source of referral.

Approaching prospective sponsors

Throughout this book we've emphasized that sponsorship is a partnership. In the context of leisure studies, Uhlik (1995) defines partnership as 'a dynamic arrangement between two or more parties, based in satisfying mutually recognized needs'. Hence, as Daellenbach (2012: 365) points out, sponsorship is not just a simple transactional relationship based on the purchase of product and/or services; 'it involves individuals with their own views, power, negotiations, levels of trust and so on'. What this tells us is that establishing positive personal relationships is important in sponsorship.

Farrelly and Quester (2003) examined the relationship between the sponsor and the sponsored organization in terms of trust, commitment and market orientation and how these affect sponsorship renewal. Their research found that trust is an antecedent to commitment, which in turn determines a sponsor's intention to renew the relationship. These conclusions support Skinner and Rukavina's (2003: 120) advice that 'before you approach potential sponsors you should get to know them', with a view to developing long-lasting trust and ties. On the one hand this involves the process of researching the company background that we have already discussed; on the other hand, it also means making an effort to develop a professional relationship with the person you are presenting the opportunity to, which is better done through face-to-face meetings. For effectiveness and efficiency it is important to identify and approach the key decision maker/s in the company, noting that companies may have different departments tasked with dealing with sponsorship proposals. Generally, however, these individuals are found in marketing and related departments.

The initial contact is usually via a call or short email briefly outlining the available opportunity and its relevance to the potential sponsor. As mentioned earlier, the intention is to create interest and to instigate a face-to-face meeting so that exploratory discussions can take place. The conventional wisdom is that a pre-proposal meeting is advantageous in an effort to determine the specific needs of the potential sponsor, as only then can an effective sponsorship proposal be developed. Event managers/marketers will be at an advantage if they have fully engaged with the previously discussed preparatory stages, and hence have worked hard to research and understand the company that they are approaching and, as stressed by Masterman (2007), can demonstrate that there is a match between the mutual target audiences. Confirmation of the accuracy of this claim and of the organization's marketing/sponsorship objectives should be obtained at this meeting, as well as information on past/current campaigns and future plans, which will inform the creation of the actual sponsorship proposal.

Building a custom package

Sponsorship opportunities are conventionally presented in sponsorship proposals as sets of benefits/rights packages that command specified fees depending on the value of the assets that they include. Crafting custom packages is essential when developing sponsorship offerings that are tailor-made and hence more likely to succeed in attracting partners, as previously discussed. Indeed, experts at Eventbrite (2017) advise parting ways with the long-standing tradition of tiered sponsorship (eg gold, silver and bronze packages) and instead recommend giving prospective sponsors a menu of assets to chose from, believing that this 'would lead to bigger sponsorship deals and longer lasting partnerships with valuable sponsors' (see Professional insight 3). What appears evident is that at the very least the sponsor should be offered a package exclusively designed for them that remains open to negotiation. Collett and Fenton (2011) note that events may offer packages of rights that include less attractive rights along with those that are more attractive to try to increase the value of the package and command a higher sponsorship fee. However, the potential sponsor would not be interested in the assets that are not relevant to achieving their objectives, hence they may want them removed from the offer.

With regard to pricing the opportunity, which seems to be unanimously considered one of the trickiest aspects of developing sponsorship propositions, Eventbrite (2017) suggests a value-based approach founded on finding the 'sweet spot' between the actual cost of the asset and the perceived value of it based on the outcomes that it will deliver to sponsors. In assigning a value to each asset and/or opportunity it is important that this is compared to the cost of similar sponsorships in the marketplace with a view to remaining competitive but also as a starting point for understanding how much an asset may be worth to the market it is being offered to (Ferrier *et al*, 2013). Many sponsorship valuation formulae exist and there is no consensus on one that would suit all circumstances. IEG (2017) provides a list of variables that may impact on price and other factors that would need to be taken into account, such as market factors (as seen in Table 6.1).

Table 6.1 Variables that impact price

Tangible

- Value of sponsor ID on event broadcast
- Value of sponsor ID in property's media buy
- Guaranteed non-measured media with sponsor ID, eg banners, scoreboards, ticketbacks, schedules, announcements, website, etc
- Value of tickets and other hospitality
- Value of on-site sampling
- Value of mailing list
- Value of booth/display space
- Value of programme book adverts and other advertising

(continued)

Table 6.1 *(Continued)*

Intangible

- Prestige of sponsored property
- Recognizability of property marks and logos
- Category exclusivity
- Level of audience interest or loyalty
- Ability of sponsor to activate the tie
- Degree of sponsor clutter
- Susceptibility of property to ambush
- Networking opportunities with co-sponsors
- Media coverage of potential property or event
- Established track record property has with sponsor

Geographic reach/impact at point of sale

Global	More than 150 countries
International	More than 75 countries
Multi-regional	15 to 74 countries in multiple regions
Multi-country	2 to 4 countries
National	Relevant in at least 15 of the top 20 areas of dominant influence (ADIs)
Regional	Multiple markets within a region
Statewide	Multiple markets within a state
Local: major market	A market
Local: minor market	B or C market
Local: minor market	D or E market

Price adjusters

Desirability of property to sponsor category	+
Number of saleable categories locked up	+
Value of sponsor's proprietary component	+
On-site sales rights	+
Pass-through rights	+
Size of sponsor's promotional commitment	–
Size of sponsor's fundraising commitment	–
Multi-term contract discount	–
Introduction to new co-sponsor	–

Market factors

- Cost to sponsor of other properties in same market(s)
- Cost to buy measured media in property's market(s)
- Cost to sponsor of comparable properties in other markets

SOURCE IEG/ESP Properties, LLC (2017). https://www.sponsorship.com/IEG/files/59/59ada496-cd2c-4ac2-9382-060d86fcbdc4.pdf

Table 6.2 Key content areas in a sponsorship proposal

Topic areas	Content
The event and the host organization The purposed here is not only to provide background information and key event details but to show the event attractiveness as well as to highlight expertise, experience and credibility of the host organization.	Organizers' information may include: ● mission statement ● history ● achievements to date including accreditations and awards Event details that are necessary are: ● name of the event ● date/time/duration of the event ● location/venue ● programme of the event* ● ticket price/s ● expected attendance** ● current and past sponsors and other partners (eg government bodies). * Any special guests should be mentioned and may provide inspiration for ideas to activate the sponsorship. ** For recurring events past attendance figures and other measures of success such as press coverage and stakeholders' feedback would help conveying that the event has credibility.
The target market and the 'fit' Emphasize how the event is a unique opportunity to reach a relevant target audience and any other attributes that can highlight sponsor–event congruence.	● Present the profile of the event target audience/s, as a minimum geo-demographic and psychographic characteristics should be included. ● Explain how it fits with the prospective sponsors' market (see Chapter 4 for details of how to develop and match audience profiles). ● Highlight other evidences of fit, eg values, ethos, brand image, goals/objectives, short/long term plans.
Marketing communication plan It is essential to show the sponsor how the audience will be reached and which types of marketing communications methods will be utilized.	● Integrated marketing communications plan (including media and digital plan and PR strategy). ● Opportunities for cross promotion and partnership. ● Who is the competition? From here the main marketing benefits the event has to offer the the sponsor can be highlighted: eg publicity, advertising, promotions, hospitality, ticket allocation, etc.

(continued)

Table 6.2   *(Continued)*

Topic areas	Content
The benefits + priced opportunities Present the package of benefits that the sponsor will be purchasing for the given fee.	In addition to the list of rights being offered (eg naming rights, exclusivity, signage, hospitality) include details of: • type of investment (in-kind or cash sponsorship); • sponsorship fee; • terms (eg length of the deal). It is useful to include, where possible, the value of the benefits to justify the sponsorship fee and show return on investment.
Activation ideas With the rights/benefits being offered, what activities could the sponsor carry out that would help fulfil its corporate and brand/marketing objectives?	This should could include a combination of: • pre event; • on site; • post event.
Evaluation How does the event measure success? What indicators could the sponsor utilize to evaluate the effectiveness of the sponsorship?	Data may include: • number of attendees; • media coverage (volume and type); • new memberships; • fund raised; • sale figures.

SOURCE https://www.eventbrite.co.uk/blog/academy/new-rules-event-sponsorships/

The pitch

So far, we have looked at the preparation required to develop an effective sponsorship proposal. To succeed, a proposal must be focused on the specific requirements of the target organization/s and be informed by an understanding of the congruence must exist between sponsor and event. Masterman (2007: 141) stress the importance of developing relationships before pitching for sponsorship: 'information that [has] been researched and supplemented by initial meetings with the potential sponsor can be used to formulate potential sponsorship solutions'. These tailored solutions, which deliver added value, are communicated through the sponsorship proposal, which is presented in a pitch to the potential sponsor.

There are various ways in which a proposal can be structured, and many prescriptions on how it should appear are available in the literature and via a simple internet search. Some companies provide their own templates or set of questions that they expect the sponsorship proposal to address (see Chapter 11), in which case it is essential to ensure that the proposal communicates all of the information that the organization requires. The proposal should answer the following questions, as indicated by Gerald and Sinclair (2003, cited in Bowdin *et al*, 2006: 244): 'What is the organization being asked to sponsor? What will the organization receive for its sponsorship? What is it going to cost?' More specifically, it may be useful to address within the content of the proposal the areas outlined above in Table 6.2.

Sponsorship contract negotiation

It is essential that the sponsorship proposal presentation concludes with the provision of the event representative contact details, so that the potential partner is able to get in touch for clarifications, to provide feedback or, ideally, to accept the proposal outright. It is, however, important to be proactive in the follow-up period and contact the company within a reasonable time frame, usually after 10–14 days. If the proposed package is of interest to the organization but they wish to 'customize' it further then negotiations would start.

Stotlar (2005) insists that discussions following the presentation of a sponsorship proposal are often aimed at addressing concerns about the pricing of the opportunity. He advises that a successful strategy to deal with instances like this is to reinforce the message by reiterating 'the benefits and price value relationship previously presented' (Stotlar, 2005: 10). In order not to be caught off guard, Bowdin *et al* (2006) recommend that the event managers should have decided on a minimum payment they are prepared to accept for the assets on offer and that it is vitally important not to undervalue these, to avoid the tension that may result from having to implement price corrections at a later stage. Stotlar (2005) advises that an alternative course of action is to offer a reduced package by eliminating some of the previously offered benefits or to propose that a co-sponsor comes on board to share the cost.

If the negotiations are successful and an agreement has been reached, the next step is to draft a written contract. Indeed, in order to avoid misunderstandings the sponsorship contract should always be in writing, no matter the size of the event and the monetary value of the deal being struck. A letter of agreement should secure the deal while the content of the contract is being finalized. For larger, more complex sponsorship deals a contract would always be necessary (Skinner and Rukavina, 2003).

There are various sponsorship contract templates available in textbooks and on the internet that may prove particularly useful for those events with limited a budget available to utilize to cover legal costs. It is nonetheless necessary that any drafted agreement be reviewed and approved by a legal advisor. Usually, the content of the contract would include: the objectives and responsibilities of both parties, benefits to be obtained by the event and the sponsor, termination conditions, ambush marketing protection, details of media, branding and leveraging, the promised exclusivity, marketing and sponsorship servicing, and insurance and indemnity required (Bowdin *et al*, 2006). In this book, legal and ethical consideration emerging from the needs of a sponsorship contract are discussed in detail in Chapter 7.

Sponsorship servicing

Maintaining a positive ongoing relationship with sponsors is a critical factor to the success of any sponsorship. McDonnell and Moir (2013: 80) concur and stress that 'sponsorship works best when nurtured and developed over a period of time'. Indeed, as stated by Sam *et al* (2005), signing of the contract should not be regarded as the terminal consummation of the relationship between event and sponsor. What follows is the sponsorship implementation phase, or *fulfilment*, consisting of the following elements: activation, evaluation and servicing. O'Reilly and Huybers (2015: 155) highlight the importance of sponsorship servicing being concerned with 'providing the resources to ensure the stipulations of the sponsorship contract are met'. Supporting the sponsor's achievement of their objectives is the principal aim of sponsorship servicing.

Sam *et al* (2005) draw attention to the fact that there are a number of additional transactional costs that occur as a result of the rights holder's work to fulfil its relationship with the sponsored organization. Such costs are likely to include those associated with maintaining regular communication with the partner organization, those resulting from the necessary coordination of the implementation of the sponsorship and associated use of the rights, as well as those emerging from the various monitoring strategies that need to be put in place. Indeed, research shows that measurement is considered an important sponsor service (IEG, 2017; Crompton, 2004). It is advisable to estimate these costs at the proposal development stage so that they can be built into the sponsorship investment sought or the event must be prepared to provide relevant extras at no additional cost.

Measuring and evaluating sponsorship

Skildum-Reid (2014b) insists that measuring sponsorship is not the event manager's job and that it is the sponsor who is 'best placed to measure the sponsor's return, against the sponsor's objectives, from the sponsor's benchmarks'. In her popular blog Skildum-Reid argues that good sponsorship is about changing people's perceptions and behaviour, hence the focus should be on achieving return-on-objectives (ROO). Accordingly, it is the sponsor's leverage programme that provides the results against objectives, not the kind of information that the event is able to provide to the sponsor post-event such as exposure, website clicks, attendance numbers and the like. Skildum-Reid (2014b) clarifies this assertion by stating: 'they may get a million impressions, but does their target market trust them more? You may have got 200k people at your event, but did they change their purchase intent?' This view aligns with the findings of Cornwell *et al*'s (2001) examination of managers' perceptions of sponsorship impacts, which highlights the importance of leveraging sponsorship as it is an indicator of perceived success. There is nonetheless an expectation on the part of sponsoring organizations that they will receive an account of whether the sponsorship fulfilled its promises. Scriven (1998, cited in O'Reilly and Madill, 2012: 53) defines 'evaluation' as 'the process of determining the worth, merit, or significance of entities'. More specifically, sponsorship evaluation is the process of determining the effectiveness of a sponsorship (O'Reilly and Madill, 2012). A sponsorship evaluation report will provide details of event outcomes and showcase measurements of how the sponsorship delivered on the proposal. It is advisable to reach out to sponsors two weeks after the event to thank them for their involvement and to arrange a meeting to discuss the outcomes of the partnership. A fulfilment report should be produced at this meeting. Steps to quantify the value that the event generated for the sponsor are as follows:

1 Quantify the ROI: More than anything, your sponsors will want to know the partnership was effective. Report on the measurements of success that were agreed upon during the proposal process. For instance, if your sponsor's objective was to hand out 500 free samples, make sure you keep close track of how many were distributed.

2 Leave a paper trail: Don't assume that a sponsor was tracking all the support you gave them in the months leading up to your event. Take screenshots of social media posts that mention them, especially if they have positive responses from attendees. Save clips from press releases and news articles — anything that demonstrates your support.

3 Track online and social activity: Measure every form of engagement, including number of visits, downloads, likes, and sharing activity, to help sponsors understand the potential reach their participation has given them. Encourage this engagement by asking attendees to comment on their experience, including their interaction with your sponsors' products.

4 Measure brand awareness and perception: In your post-event survey, include questions that will prompt attendees to comment on their experience with your sponsors. If your sponsors conducted sessions at your event, consider asking attendees to rank their favorite sessions. Summarize the results and include the demographics of those who answered.

5 Communicate changes in your event data: Did a sponsor's target demographic grow since your last event? Look back at your event data to see how the demographic makeup of your attendees changed and report those metrics. As your sponsors do their own evaluation of their efforts, this information will help them understand their results.

SOURCE Eventbrite (2016). www.eventbrite.co.uk/blog/academy/new-rules-event-sponsorships

It seems reasonable to think that the overall outcomes of the partnership should be a shared responsibility of the sponsor and the sponsee, as Bowdin *et al* (2011) suggest. Moreover, the event manager should be proactive in facilitating this process. Besides, it is always good practice for any event to engage in a thorough process of evaluation involving the various stakeholders (O'Toole and Mikolaitis, 2002). It is also wise to consider evaluation not as an afterthought but to decide on evaluation measures during the initial stages of event planning to ensure accurate monitoring pre, during and after the event. This is also true when developing sponsorship. Indeed, measurements of sponsorship effectiveness should be discussed at the outset of the relationship, which in turn would help managing sponsors' expectations and avoid misunderstandings. Skildum-Reid (2012) explains: 'the issue with expecting a report outlining the value of media exposure usually starts during the sales process. If you sell on the basis of logo exposure, they'll expect you to prove how much exposure they received'. This validates Crompton's (2004) view that due to increased pressures on companies to demonstrate return on investment, evaluation measures would be included in proposal packages. Notably, among the reasons why measuring the impact of sponsorship is important, Farrelly and Quester (2003) propose that it plays a role in sponsorship renewal. This is confirmed by research from IEG (2013), which shows that post-event reports are one of the most sought after property-provided services while helping properties in the following ways:

- help sponsors justify their investments;
- build internal support at sponsoring companies;
- demonstrate how rights holders have gone beyond terms of a contract;
- set the stage for renewal discussions.

The body of academic literature concerning sponsorship evaluation has continued to grow since Cornwell and Maignan (1998: 13) reflected on the fact that 'demonstrating the commercial impact of sponsorship is probably the best way to legitimize it as a marketing technique'. Research streams have included studies focusing on the development of sponsorship evaluation frameworks (eg O'Reilly and Madill, 2012) and studies stressing the need for improved measurements (Crompton, 2004). Today, attention has shifted from evaluation measures of media exposure, the impact on awareness and image enhancement, to a focus on intent to purchase, product trial and sales increase. These issues will be further explored in Chapter 9, which is dedicated to how to measure the return on sponsorship using digital as well as more traditional methods.

Conclusion

In this chapter we have endeavoured to illustrate the complexity of the process involved in selling sponsorship, of which the sponsorship proposal constitutes a fundamental component. Importantly, the event manager/marketer will have to engage in a series of tasks in order to develop and present sponsorship opportunities that are attractive to potential partners and have greater chances of securing sponsorship agreements. This chapter has also emphasized the importance of full engagement with preparatory activities such as identifying suitable assets, creating detailed target audience profiles and identifying where congruence exists between event and potential sponsoring organization. Diligent preparatory research will lead to forming an in-depth understanding of how the event can deliver value to its potential partners and to the development of a range of sponsorship opportunities that satisfy the specific needs and requirements of prospective partners.

The sponsorship proposal, as the principal means by which sponsorship opportunities are presented to potential partners, must be effective in illustrating what the event promises to deliver and how. Furthermore, any effort made to develop a working relationship and to establish two-way communication with potential sponsors during the proposal development process would most likely pay off, as it would result in sponsorship propositions that are tailor made and unique for each specific partnership being sought. Indeed, sponsorship seeking should not just be understood as a formulaic process but as a creative task that would also benefit from the establishment of a personal connection with the prospects. It should also be recognized that well-connected, tenacious, bright and enthusiastic individuals who are resilient in the face of repeated rejection are most likely to succeed in securing sponsorship.

Discussion questions and activities

1 Using examples, explain why it is important to develop customized sponsorship opportunities.
2 Identify an event that you are familiar with and do an internet search to find background information and to identify a potential partner. What will each get out of the partnership?
3 Using the event that you have researched:
   – Prepare an initial proposal following the guidelines provided in this chapter.
   – What specific information would you seek from a potential sponsor at a pre-proposal meeting to inform the development of the actual sponsorship proposal?
4 What are the steps involved in making an approach to a prospective sponsor?

Further reading

Daellenbach, K, Davies, J and Ashill, N (2006) Understanding sponsorship and sponsorship relationships: Multiple frames and multiple perspectives, *International Journal of Nonprofit and Voluntary Sector Marketing*, **11** (1), pp 73–87

This paper reviews and applies multiple organizational behaviour frameworks, namely lifecycle theory, resource based view of the firm, resource dependency theory, institutional theory and social network theory, to examine the role of sponsorship relationships.

Farrelly, F and Quester, P (2003) The effects of market orientation on trust and commitment: The case of the sponsorship business-to-business relationship, *European Journal of Marketing*, **37** (3/4), pp 530–53

Here agency theory is utilized to examine the relationship between the sponsor and the sponsored party, especially focusing on the effects of market orientation, trust and commitment, and whether they drive sponsorship renewal.

Eventbrite: eventbrite.com and eventbrite.co.uk

The world's fastest growing registration and ticketing platform also serves as an event management services website. Among its varied content it includes a wealth of practical information on how to go about seeking event sponsorship. Free resources available include prospectus and proposals templates, guides and original research on the sector.

References

Baylis, C (2016) Sponsorship inventory and asset development essentials, The Sponsorship Collective, 3 June [Online] https://sponsorshipcollective.com/sponsorship-inventory-asset-development-essentials/ [Accessed 02/07/18]

Bowdin, G, Allen, J and Harris, R (2006) *Events Management*, 2nd edn, Butterworth-Heinemann, Oxford

Bowdin, G, Allen, J and Harris, R (2011) *Events Management*, 3rd edn, Butterworth-Heinemann, Oxford

Collett, P and Fenton, W (2011) *The Sponsorship Handbook: Essential tools, tips and techniques for sponsors and sponsorship seekers*, Jossey-Bass, San Francisco

Cornwell, TB and Maignan, I (1998) An international review of sponsorship research, *Journal of Advertising*, 27 (1), pp 1–21

Cornwell, TB, Roy, DP and Steinard, EA (2001) Exploring managers' perceptions of the impact of sponsorship on brand equity, *Journal of Advertising*, **30** (2), pp 41–51

Crompton, JL (2004) Conceptualization and alternate operationalizations of the measurement of sponsorship effectiveness in sport, *Leisure Studies*, **23** (3), pp 267–81

Daellenbach, K (2012) Understanding the decision making process for art sponsorship, *International Journal of Nonprofit and Voluntary Sector Marketing*, **17** (4), pp 363–74

Eventbrite (2016) *The New Rules of Event Sponsorship*, Eventbrite

Eventbrite (2017) *Guide to Event Sponsorship: The current trends and best practices for success*, Eventbrite

Farrelly, F and Quester, P (2003) What drives renewal of sponsorship principal/ agent relationship? *Journal of Advertising Research*, **43** (4), pp 353–60

Ferrier, S, Waite, K and Harrison, T (2013) Sports sponsorship perceptions: An exploration, *Journal of Financial Services Marketing*, **18** (2), pp 78–90

Frericks, M (2016) Which sponsor will win Wimbledon? *Media Monitoring*, 8 July [Online] https://bis.lexisnexis.co.uk/blog/posts/which-sponsor-will-win-wimbledon [Accessed 25/06/17]

Gerald, E and Sinclair, L (2003) *The Sponsorship Manual: Sponsorship made easy*, 2nd edn, Sponsorship Unit, Victoria, Australia

IEG (2013) The key to sponsor servicing: Post-event fulfillment reports [Online] http://www.sponsorship.com/iegsr/2013/04/15/The-Key-To-Sponsor-Servicing--Post-Event-Fulfillme.aspx [Accessed 26/06/17]

IEG (2017) *IEG's Guide to Sponsorship* [Online] www.sponsorship.com/IEG/files/59/59ada496-cd2c-4ac2-9382-060d86fcbdc4.pdf [Accessed 25/01/17]

McDonnell, A and Moir, M (2013) *Event Sponsorship*, Routledge, London

Masterman, G (2007) *Sponsorship for a Return on Investment*, Butterworth-Heinemann, Oxford

More, G (2008) The rights holder guide to successful sponsorship sales, *Journal of Sponsorship*, **2** (1), pp 67–76

O'Reilly, N and Huybers, T (2015) Servicing in sponsorship: A best–worst scaling empirical analysis, *Journal of Sports Management*, **29**, pp 155–69

O'Reilly, N and Madill, J (2012) The development of a process for evaluating marketing sponsorships, *Canadian Journal of Administrative Science*, **29** (1) pp 50–66

O'Toole, W and Mikolaitis, P (2002) *Corporate Events Project Management*, Wiley, New Jersey

Sam, MP, Batty, R and Dean, RGK (2005) A transaction cost approach to sport sponsorship, *Sport Management Review*, 8, pp 8–17

Skildum-Reid, K (2012) How to shift a sponsor's mindset on measurement [Online] http://powersponsorship.com/how-to-shift-a-sponsors-mindset-on-measurement/ [Accessed 25/06/17]

Skildum-Reid, K (2014a) Can't keep up? 5 ways to simplify sponsorship servicing [Online] http://powersponsorship.com/cant-keep-up-5-ways-to-simplify-sponsorship-servicing/ [Accessed 26/06/17]

Skildum-Reid, K (2014b) What should a sponsee include in a year-end ROI report? [Online] http://powersponsorship.com/year-end-roi-report/ [Accessed 25/06/17]

Skildum-Reid, K (2016) Don't send a sponsorship proposal until you read this [Online] http://powersponsorship.com/dont-send-a-sponsorship-proposal/ [Accessed 17/06/17]

Skinner, BE and Rukavina, V (2003) *Event Sponsorship*, Wiley, Hoboken, NJ

Stotlar, DK (2005) *Developing Successful Sport Sponsorship Plans*, Fitness Information Technology, Morgantown, WV

Uhlik, KS (1995) Partnership, step by step: A practical model of partnership formation, *Journal of Park and Recreation Administration*, 13 (4), pp 13–24

Ukman, L (2012) 11 basics of successful sponsorship sales [Online] http://www.sponsorship.com/About-IEG/Sponsorship-Blogs/Lesa-Ukman/June-2012/11-Basics-Of-Successful-Sponsorship-Sales.aspx [Accessed 20/06/17]

Virgin Money London Marathon (2016) Latest news: Lucozade extends Virgin Money London Marathon partnership [Online] https://www.virginmoneylondonmarathon.com/en-gb/news-media/latest-news/item/lucozade-extends-virgin-money-london-marathon-partnership/ [Accessed 27/06/17]

Wimbledon (2017) Official suppliers [Online] http://www.wimbledon.com/en_GB/atoz/official_suppliers.html# [Accessed 27/06/17]

Managing relationships with sponsors and funding bodies

LEARNING OBJECTIVES

Having read this chapter and worked through the questions and activities you should be able:

- to discuss the relationship between sponsors and event properties;
- to examine the nature of sponsorship agreements and relationships from a legal perspective;
- to examine how sponsors are managed by event properties;
- to evaluate ethical issues relating to event sponsorship.

Introduction

In any event context there will be a legal framework – a set of rules and regulations – that ensures that all those involved in the event are treated fairly according to the law of a particular country or jurisdiction (eg a city, state or country). This chapter examines how relationships between sponsors and event properties are managed and focuses on legal aspects before moving on to discuss how event managers can work with sponsors so that both parties get the most out of the relationship. Ethical issues such as corporate social responsibility (CSR), ambush marketing and reputation management are also assessed.

Bowdin *et al* (2011) highlight the importance of identifying the legal owner(s) of an event. This could be:

- an individual such as the event manager;
- a group of individuals, for instance an event committee;
- a separate legal entity such as a company or charity;
- the sponsors of the event.

Establishing ownership of the event has significant implications as the owner is legally responsible for the event and therefore liable in the unfortunate situation where legal action is taken. In the sponsorship context, ownership of the event needs to be clearly delineated, and contracts between a sponsor and an event property will contain a statement or clause that sets out the sponsor's liability. The level of each party's liability in effect sets out how much of the event property the sponsor owns in relation to the others.

It is important to recognize that legal frameworks apply at city, state and country levels and will vary between these jurisdictions. This chapter should not be read and followed as a legally authoritative guide but as a broad overview of the key issues relating to the laws that an event manager will face in relation to sponsorship.

Sponsorship agreements

Sponsorship agreements take various forms. A memorandum of understanding or letter of sponsorship can be used to set out in writing the terms of the deal. Skinner and Rukavina (2003) identify three types of sponsorship documentation:

- the confirming letter;
- the letter of agreement;
- the formal contract.

McDonnell and Moir (2013) set out four types of agreement:

- drawn up by a lawyer and signed by both parties with a company seal;
- proforma signed by both parties with a company seal;

- letter of agreement signed by both parties;
- confirmation letter.

A confirmation letter is not a contract; rather, it is a statement of an oral/verbal contract between parties (Martin, no date, cited by Skinner and Rukavina, 2003). At the same time, it's important to realize that a confirmation letter may be used as evidence in court that a contract exists. A letter of agreement is, when properly drawn up, a contract. The main differences between a letter of agreement and a contract are the levels of formality, detail and cost (a contract is more expensive to draw up). At the same time, it's important to note that according to Skinner and Rukavina (2003: 134) while a contract is 'more detailed and more intimidating, [it] is no more enforceable than a letter of agreement'.

Contracts

A working definition:

> A contract is a legally enforceable promise or undertaking that something will or will not occur. The word 'promise' can be used as a legal synonym for contract; although care is required as a promise may not have the full standing of a contract, eg when it is an agreement without consideration.

(McDonnell and Moir, 2013: 89)

It is important to understand the meaning of the term 'agreement without consideration'. Consideration is the benefit that each party receives or expects to receive from the contract – in this context the sponsored property receives a payment or in-kind goods and the sponsor receives agreed opportunities to promote their brand. For a contract to be valid it must have consideration; that is, the sponsored property and the sponsor must make a change to their 'position'. A change of position and therefore consideration are usually the result of either:

- a promise to do something one is not legally obligated to do; or
- a promise not to do something one has the right to do.

Figure 7.1 The components required for a valid contract, and factors that will invalidate a contract

A second and key legal theory relating to contract is that of 'promissory estoppel'. The central rule of promissory estoppel is preventing a promisor from going back on their word where there has been no consideration by the promise.

Promissory estoppel key points

- Promissory estoppel is a doctrine that provides an equitable defence, preventing a party who has made a promise to vary a contract for the other party's benefit from later reneging on it and attempting to enforce the original contract.

- Promissory estoppel suspends a right; it does not usually extinguish a right.

- A promise or assurance that is inherently vague or uncertain will not be sufficient for the purposes of promissory estoppel.

- There must be a clear and unequivocal promise or representation that existing rights will not be fully enforced. This representation can be implied.

- The representation or promise was intended to be binding and acted upon. The representation was then acted upon.

Notable case law in the area of promissory estoppel are the cases of *Central London Property Trust Ltd v High Trees House Ltd* (1947) and *Virulite LLC v Virulite Distribution Ltd* [2014] EWHC 366 (QB).

(With thanks to Stephen Dale, Barrister and Senior Teaching Fellow, University of Surrey Business School)

Taking an example, if a company promises to sponsor an event with no conditions attached and then changes their mind the event manager cannot force the company to do so. This is because the event property has not made a change to its position. However, if the event manager had put down deposits for stage hire based on the company's promise and the company knew about this a court may enforce the original promise. This is because the law recognises that when a party makes a promise on which another party takes action it is important to hold the company or individual to their promise.

Drafting a contract

When drafting a contract the following points need to covered:

1 The parties to the agreement must be clearly specified. This could be persons or organizations.

2 The title of the agreement – 'This is a contract between…'.

3 The objectives of both parties and the benefits to be exchanged should be clearly stated:

   – Who does what for whom?

   – When will the contract be executed? In particular, when will payments be made and, vitally, for how much, and when will the performance take place?

   – The location of the performance should be specified.

   – The methods of performance must be clearly set out. This is the 'consideration' element of the contract, which must set out what both parties are committing to (how their position will change).

4 The procedures for communication between partners – who will be responsible for reporting, and how often?

5 Similarly to 4, the procedures for evaluating the sponsorship. Who will be responsible? When and how will the evaluation take place?

6 The sign off process for approving marketing materials such as signage.

7 The process for resolving disputes between parties.

8 The length of the agreement and the process for ending the contract.

In addition to 1–8, McDonnell and Moir (2013) highlight the importance of factoring in:

- Exclusivity in category – This must be very clearly specified, as a category can be very broad. For example, a soft drink manufacturer may see their category as all beverages unless the contract specifies non-alcoholic carbonated beverages.

- Exclusivity in territory – The contract should consider whether it is binding nationally, internationally or across another geographic area. The larger the territory, the greater the sponsorship fee. The implication is that there may be more than one partner in the same category in different areas.

Another fundamentally important aspect of drawing up a contract is that the terms used should be defined clearly. For example, what exactly do the terms name sponsor, official partner and official supplier mean? Each term must be agreed by both parties and set out in the contract.

A useful checklist for preparing a sponsorship contract is provided by IEG and is set out below.

Checklist for preparing a sponsorship contract

When it comes to sponsorship contracts, the devil is the details. To gain the most out of contracts, buyers and sellers need to be as explicit as possible on topics ranging from the most basic (sponsorship fees) to the complex (pass-through rights, content ownership, future options, etc).

Sponsorship rights
- On programme cover?
- In programme adverts?
- In all advertising?
- In all print advertising only?
- On television billboards?
- On merchandise (T-shirts, bumper stickers, etc)?
- In press releases?
- On stationery?

Sponsorship fee
- How paid?
- When paid?
- Secured by letter of credit or escrow?

- Refundable if TV ratings or other performance indicators are poor?
- Rights fee is unrestricted?
- Penalty for late payment?
- Who pays for promotional collateral, logistical support, etc?

Merchandising rights

- Can the sponsor sell T-shirts, mugs and similar souvenirs?
- Can the sponsor manufacture its own souvenirs or buy from the property at cost?
- Who gets the profit on merchandising efforts?

Pass-through rights

- Which categories are pre-approved?
- Which categories are off limits?
- What is the approval process and timeframe?
- Which rights and benefits can/cannot be passed through?
- Who will be responsible for servicing the pass-through relationship?

Ownership of television rights

- Who owns and controls?
- If the organizer owns, does the sponsor have right of first refusal on available spots?
- Is there an estimated rating and/or a rebate for low ratings?
- Does the sponsor get opening/closing credits or billboards?
- Does the sponsor have rights to use footage of the event for current and/or future advertising?
- Will the property get all rights necessary from participants to allow use of clips in commercials without further compensation?

Control over programming/content

- What programming/content does the property control?
- What programming/content does the sponsor control?

Public relations and personal appearances

- Can the property commit key personnel or talent to personal appearances on behalf of the sponsor?
- Can the property commit its spokespersons to mention the sponsor's name whenever possible?

- Does the sponsor have the right to erect a courtesy tent?
- Can the property commit the key personnel participating in an event to attending post-event parties in their honour?
- Does the sponsor get free tickets (for key customers, tie-in contests, etc)?

Future options

- Does the sponsor have the right to renew its sponsorship on the same terms and conditions (plus a fixed increase in the price)?
- Does the sponsor have the right of first negotiation for subsequent years?

Fulfilment report

- When will it be delivered?
- What elements will be included?

Trademarks

- Sponsor's quality control.
- Property's quality control.
- Ownership of special logos.

Liabilities

- To observers.
- To participants.
- To the site.
- To innocent bystanders.
- For infringement of trademarks.
- For contractual commitments in the event of rain, broadcast interruption, force majeure events.

SOURCE IEG Legal Guide to Sponsorship (no date)

Issuing your own contracts may seem daunting; however, remember the definition of a contract given at the start of this chapter, 'A contract is a legally enforceable promise or undertaking that something will or will not occur' (McDonnell and Moir, 2013: 89). In other words, it is an agreement that is written down and which both parties sign. When formalizing an agreement as a contract the following advice from EventScotland (EventScotland, no date) is very useful.

Checklist for preparing a contract – EventScotland

1 Keep it simple – there is no need to write in legalese.

2 Always include the full contact details of both parties and name a representative for each.

3 Ensure that the signatories have the power to sign on behalf of their respective organizations.

4 Date the contract and state a return date as appropriate.

5 Include full and clear details of what you expect to receive.

6 Include full details of what you will provide.

7 Include specific detail of the financial agreement and remember to be clear if VAT is included.

8 If you are dealing with a foreign company, be clear under which country's law the contract is drawn up and the rate of exchange applied to the fee.

9 Include a statement about what happens in the event of cancellation or if either party is unable to deliver to the agreement.

10 Include a statement about any insurance requirements.

11 At the end provide a section that allows each party to print their name, provide a signature and date their agreement.

12 Send two signed copies to the other party in order that one can be returned signed by them.

Ensure you keep copies on your computer as well as a hard copy in a 'contracts' file. Finally, always ask a lawyer (perhaps there is one on your committee or board) to have a look at any documents that you are unsure about. Where a significant amount of risk is involved always seek legal advice.

While it is important to codify the relationship between a sponsor and sponsorship property in the appropriate way with sufficient detail, the success of any sponsorship relationship will depend on how effectively it is managed. In particular, ensuring that sponsors get the best out of their investment is vital to the success and longevity of sponsorship partnerships. Moreover, ethical issues such as ambush marketing and CSR are central concerns to sponsorship managers.

Managing the sponsorship relationship

The importance of understanding not just a sponsor's business objectives but also the characters who make decisions and the processes that are followed in decision making cannot be understated. A good event sponsorship manager recognizes that it is far easier to maintain a relationship with an existing sponsor than it is to acquire new sponsors. Therefore, demonstrating a commitment to the sponsor by advising on how to get the best from their sponsorship investment is fundamental to the foundation of a successful sponsorship relationship.

In particular, it's important that the event manager is candid with the sponsor about the level of investment required. Reic (2017) suggests that sponsorship activation budgets are normally two to six times the amount spent on the rights to the sponsorship property itself and that the sponsorship relationship normally lasts between two and five years. Given this, Reic (2017: 218) observes, 'currently most of the sponsorship activation is initiated by the sponsorship brands, rather than the sponsored properties themselves, this is an area that event marketers could place much more emphasis on.' McDonnell and Moir (2013) concur that both sides need to invest time in the sponsorship relationship and suggest that this is done through regular meetings and keeping accurate records of what was discussed and agreed. Moreover, they suggest that where a close relationship is formed it is less likely that the sponsor will withdraw as they feel part of the event.

When seeking applications from sponsors or grant makers for the first time it is vital to recognize the importance of forming a relationship with the sponsor or grant maker in advance of submitting an application. Approaching potential funders informally to ascertain the appropriateness of an application and to establish a relationship with the funder that will hopefully lead to an application standing out is an important part of the process. Indeed, for some organizations it is encouraged. For example, the Caterpillar Foundation (Caterpillar Foundation, no date) state on their website 'Unsolicited proposals from organizations that have not engaged in a dialogue with Foundation representatives regarding the relevance of their programs are discouraged'. Engaging with the potential funder in advance can save time through the avoidance of making inappropriate or unrealistic applications.

Research insight 5: sponsoring a festival – it's not just a contract, it's a networked relationship...

Luonila (2016) examines the nature of collaboration between festival organizers and sponsors in networked, project-based festival production. The researcher asks why and how sponsorship is used at festivals, from both festival manager and sponsoring business perspectives. The overall aim of the research is to comprehend the role of sponsorship as a resource and a strategic marketing choice. Moreover, the research is particularly focused on the goal of collaboration, which both festival organizers and sponsors say they want.

The researcher examines four festivals and two companies that sponsor festivals in Finland, which has a vibrant festival scene. Using a qualitative, case study approach she takes a discursive view that analyses the ways the interviewees use language and the meanings they make in relation to wider themes and trends in society. Twenty-three interviews, lasting between 45 minutes and two hours, were conducted with key persons involved with the artistic, technical and administrative aspects of the festivals. Other data included in the case studies included material from websites, marketing brochures, onsite observation and a research diary.

The research concludes with multiple insights, some of which confirm what other studies have found – for example, the move away from philanthropic methods or logo visibility as an investment, towards an emphasis on partnerships, interactive activities and innovation through collaboration. The value of festivals for sponsors is in their uniqueness and in their offer of experiences not directly related to the sponsors' business. Moreover, the researcher found that sponsors are often interested in sustainability and the benefits to the region that a festival brings.

One of the main issues that both festival organizers and sponsoring businesses face is finding the human resources to properly sustain the relationship and ensure continued success. However, the research concludes that it is not just the ability of festival organizers and the sponsoring businesses to manage their relationship productively but their ability to network more widely in the multiple layers of the festival's ecosystem. In other words, sponsors need to engage with the multiple festival stakeholders to get the most from their sponsorship investment.

Luonila, M (2016) Sponsorship thinking: A creator for collaborative undertakings in the festival context, *Event Management*, **20** (2), pp 267–84

Ethical knowledge – the central event management competence

So far in this chapter we have discussed legal matters relating to event sponsorship. At the same time, event managers should be aware that there is a range of ethical issues that can affect them. Perry *et al*'s (1996) survey of event managers fount that, when prompted, event managers ranked ethical knowledge twelfth out of sixteen areas of competence. Moreover, their study placed ethics with contextual knowledge as the least important knowledge area. More recent research focusing on the text of job advertisements, such as Arcodia and Barker (2003), shows that an understanding of ethical issues or corporate social responsibility is not seen as important as no advertisements mention these terms. Arcodia and Barker (2003) note that 5 per cent of the advertisements analysed identify 'trustworthiness/responsibility' as an employee attribute they are looking for. At the same time, in his literature review Tang (2014) identifies professional ethics as an important attribute for tourism and hospitality professionals, although it does not figure highly in the competence framework his paper goes on to present.

In this section we first examine the nature of ethics and then establish a framework for evaluating ethical issues before discussing specific ethical issues in event sponsorship contexts. Finally, we will argue that the ability to adopt an ethical approach in event sponsorship and fundraising activities is a core competence for an event manager. Taking decisions based on a sound understanding of CSR is the central competence that underpins all other event management competencies and is particularly relevant in event sponsorship contexts.

Ethics, specifically business ethics, refer to a set of moral principles and values that guide the actions of businesses and other organizations. Business ethics set standards relating to acceptable behaviour, particularly when the decisions of a business lead to actions that have negative or harmful outcomes for stakeholders.

Business ethics and ethical decision making can be understood more clearly if they are placed in context. Daftet *et al* (2010) outlined three domains of human action – codified law, ethics and free choice – and set them on a continuum relating to the degree of explicit control. Codified law has the highest level of explicit control as it relates to legal standards.

Ethics, which relates to social standards, has some control. Free choice relates to personal standards and so has a low level of legal control.

The codified law domain relates to behaviours that are subject to legislation, and to ignore them would lead to court actions. For example, if an alcohol sponsor knowingly gave out samples of its product to children at an event it would be breaking the law. At the other end of the continuum is the domain of free choice, where it would be argued that adults are free to decide whether to drink alcohol or not, regardless of its harmful effects on their health.

An ethical business decision is one that is both legal and fits with the shared standards of the community. The problem of ethical dilemmas often occurs when there are both harmful and beneficial outcomes as a consequence of a business decision. Furthermore, because funding is involved that may ultimately allow an event to go ahead or not, ethical decisions can be particularly difficult.

What is also important to bear in mind is the potential for mixed and contradictory messaging that may result from a lack of ethics in business decision making relating to event sponsorship. Poor, ill-judged decisions may lead to legal action or a loss of event authenticity that undermines an event's credibility. In a sponsorship context and following from the alcohol example above, if the event is sporting related there is an ethical dilemma in that the community will benefit from the sporting event taking place but the sponsorship by an alcohol brand may lead to negative health outcomes for the community that outweigh the benefits.

One example given by McDonnell and Moir (2013) is that of Dow Chemical, who in 2012 were a TOP level Olympic sponsor. Dow Chemical acquired Union Carbide in 2001. In 1984 a chemical factory in Bhopal, India that was part owned by Union Carbide leaked deadly gases into nearby communities, killing 20,000 people. In 1989 Union Carbide paid the Indian Government $470 million in compensation. Since then there have been further claims and appeals in relation to compensation, all of which up to 2016 were rejected by courts in the US and India.

Dow Chemical's sponsorship of the 2012 Olympics and ongoing sponsorship to 2020 led to significant negative coverage during the 2012 London games. In Bhopal a 'special' Olympics was held for children affected by the disaster to draw attention to the community's belief that Dow has an ongoing responsibility for the disaster that it was avoiding.

The contentious nature of Dow's link with Union Carbide was something that the organizers of the Olympics were aware of. Indeed Lord Coe, Chair of the London Organising Committee of the Olympic Games, defended the sponsorship deal, highlighting that Dow had not been involved with Bhopal at the time of the disaster or when the final compensation settlement was agreed. However, Dow's sponsorship led to the resignation of Meredith Alexander from the Commission for Sustainable London 2012 (Hart, 2012). Moreover, a motion in the London Assembly to terminate Dow's sponsorship and demand an apology from the London Organising Committee for the Olympic Games to the victims of Bhopal was narrowly defeated by 11 votes to 10 (Magnay, 2012).

When considering the ethical implications of a business decision in relation to sponsorship, it's useful to factor in the motivations of the sponsor. The question is, why does this organization want to sponsor the event? Often, a potential problem may then present itself. If we consider IEG's list of sponsor motivations set out in Chapter 4 we can see that showcasing community responsibility – well-focused sponsorships that deliver tangible benefits to communities – can have significant impact. Sponsors who are able to demonstrate integrity through CSR will have a very positive impact on consumer impressions of their brand. In the case of Dow Chemical the issues relating to Union Carbide led to the integrity of the sponsor and the event itself being called into question.

The term 'corporate social responsibility' is mentioned in IEG's sponsor motivation above and it's important to define what the term means. CSR is:

> the voluntary dedication of business towards sustainable development, resulting in benefits for society (people), environment (planet) and the economy (profit). At the level of consumers, sustainability requires the consideration not just of the price of a particular good or service, but also of its impact on people and the natural environment.
>
> (Ferdinand and Kitchin, 2012: 201)

When CSR is brought into ethical business decision making on sponsorship, a complex range of issues needs to be considered. As the Dow Chemical example above shows, a potential sponsor's business background and the values it stands for should be considered. In this case a company that had a tarnished reputation from a disaster nearly 30 years prior to the event came back to haunt Dow Chemical and the London Organising Committee of the Olympic Games. Another related area is linked to event suppliers and whether the practices and materials used by a supplier are in keeping with the values of the event being sponsored. So, for example, if a sponsor supplies branded T-shirts for the event, does it matter if they have been produced by women and children in poor conditions somewhere in the developing world?

Sponsorship insight 3: where did you get that T-shirt?

When moving from one event management role to another it's really important to understand the different values of the organization you are entering. Tom Lunt recalls a conversation with a former colleague.

'In my first role as an event fundraiser we were not too worried about where the sponsorship and other non-ticket revenues came from. For some of our big-ticket events we had sponsorship from drinks brands and genetic engineering companies. Often these came through personal contacts with senior executives who supported the work the charity did.

'However, when I moved to a new organization I soon realized that this would no longer be acceptable practice. On two separate events I had to say no to sponsorship from a major entertainment company from the United States and a petrochemical corporation as well. This was because to accept financial support from such organizations would have contradicted the organization's values.

'I did slip up one time early on in the role. We were doing a big event and we needed branded T-shirts. I called a few suppliers and got a good quote, and the T-shirts arrived a few days later. However, as I was returning from a staff conference some time after the event had taken place a colleague gently asked me where the T-shirts had come from and whether they were sustainably sourced and guaranteed not to involve child labour. I had to admit that I didn't know. Next time I ordered T-shirts I made sure the merchandise had been produced to the proper ethical standards.

'It's so easy in the rush to achieve deadlines and get things done ready for an event to overlook things like this. Having a clear CSR policy in place that gives guidance on suppliers should prevent internal contradictions that could prove embarrassing or worse if widely reported.'

Recently, BP's sponsorship of cultural institutions such as the British Museum and Royal Shakespeare Company led to a letter signed by 214 prominent artists including the actor Mark Rylance (Khomami, 2016) which called for the corporate's five-year sponsorship deals to be ended. The protest was based on BP's record on climate change and human rights. While it is unclear how much impact the letter has had, Brown (2016) notes that BP ended its 34-year sponsorship of the Edinburgh International Festival. BP said this was due to the extremely challenging business environment. However, the previous year there had been significant pressure for the festival to sever ties with BP because it was damaging the event's reputation.

What is clear is that in balancing the interests of people, planet and profit event managers have to balance a range of competing needs. For example, sponsorships such as BP can allow access to what would otherwise be very expensive events, museums, performances and exhibitions.

Research insight 6: corporate social responsibility – moving beyond the checklist

Musgrave and Woodward (2016) take the concept of CSR and examine how it has been applied in the meeting planning industry. This is particularly important given the growth and size of the meetings industry, which is estimated to be worth in excess of $1.1 trillion. The researchers suggest that, given the potential impact of the meetings industry on the environment and society, how meeting planners, venues and their clients address CSR will be key to the credibility of the sector in the future.

The meetings industry, and in particular industry associations like Meeting Professionals International and the Association of Exhibitions and Events, have made CSR part of their work. A wide range of guides, standards and other documentation is available. However, this material views CSR in a range of ways from ethical practice to environmental sustainability and there has been limited progress to define and simplify the complexity and context driven nature of CSR at an industry-wide level.

The researchers examine the contextual application of CSR and variable uptake and practice of CSR in the meetings industry. This is done through the application of an ecological systems theory framework first developed by the developmental psychologist Urie Bronfenbrenner. This framework has four levels:

1 The microsystem – family, peers, community groups, health services and school.
2 The mesosystem – personal values and CSR activities.
3 The exosystem – industry, mass media, local politics and neighbours.
4 The macrosystem – societal forces, class, race, gender, culture.

Using this framework as a guide, the researchers invited 20,000 meeting planners to be interviewed. This led to 90 semi-structured interviews with meeting professionals that were conducted either over the telephone or via Skype. The constant comparison process was used by the researchers, meaning that the interviewers closely read the first four or five interview transcripts and open coded them. This means summarizing the content into short sections of text or 'units' of meaning. The next stage involved the researchers discussing the open codes and grouping them into broad categories that reflect their importance to the interviewees or help to explain how the interviewees described their views. These categories are then formed into a coding frame that is then applied to the analysis of the rest of the interview data. Qualitative software such as NVIVO can be used to apply the coding frame systematically. The final stage of constant comparison is summarizing and interpreting the findings.

The researchers found 12 codes that they linked to the ecosystems theory framework in the following way:

- microsystem;
- non-financial donations;
- workforce;
- macrosystem;
- green technology;
- legislation;
- transparency and reliability;
- exosystem;
- community engagement;
- supply chain management;
- mesosystem;
- volunteer labour.

The researchers suggest that using the ecosystems approach to CSR implies a flexible approach and that the application of different values and implementation approaches can have similar results. This is important because placing context at the centre of CSR practice may encourage event planners to move beyond checklist approaches to accept national and international standards such as ISO 20121.

Musgrave, J and Woodward, S (2016)
Ecological systems theory approach to corporate social responsibility:
Contextual perspectives from meeting planners, *Event Management*, **20** (3), pp 365–81

Conclusion

Central to the management of a relationship between an event property and a sponsor is the legal framework that is negotiated and agreed in the contract. First and foremost, the ownership of the event property must be established. When preparing and examining a contract the term 'consideration' is very important as it sets out what each party expects to receive from the agreement. In Professional Insight 4 James Tibbetts describes what consideration is very succinctly: 'we provide this, you provide that'. If this is done concisely and precisely a firm foundation will be put in place for a successful relationship between the event property and the sponsor. The IEG checklist and sponsorship template will help you to prepare a sound contract.

Ethical considerations have not been identified in past research on event manager competencies. However, we argue that this is because research (in particular the content analysis of job advertisements) has led to a focus on practical competencies. Clearly, when considering a brand as a potential sponsor for an event property it's vital that the brand will not detract from the integrity of an event, or vice versa.

In the next chapter, we will examine the phenomenon of ambush marketing, which has become increasingly prominent in events management. The term encompasses a wide range of activities, from leafleting a rival event, large stunts such as Paddy Power flying aeroplanes over the Ryder Cup (Sweeny, 2012) to the use of Adwords online. In Professional Insight 4 James Tibbetts, who has worked as Operations Director on a range of major sporting events such as the Tour of Yorkshire, offers advice on what to do if ambush marketing is encountered. In a wide-ranging interview James offers unique insights into many of the topics we have covered in this chapter as well as the practicalities of writing sponsorship contracts so that they work with the overall event business model.

Discussion questions and activities

You are an event manager of a large festival. Consider the following issues:

1   Your sponsorship manager is very upset. Having received emails from a brand saying they would take a sponsorship package that included hoardings on either side of stage, she hired additional scaffolding for the stage to display the sponsor's branding. The sponsor is attempting to back out of the agreement and she is concerned that the festival will be out of pocket. What is your opinion on the brand's

legal position – have they entered into a legally binding contract with the festival? Justify your answer with reference to the appropriate legal frameworks.

2 The festival has recently agreed a contract with a new sponsor that guarantees exclusivity in that product sector. On the first day of the event you're informed that a rival brand is organizing an 'activation' in one of the camping fields. What actions would you take?

3 Using this chapter and examples from your own experience, discuss whether ethical competence is just as important for an event manager as legal, financial, PR and marketing competencies.

Further reading

IEG: www.sponsorship.com

This website is very useful for getting up-to-date information on sponsorship, insights, trends and events.

Mullins, LJ (2013) *Management and Organisational Behaviour*, FT Publishing International, London

This is a general management text that covers a range of issues including a comprehensive and thorough discussion of ethics and corporate social responsibility in Chapter 17.

References

Arcodia, C and Barker, T (2003) The employability prospects of graduates in event management: Using data from job advertisements, in *Riding the Wave of Tourism and Hospitality Research*, CAUTHE, pp 19–34, Southern Cross University, Lismore, NSW

Bowdin, G, Allen, J and Harris, R (2011) *Events Management*, 3rd edn, Butterworth-Heinemann, Oxford

Brown, M (2016) BP ends sponsorship of Edinburgh International Festival after 34 years, *Guardian*, 6 April [Online] https://www.theguardian.com/culture/2016/apr/06/bp-ends-34-year-edinburgh-international-festival-sponsorship [Accessed 28/06/18]

Caterpillar Foundation (no date) [Online] http://www.cybergrants.com/pls/
cybergrants/quiz.check_answer [Accessed 15/06/17]

Daft, R, Kendrick, M and Vershinina, N (2010) *Management: International
edition*, 10th edn, Cengage Learning EMEA, Hampshire

EventScotland (no date) Event management guide – EventScotland [Online]
http://www.eventscotland.org/development/our-key-publications/event-
management-a-practical-guide/ [Accessed 26/02/18]

Ferdinand, N and Kitchin, P (2012) *Events Management: An international
approach*, Sage, London

Hart, S (2012) London 2012 Olympics: Watchdog commissioner resigns
over Games' sponsorship link with Dow Chemical, *Daily Telegraph*,
25 January [Online] http://www.telegraph.co.uk/sport/olympics/9039749/
London-2012-Olympics-watchdog-commissioner-resigns-over-Games-
sponsorship-link-with-Dow-Chemical.html [Accessed 15/06/17]

IEG (International Events Group) (no date) IEG's sponsorship contract checklist
[Online] http://www.sponsorship.com/iegsr/2014/04/07/IEG-s-Sponsorship-
Contract-Checklist.aspx [Accessed 03/07/18]

Khomami, N (2016) Mark Rylance heads list of artists calling for end to BP
cultural sponsorship, *Guardian*, 2 August [Online] https://www.theguardian.
com/environment/2016/aug/02/mark-rylance-heads-list-of-artists-calling-for-end-
to-bp-cultural-sponsorship [Accessed 28/06/18]

Luonila, M (2016) Sponsorship thinking: A creator for collaborative undertakings
in the festival context, *Event Management*, 20 (2), pp 267–84

Magnay, J (2012) London 2012 Olympics: Dow Chemical puts blame for
ongoing crisis in Bhopal at Indian government's door, *Daily Telegraph*,
8 March [Online] https://www.telegraph.co.uk/sport/olympics/9130231/
London-2012-Olympics-Dow-Chemical-puts-blame-for-ongoing-crisis-in-
Bhopal-at-Indian-governments-door.html [Accessed 28/06/18]

McDonnell, A and Moir, M (2013) *Event Sponsorship,* Routledge, London

Musgrave, J and Woodward, S (2016) Ecological systems theory approach to
corporate social responsibility: Contextual perspectives from meeting planners,
Event Management, 20 (3), pp 365–81

Perry, M, Foley, P and Rumpf, P (1996) Events management: An emerging
challenge in Australian higher education, *Festival Management and Event
Tourism*, 4 (3), pp 85–93

Reic, I (2017) *Events Marketing Management: A consumer perspective*, Routledge,
London

Skinner, BE and Rukavina, V (2003) *Event Sponsorship*, Wiley, Hoboken, NJ

Sweeny, M (2012) Ryder Cup 2012: Paddy Power tees up ambush plan, *Guardian*, 1 October [Online] https://www.theguardian.com/media/2012/sep/29/ryder-cup-2012-paddy-power-ambush [Accessed 28/06/18]

Tang, H-WV (2014) Constructing a competence model for international professionals in the MICE industry: An analytic hierarchy process approach, *Journal of Hospitality, Leisure, Sport & Tourism Education*, **15**, pp. 34–49

Legal issues in event sponsorship and fundraising

08

LEARNING OBJECTIVES

Having read this chapter and worked through the questions and activities you should be able:

- to examine how ambush marketing can be managed by event managers;
- to assess the importance of event insurance;
- to compare the differences between sponsor and grant-maker requirements;
- to examine the legal aspects of developing a sponsorship partnership.

Introduction

In this chapter we will see how some of the central points made in Chapter 7 actually work in reality. The Professional insight interview with James Tibbetts covers a great deal of ground, including the relationship between sponsors and event properties. He also offers valuable advice and insight into how to approach legal considerations when entering into sponsorship agreements.

Before James' interview we will examine an important area of sponsorship that can work both for and against event managers and event sponsors. Ambush marketing is a well-established technique that is used widely in the events sector.

As with Chapter 7, this chapter should not be read and followed as a legally authoritative guide but as a broad overview of the key issues relating to the law that an event manager will face in relation to sponsorship.

Ambush marketing

Ambush marketing is not a new phenomenon, having been identified as far back as the 1984 Olympics when Kodak announced they were the proud sponsors of ABC's broadcasting of the Olympic Games and secured the role of official film-maker for the US track team. No one was in any doubt that Kodak had 'ambushed' Fuji's sponsorship of the Los Angeles Olympics (Sandler and Shani, 1989).

Ambush marketing can take several different forms; what they have in common is the intention to benefit from a sponsorship property in a way that has not been agreed through a sponsorship contract. Chadwick and Burton (2011) set out a typology of ambush marketing strategies. At the same time, Koenigstorfer and Uhrich (2017) suggest a range of counter-ambush strat egies. The relationship between ambush and counter-ambush marketing is set out in Figure 8.1, which should also be considered in relation to the comments made by James Tibbetts in the following Professional insight interview.

Figure 8.1   Ambush and counter-ambush marketing strategies

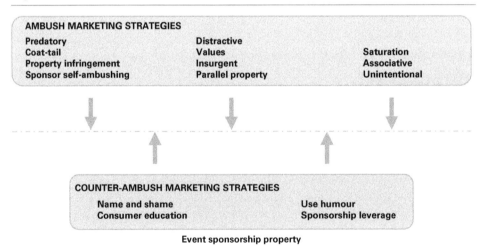

SOURCE Adapted from Chadwick and Burton (2011) and Koenigstorfer and Uhrich (2017)

Professional insight 4: managing relationships with sponsors – interview with James Tibbetts, Chief Operations Officer, Female Sports Group

The Female Sports Group (FSG) generates revenue, raises awareness and delivers consultancy services in women-led sport, mixed gender sport and community sport. Some of the projects the FSG works on are Badminton England, the Vitality parkrun UK and the Commonwealth Games England. As Chief Operations Officer (COO), James' main responsibility is to set up the events side of the business, which is not something the company has done before. The main project he is currently working on is the delivery of FSG's first major event property, the P&P World Cycling Revival.

Talk me through the legal considerations you have to think about when establishing a sponsorship property, preparing and agreeing a sponsorship contract and the legal aspects of working with sponsors to put on a live event.

In terms of establishing an event like the Cycling Revival, it's not just a sponsorship property, it's a hospitality property, a ticket revenue driving property. The key initial consideration is having your house in order in terms of delivering the event. Have you got a contract with the venue? Have you got a plan for insurance? The level of appropriate insurance will be one of the first legal considerations an event manager will need to think through with the venue and sponsors. If you are going to go out and sell sponsorship, how will you protect yourself if things go wrong? It's a big thing to think about in our context. We are going to deliver a big outdoor event – what happens if it pours with rain? What happens if there's an accident and the track is damaged? So the legal framework needs to be put in place through proper planning and insurance so that if a sponsor invests £250,000 or whatever and then the event doesn't deliver the correct insurances will cover it.

The core insurances to operate as a business are employer's liability and professional liability insurance. For an event company, over and above that you need to have public liability insurance in relation to the type of event you are running. For cycle racing, the public liability insurance will cover your operations as a business – running an event – so protecting the people putting barriers out and building structures and also protecting the public in and around the event. At a cycling event you may need to have third party cover for the racing and third party cover for riders having crashes. I have been at events where there have been crashes and bicycles have flown into the crowd and hit someone on the head!

Getting advice from an experienced broker is vital. There are several that operate in the sports events space. JLT operate in this area, and also Miller. There are different policies out there, which are underwritten with Lloyds of London or Sports Cover. With Cycling Revival we have found when trying to get cover, because we are partly a live music event and partly an exhibition, we probably fall into a grey area between sport and live entertainment. So, probably more of a festival than a traditional cycle race. We have to negotiate a hybrid policy specifically put in place to cover all these risks.

Another consideration if you're working in an existing venue is that the venue may have predetermined insurance policies in place that will apply to the event contract. For example, having worked in velodromes before, each of the venue owners had different legal requirements of you in terms of the level of insurance cover that needed to be in place. So before going out and approaching potential sponsors it's important to know what level of cover you can get and that the insurance broker will actually sell you that level of cover. Brokers can and do turn round and say 'You're not experienced enough to deliver an event with that level of complexity.' Insurance is a hefty cost, so an event manager will need to know what that is when planning the financials of the wider event, including the value of sponsorship packages.

If you go to the Glasgow Velodrome they'll require a £5 million public liability policy. Whereas the Lee Valley Velopark in London requires a £10 million policy. When the Lee Valley Velopark opened they asked for £20 million cover, which wasn't available on the insurance market, and we had to get two £10 million policies to run one after the other! So you need to know you can get it. One of the challenges I had when I was Event Director for the Tour de France in Yorkshire was getting the appropriate level of insurance. It was one of the big costs on the budget. Underwriters will send you a form to fill out where you have to prove your ability and track record. How many claims have got on your policy in the last 10 years? That sort of thing.

This may sound difficult but it's quite straightforward – have a conversation with a broker, explain what you want to do, and they'll walk you through it and find the best deal on the market for you. Then you can draw up an agreement in principle that can be presented to a sponsor to help build confidence.

The other important consideration when you're establishing a sponsorship property is how you protect your intellectual property (IP) around a sponsorship property. The problem is, you can't really protect an idea under IP law. The ways you can do it depend on where in the world you are: the West, the UK, USA and Europe is very different landscape to, for example, China, where, historically, IP law hasn't existed (please see Author's note at end of interview). You need to think about the markets you want to protect in. It's very difficult to protect a format at an event. First, you need to come up with a name, brand name and logo and go down the traditional copyrighting process with those. Lock down IP assets associated with the brand – the Facebook, Twitter, Instagram and Snapchat social media addresses – so no one can get in that space and take those assets. It's almost first come, first served – same with internet addresses. The last thing you want when you've just sold a sponsorship package is to find that someone else has bought the website address and can hold you to ransom with it. That's more a practical than legal consideration, but it may lead to legal issues further down the line if you don't sort it out.

The IP side is to ensure that you get your trademark registered in the correct class. For the events I have been involved with over the past few years that's Class 41 Sporting Goods and Entertainment. There are several categories that are relevant, and it can get complicated. In my previous role I had a lot of discussion with UEFA over the name of the Revolution track cycling event that the FACE Partnership ran. FACE tried to trademark the Revolution Champions League. The rationale for going after that brand name was that the term 'Champions League' exists in a lot of other sports. There is a boxing champions league and a poker champions league. So we thought, going for champions league with Revolution in front of it, we would get away with that. However, we got a 'cease and desist' letter from UEFA pretty quickly. I got a letter from a lawyer in Madrid stating their IP over the name and a copy of their trademark. Our lawyers then responded and at the same time I got a letter from UEFA's lawyers in Geneva also requesting we cease use of the name. We then responded to Geneva who then stopped the lawyer in Madrid. We then spoke directly with Geneva and said look this isn't about football. Can we have a co-existence agreement? Which they quickly agreed to on the proviso that we called the event the Revolution Cycling Champions League. So there was a compromise, which made sense.

So, by going through the trademarking process, you can flush out all those potential issues. When establishing an event and coming up with ideas that you hope will be a significant brand you don't want somebody approaching you five years down the line saying 'I trademarked that name, can you change yours please.' A practical step for anyone looking to trademark is to go onto the Intellectual Property Office website. The website is free to access and you can you can search all the trademark applications for the last 70 years or so. You can look at logos and brand names, and it will tell you whether the trademark exists, and whether an application has been rejected or withdrawn.

In terms of preparing sponsorship contracts, the contract is king for me. You've got to have the rights, the wherewithal and the backup to deliver the contract. That's easier when you own the event, but there are situations where you may be working for an agency selling a sponsorship on behalf of someone else. We find this with the parkrun event. We don't own parkrun so we have to have a contract to flow down rights to third parties. We will do the sponsorship contract, so the sponsor has a contract with FSG, but there is also a contract between FSG and parkrun that says we have these assets and have the rights to sell them. You have to prove that you can sell the rights.

In terms of agreeing contracts you have to be really clear and concise about what rights somebody gets. The way I like to think about it is we provide this, you provide that and you break it down into 'these are the parties, this is the background to what we are doing'. FSG will provide the following, point by point, here's your rights – those rights may be X number of logos on a podium backdrop, X number of logos printed onto the track, X number of logos on banners, inclusion in emails, the bottom of the website. Break it down and be as specific as you can and then in return they provide whatever they've agreed to provide back. Traditionally that will be money, but what is more common these days is more than just cash. You might be getting a combination of cash and product.

So, hypothetically, say you are doing a sponsorship deal with BMW or another car dealer. They may love the package with logo inclusions, tickets and hospitality. Generally, it's not just for branding – it will be two or three things tied in together. They'll offer to give you the million pounds you want for it but actually what they'll offer to do is give you three-quarters of a million and the rest in cars. And you have to put the cars in prominent places, and they must be used by event staff and as prizes.

In this way money is saved against another budget line. Product is quite a simple one to equate but there are softer things. For example, when I worked on the Tour of Britain, Honda had a huge database of customers. They may give you the right to email all their customers with details of your event. They may want to promote the event through their own social media, things like that. The traditional model of 'you get these rights for this amount of money' doesn't exist in the same way anymore. There's normally some money that changes hands but it's money plus – a plus that becomes far more worth it. And brands are recognizing this; it's product placement, essentially. Particularly with car brands, it's quite straightforward. Going back to the Honda example, they didn't just give us the cars, they gave us fuel cards so every time I went to a meeting it was free. The moment you did over 5,000 miles they gave you a new car and fuel card. Those deals are gold dust. Another example is clothing. I was involved in an event where Jeff Banks gave us suits and uniforms for all the staff on the ground; that was a significant saving off our bottom line.

So going back to contracts: lock down the rights, specify clearly what they get and what you get. I think it's incredibly important to specify when payment will be made. Cash flow is very important to events and the timing of when sponsorship revenue is paid will have a big impact. So when planning an event like the PP World Cycling Revival we've got overheads, we've got an office, people and so on. You need to lock down when that money's going to be paid. Legal agreements need to be aligned with the cash flow, so that has to be locked down in the contract. I like to put in the payment terms, not just the payment methods. Include details such as what account they pay into, account number, sort code, etc.

Cancellation and termination of the contract are the final pieces of the jigsaw for me. How do we get out of this deal if it is not working for us, or how do they get out of it in such a way that it protects the business and their interests as a sponsor? One way of doing this is to have a set of key performance indicators (KPIs) that are agreed and set down in the contract. This would be a set of minimums for the sponsor, where the event organizers undertake to get the sponsor's logo in front of a certain amount of people and on TV for a specified period of time, and so on. Then, if the KPIs aren't achieved, there may be a phased way of terminating the contract or the way the payments are made may be altered. So there may be a success fee or bonus.

There are some practical things that you need to ensure the sponsor has, and these need to be stated in the contract. They need to have public liability insurance and health and safety procedures and paperwork – risk assessments and method statements. Otherwise, they cannot come on site and deliver the activations they have planned. The contract can also be very useful for ensuring that everyone's role is clearly defined. I always want it put in the contract who the main point of contact is. Otherwise you can be going round in circles looking for people.

Can you offer any insights into events and broadcasting?

My experience of broadcasting rules and regulations in relation to events is that there are certain rules, particularly in the UK with Ofcom (the communications regulator). There are certain amounts of airtime during programming that can be given to commercial topics. It will vary from broadcaster to broadcaster. If you are on ITV or Sky (commercial TV stations) the rules are a lot more flexible than if the broadcast is on the BBC (the British public service broadcaster). When you're broadcasting on the BBC, incidental branding seems to be OK, but showing anything that's like the Right Guard Challenge as part of *A League of Their Own* on Sky would not work on the BBC. It's very rare that you will produce a TV programme dedicated to an event. In the future this may change, but at this moment in time you'll generally work with a TV production company who will know the rules and advise you accordingly.

If you go in on the BBC you'll provide them a theme; it will all have to look like a BBC programme and you won't get access to break bumpers, no product placement, and you'll probably have to use their presenters. ITV is a lot more flexible; at the beginning and end of programmes there are little adverts tied specifically to that programme – called 'break bumpers'. You may negotiate the right to sell those as part of your sponsorship packages. Or if Sky or ITV are paying you they may retain them to sell, to recoup some of the cost of the programme. Within the programmes themselves there are strict limits on what you're allowed to do regarding product placement in the UK. And events are completely subject to the rules relating to tobacco and alcohol as well.

How do you go about valuing a sponsorship opportunity at an event?

It very much falls back to looking at what the rest of the market is doing. Actually looking at your nearest competitors and partners. In my sector I know a number of companies organizing similar events and working in particular sponsorship markets. A lot of big properties operate by selling rights through agencies. There are a lot of traditional ways to evaluate an already existing property through media analysis using Kantar Media. Kantar would look at the number of eyeballs. Let's say Epson, as a printer brand, sponsor a football match. Kantar would watch all of the footage of that football match and measure the amount of time the logo was on the screen. That would then quantify into media value. They'd also look at the spread of social media reach. These figures would then be put together and a multiplier included, because one person watching may mention it to a friend or colleague, that sort of thing. They will come with numbers and then look at the market and compare what others are paying for those sorts of numbers for similar events.

With smaller independent sponsorship agencies, they'll say something like 'The Cycling Revival's going to get 15,000 people in the AB demographic over this amount of time, in these proportions of men and women.' This could then be compared to a similar event like the Goodwood Revival. We know Goodwood Revival sold sponsorship packages for the following values. So it's benchmarking against others in the market.

How would an agency know what a brand had paid for a sponsorship?

This information is not published – it tends to be a lot of word of mouth. The industry isn't huge. There are a lot of good tools to help, such as Pearlfinders, who amalgamate information on brands across various markets: what they've said in an interview with an industry magazine, what they're interested in, etc. They'll amalgamate all that data. Also, people talk off the record. In some cases it's easier to calculate. For example, hospitality is quite easy to do as the price of a ticket can be calculated. Sponsorship isn't quite the same; you might create a menu of items and you can factor in the hospitality cost and end up with some unknowns. There's no hard and fast rule – it comes with experience and knowledge of the business.

How do you work with sponsors to help them maximize their sponsorship investments?

A sponsorship management plan will generally be set out and overseen by an account manager in the team. Once the contract is signed there will be a matrix of assets that have been promised and the event team will focus with the account manager on delivering those assets. Generally, with a big sponsor there will be a monthly progress meeting. It is often forgotten that the earlier a sponsor signs up for an event the longer they get the benefits of the partnership, because they'll be included in activities for a longer period of time. This is what is missed by those who sign up at the last moment because it's a bit cheaper.

When we pitch to a brand, part of the pitch will be about how the activations will work. For example, with a champagne brand we'd say we'll give everyone who comes to the event a free glass of champagne and we will create this amazing experience as part of the event. We'll take a revenue share but the focus is on maximizing their exposure to the audience. Normally a sponsor can expect to spend the same again on their activations at the event as they paid for the sponsorship rights. So the sponsorship budget should essentially be double. It's like in exhibitions where you pay for the space but then have to build the stand. That said, with digital technology some of the additional activities can cost less.

In terms of good activations, I saw an amazing one at the Eroica Britannia vintage cycle ride. Hendrick's Gin came up with a completely immersive experience. They had a marquee with a 'mad scientist' experiment set up with actors dressed up in theme – full tweed – and when you walked into the tent you were brought into the experience with the actors. They started this story about how they were doing experiments with cucumbers (with Hendrick's Gin you're supposed to have a cucumber), they spun this story about how they were experimenting to find out if cucumber growth was affected by what type of music was played. They'd wired up these trays of cucumbers around this bench, with these 'mad scientist' actors behind spinning this story, and you put on safety goggles which had a metal connection and a wire – the cucumbers were also wired up. They got you to touch the cucumbers, and when you did it completed the circuit and played a different instrument or beat. Between the six of us we played about two minutes of jazz, which was recorded and uploaded to their website. I thought it was so cleverly done. At the end this a lady came in with a tray of Hendrick's Gin and tonics that we had in the sunshine. Looking back at going to Eroica, that's one of the experiences that I remember as being really, really cool.

You see good and bad sponsorship activations. Some just don't bother – they've spent money and got branding up. The worst I've seen is where brands just buy advertising and do nothing else, because you don't know why the brand is involved. Football, I think, is a prime place where they are getting this wrong. There is a lot of advertising revenue but you don't know half the time what these brands do.

What do ethics and corporate responsibility mean to you in a sponsorship context?

FSG is all about women's sport, so we've come across the 'prize money' issue that exists in cycling. It's an ethics thing around paying men and women equal prize money. That's a big issue in some sports these days. Another issue is the use of podium girls. For example, the Tour de France has very pretty girls handing out the jerseys at the end of each stage. This is an underlying debate that's going on in cycling. We're very aware of that and we've had sponsoring brands who've fed back saying 'We don't want podium girls – we want a boy and a girl.' You see that when you look back at the podiums from London 2012.

Have you ever organized an ambush marketing campaign?

Not particularly. The only thing I've done is sent leafleting teams into or around other events, which was some time ago. That's quite standard – most events will leaflet to give people an idea of what similar events are going on. Also it's not necessarily ambush marketing. We sent in people to leaflet as an event finished and as people were leaving we were handing out a ticket offer to our event.

But a lot of the digital stuff you can do around Google Keywords and AdWords is quite clever. You can make sure your event appears at the top of the list when people are searching for similar events. That happened a few years ago with the track cycling events I was involved in where another track event bid consistently to be above us on the Google list, to be at the forefront of people's thinking.

Have you had to deal with ambush marketing at an event you've organized?

I haven't had to deal with anything other than contingency planning. So one of the big things we contingency planned for on the Tour de France in Yorkshire was a big Paddy Power stunt. The last thing you want is to be on the end of one of their stunts because they just don't care. They're very effective at what they do (see Author's note at end of this interview). However, as hosts and rights holders in the UK we had to be able to commit to being able to deal with things like that. We came up with a contingency plan that involved various different groups and authorities to make sure that, if something did appear, it had as little impact as possible. That went as far as physically stopping people and getting intelligence ahead of the event. We knew of two or three things that were planned, which we headed off at the pass, so to speak. We also had plans in place for spotting stuff in advance. So if Paddy Power had put a big figure up on a hillside that was trying to attract the TV cameras we'd know about it and be able to brief the client and encourage the TV stations not to show it.

The key thing is not to sit back and do nothing. As the event manager, it may be possible to embrace it and turn it to your advantage. There are subtle things you can do as an organizer to take attention away from an ambush stunt without being heavy-handed. If you look after the press and present good content about the stories you want to tell about the event, they are less likely to be diverted by ambush activities. So, sensible briefing of suppliers and the press is far more effective than a heavy-handed approach. A light touch, such as a steward, or even someone not in uniform, approaching those putting on a stunt and having a quiet word to say that's really not appropriate, can you stop please, is often enough.

What would you say are the main differences between managing a commercial sponsorship relationship and a relationship with a grant maker or funding body?

Funding bodies are very different to commercial sponsors. Public bodies like EventScotland, UK Sport or the Department for Digital, Culture, Media & Sport have different rules of play in terms of the use of funding. If you bring in private sector funding through a sponsor, ticket revenue or hospitality you can spend it on whatever you want. However, funding granted by public bodies will have a use tied to it. For example, if you bring in EventScotland funding you may be required to use that money to market the event to international audiences. A common one is funding being granted specifically to bring in stars, eg you might want to use public money to incentivize the stars to travel to a certain region, either by offering a bigger prize pool or an appearance fee. Public money tends to come with more red tape and things tied to it.

Furthermore, there tends to be a reporting method. So with EventScotland or London & Partners, the London Mayor's office, you'll be expected to do some form of economic impact reporting. There are a number of tools available. For example UK Sport has an event metrics part of its website, which you can use to build up a picture of how much the public have spent coming to an event, which can then be used to justify the investment they have made. Politically, that goes back to the powers that be and the taxpayer. So the reporting structures, accountability and governance that go with public funding make it very different to commercial sponsorship.

This is where event safety standards and sustainability come into play: BS 8901 and ISO 20121. The event's commitment to the national living wage. All this will need to be considered with a public sector contract as they'll expect you to comply with these rules. With public funding a major factor is, how does this event give back to the local community? As well as on a global stage, if you're thinking about London & Partners, for example. So that links back to the whole CSR agenda. When I was working on the Tour de France one of the key metrics was the net/gross economic impact, and then how many full-time equivalent jobs was the event generating? And it's really hard to measure and quantify, but to qualify for funding you have to do it. It's a different avenue of funding that people don't really consider and think through properly. If you do it wrong you can be accused of misappropriating funds and ultimately be asked to pay the money back. At the same time, grant funding, properly administered and accounted for, can make the difference between an event going ahead or not, so it can be well worth the extra effort involved.

Author's note

James Tibbetts' comments in relation to IP and copyright law in China reflect the situation historically. However, the situation in China is changing – see for example Mostert (2017).

An example of Paddy Power's publicity stunts is the defacement of the Cerne Abbas Giant, where the club was replaced by a tennis racket during the Wimbledon tennis tournament (Simmons, 2017).

Conclusion

The issue of ambush marketing has become increasingly prominent in events management. The term encompasses a wide range of activities, from leafleting a rival event, to large stunts such as Paddy Power flying aeroplanes over the Ryder Cup (Sweeny, 2012), to the use of AdWords online. As James Tibbetts suggests, contingency planning is very important in such situations so that a measured and appropriate response may be adopted if ambush marketing is encountered. In such situations a proportionate response that doesn't give undue prominence to the ambush is key. Using humour and diverting attention by putting out more interesting content is likely to be most effective.

Discussion questions and activities

Go to the Hiscox event insurance webpages www.hiscox.co.uk/event-insurance where you will find generic policy documents and insurance application forms that you can download.

1 You are the lead event manager for a major financial conference that takes place each year. A significant attraction of the conference is the exotic locations in Africa, South America and South East Asia. Delegates are also attracted by the programme of speakers that the conference advertises.

   – Study the conference policy document. What extensions to the basic cover for your conference would you want to add?

   – You have secured a really good deal for a conference venue in Freetown, Sierra Leone. The venue manager asks you to confirm your booking and pay a deposit. What should you check before you confirm and send the deposit?

2   James Tibbetts suggests that one way of countering ambush marketing is by providing good content that will keep media interest in the event and not in the ambush publicity stunt. Have a look at the following events' web pages – how well do you think they do in providing good content around their event?

   –   The Cycle Show;

   –   The London Art Fair;

   –   The Virgin London Marathon;

   –   Glastonbury Festival of Performing Arts;

   –   The Guildford Book Festival.

   What other reasons are there for providing good content around an event?

3   You have been approached by a broadcaster who would like to televise the event. A big discussion takes place in the office regarding whether this would be possible and what steps the event manager would need to take, particularly as the broadcaster wants to show coverage before and after the 9 pm 'watershed'. What advice would you give in this situation?

4   Grant funders often require detailed impact reporting. Read through the guidelines and review the impacts calculator available from www.eventimpacts. com then identify an event in your local area. Contact the organizers and see if they are able to provide you with the information needed to prepare an impact assessment report for their event.

Further reading

Chadwick, S and Burton, N (2011) The evolving sophistication of ambush marketing: A typology of strategies, *Thunderbird International Business Review*, **53** (6), pp 709–19

This is a comprehensive article that examines the genesis of ambush marketing, how it is defined and the ways in which it can be managed. The authors present a typology of different ambush marketing techniques and provide examples from major sport events.

Duxbury, R (2015) *Contract Law*, 10th edn, Sweet and Maxwell, London

Hiscox Insurance website: www.hiscox.co.uk/event-insurance

This website gives good advice on securing event insurance. There are draft policies and application forms for conferences, exhibitions and special events to download.

Ofcom: www.ofcom.org.uk

The government agency Office of Communications website sets out the OFCOM Broadcasting Code, which includes the Cross-promotion Code and Commercial References on TV.

Eventbrite has a range of useful advice guides and interviews with experts on a range of important event management topics, including event insurance. There is a good interview with Martin Linfield, Head of Hiscox's Event Insurance on this link: https://www.eventbrite.co.uk/blog/event-insurance-explained-ds00/

References

Chadwick, S and Burton, N (2011) The evolving sophistication of ambush marketing: A typology of strategies, *Thunderbird International Business Review*, 53 (6), pp 709–19

Koenigstorfer, J and Uhrich, S (2017) Consumer attitudes toward sponsors' counterambush marketing ads, *Psychology & Marketing*, 34 (6), pp 631–47

Mostert, F (2017) China clamps down on pirate trademark ransoms for famous brands, *Financial Times*, 29 June [Online] https://www.ft.com/content/3f580c34-4c70-11e7 a3f1 c742b9791d43 [Accessed 28/06/18]

Sandler, D and Shani, D (1989) Olympic sponsorship vs ambush marketing: Who gets the gold? *Journal of Advertising Research*, 29 (4), pp 9–14

Simmons, R (2017) Paddy Power under fire after Wimbledon publicity stunt [Online] https://www.gamblinginsider.com/news/3626/paddy-power-under-fire-after-wimbledon-publicity-stunt [Accessed 08/01/18]

Sweeny, M (2012) Ryder Cup 2012: Paddy Power tees up ambush plan, *Guardian*, 1 October [Online] https://www.theguardian.com/media/2012/sep/29/ryder-cup-2012-paddy-power-ambush [Accessed 28/06/18]

Evaluating sponsorship and grant-making relationships

09

LEARNING OBJECTIVES

Having read this chapter and worked through the questions and activities you should be able:

- to explain why it is important to evaluate sponsorship;
- to present ways to measure the return on sponsorship;
- to introduce the use of digital metrics in sponsorship measurement and evaluation.

Introduction

As illustrated elsewhere in this book, over the last two decades sponsorship has experienced remarkable growth but it also continues to compete with other marketing communication methods for funding. Hence, understanding the role that evaluating sponsorship effectiveness can play in the success of individual sponsorship and of the sponsorship industry as a whole is paramount. Yet the study of sponsorship measurement still lags behind.

This chapter discusses the importance of sponsorship measurement and evaluation, both in terms of return on investment (ROI) and return on objectives (ROO), and presents some of the commonly used metrics to assess the return on sponsorship. The chapter concludes with a look at the growing relevance of social media in evaluating sponsorship effectiveness.

Why sponsorship evaluation?

Sponsorship evaluation is the process of determining the effectiveness of a sponsorship, its worth, merit and significance (O'Reilly and Madill, 2012). The need to understand how different marketing techniques contribute to integrated marketing communications strategy has always been important. However, as we shall see, as spending on sponsorship has increased research-ers and practitioners have focused on how to evaluate sponsorship campaigns. Research streams have included studies focusing on the development of spon-sorship evaluation frameworks (eg O'Reilly and Madill, 2012) and studies stressing the need for improved measurements (eg Crompton, 2004; Meena-ghan, 2013). While many studies have shown the positive impact of specific sponsorship campaigns, this aspect of sponsorship still appears not fully understood and, as Cameron (2008: 133) suggests, key questions remain with-out definitive answers: 'What does sponsorship do better than other forms of marketing communication? Do prevailing approaches to measurement accu-rately capture the essence of effective sponsorship?' According to Crompton (2004: 268), existing research consists mainly of 'anecdotal information and case studies from which it is difficult to make useful generalizations'.

On the industry side, statistics show that 27 per cent of sponsoring compa-nies spend nothing on sponsorship evaluation, while 42 per cent spend 1 per cent or less of their sponsorship budget on this task (IEG, 2017a). And yet, although surprisingly low these figures still represent an improvement from previous results. Overall, IEG concludes that we are now seeing a positive movement in the amount sponsors are investing in measurement of their partnerships, with the numbers of companies spending more than 1 per cent of the sponsorship budget on evaluation growing from 26 per cent in 2015 to 31 per cent in 2016. As expected, it is the larger sponsors like Coca-Cola and mega events such as the Olympic Games that lead the way in carrying out systematic and rigorous assessments of sponsorship impacts. The increas-ing recognition by sponsors of the importance of evaluating sponsorship effectiveness is also demonstrated by the fact that assistance with measuring return on sponsorship (either ROI or ROO) is considered the most valued property-provided sponsorship service by 41 per cent of companies surveyed by IEG in 2016. As Urban Kapraun (2009) explains, 'with every marketing dollar being scrutinized, in-depth measurement and analysis at all levels and on both sides is the key to the success of a sponsorship'.

Indeed, Meenaghan (2013: 388) stresses that expenditure on the scale seen in sponsorship in recent years 'demands the rigorous evaluation of its effectiveness' and draws attention to the case of the London Olympics in 2012 where each of The Olympic Partners' (TOP) 11 sponsors (Coca-Cola, Acer, Atos, GE, Dow, McDonald's, Omega, Panasonic, P&G, Samsung and Visa) contributed £64 million in sponsorship fees in exchange for exclusive global marketing rights. In addition to this, seven London 2012 Olympic Partners each paid £40 million, seven London 2012 Supporters paid £20 million each and 28 London 2012 Providers and Suppliers each paid £10 million (*Guardian*, 2012; Meenaghan, 2013). Remarkably, the top 11 biggest global sponsors – Pepsi, Anheuser-Busch, InBev, The Coca-Cola Co, Nike, AT&T, Toyota, Adidas, Ford Motor, Verizon Communications and Miller Coors – invest a staggering US$125–375 million a year in sponsorship (IEG, 2016).

Importantly, however, in a similar way as the financial crisis led to a temporary slowdown in sponsorship investment – notably the year 2008 saw the smallest growth rate in the forecast's history (IEG, 2008) – marketing spending is today being impacted to a certain extent by uncertainty linked with Trump and Brexit (IEG, 2017b). Meanwhile, according to ESP (2017), factors influencing this slowdown include the following: 'competition for dollars from other marketing channels, increased emphasis on activation spending over fee spending, and companies in major sponsor categories such as beverages and packaged goods holding tight to their purse strings in the face of little to no sales growth'. Notably, according to IEG's annual spending analysis, after a record number of companies (21) joined the list of biggest US sponsors in 2015, bringing the total number spending more than $15 million to 122, the following year, for the first time ever, no new companies were added to the list, which actually decreased to 106 companies (ESP, 2017). In the context of greater pressures on marketing budgets, demonstrating the effectiveness of sponsorship programmes compared to other promotional activities with which they compete for funding is a concern for both marketers and events managers, who should have reliable measurement tools at their disposal.

Return on investment is a commonly used financial performance measure calculated by dividing the monetary benefit (or return) of an investment by the cost of the investment (ROI = (gain from investment – cost of investment)/cost of investment), and is typically expressed as a percentage. It is a popular way to go about assigning a monetary value to sponsorship as well as of other types of investments. Collett and Fenton (2011: 102), however, warn: 'the issue with this approach is that it fails to take into consideration the multiplicity of objectives that any single sponsorship might be tasked with achieving, many of which do not have direct financial returns'. Conversely return on objectives is being advocated as a more suitable approach as it focuses on how well the specific objectives of the sponsorship have been achieved, some of which may be measurable in terms of cash return but others may not, for example an increase in brand awareness (Collett and Fenton, 2011). Skildum-Reid (2011) concurs and asks, 'How do you reflect the objective of increasing trust in dollars? How do you reflect the objective of increasing loyalty or evoking advocacy in dollars? You can't, unless you just throw an arbitrary number on it – which plenty of sponsors try, but is hardly accurate'.

While in the early days of modern sponsorship it often used to be the case that the decision to sponsor an event was made by companies merely on the basis of the personal interests of CEOs and board members, now there is increasing pressure on senior managers to demonstrate the benefits of such investments (Crompton, 2004). Indeed, as discussed in Chapter 1, sponsorship is understood as being entirely distinct from philanthropy. As an actual investment, demonstrating its return and that the sponsorship activity has met its objective/s is of paramount importance. According to Meenaghan (2013: 391), among the factors leading to increased pressure for greater accountability in sponsorship is 'the requirement for greater accountability in marketing generally and the demands for proper corporate governance and transparency in business at large'.

Meanwhile Crompton (2004) reminds us that it is the intrinsic nature of sponsorship as an exchange relationship that makes justifying a return for each party a fundamental consideration. In the context of this theory, sponsorship is seen as a transfer of value between parties (Stotlar, 2004), hence it is essential to ascertain if the benefits support the expenditure. Crompton (2004) describes this process in simple terms as consisting of two parties exchanging resources whereby the trade-off is weighed between what will be gained and what will have to be given up, and the exchange has to be perceived to be fair by both sides, which can be demonstrated by evaluating the benefits resulting from that investment.

Furthermore, among the reasons why measuring the impact of sponsorship is important, Farrelly and Quester (2003) propose that it plays a role in sponsorship renewal, as mentioned in Chapter 6, when we also highlighted how sponsors expect the event to provide an account of whether the sponsorship has delivered on its promises. Hence, as stressed by Crompton (2004: 269), 'it would appear imperative that [...] organizations incorporate measurement audits in the proposal packages that they present to prospective sponsor companies', as discussed in Chapter 6. Indeed, the general consensus is that evaluation should be an ongoing process consisting of various research interventions. As explained by Meenaghan *et al* (2013), research at the start of the relationship will serve to establish benchmarks. Tracking using agreed metrics is then carried out on an ongoing basis, followed by a final evaluation on programme completion, identifying successes achieved over the life of the sponsorship.

Measuring the return on sponsorship

Meenaghan (2013: 388) categorically concludes that there is a 'measurement deficit' in sponsorship. Indeed, as highlighted in the previous section, research shows that the majority of companies allocate little if any budget for performance evaluation – even given the increasingly greater demand for accountability. Kolah (2015) is among those that warn about the lack of a universally accepted measurement methodology. Meanwhile, according to Meenaghan and O'Sullivan (2013), the systematic take-up of a practice of evaluating sponsorship performance is prevented by issues arising directly from the nature of the metrics employed. O'Reilly and Madill (2009: 218) helpfully define 'metrics' and 'methods' in the context of sponsorship evaluation as follows: 'a metric is a way of measuring a given objective and a method is then described as the research method selected to carry out the metric (eg sampling plan, analysis plan, statistics, research methods, etc)'.

O'Reilly (2007: 5) agrees with various other practitioners and academic researchers that evaluation constitutes a challenge for the development of sponsorship. He explains that shortcomings of existing evaluation tools include: 'failure to assess return on investment (ROI) and reliance on simple measures that do not take the objectives of the sponsorship, such as sales increases and brand equity, into account'. Pearsall (2010: 115) contends that reasons for the difficulty in establishing evaluation metrics arise from issues such as 'no standard unit of measurement, no industry-wide benchmark for success and failure, limited budgets to implement research and often no call to action after the metrics are established'. In addition, he points to the issue of the lack of consensus on whose responsibility it is to measure the effects of sponsorship, whether it is the sponsor or the sponsored party.

Indeed, many companies are of the belief that evaluation should be a task for the event or sponsored organization and are disappointed that organizations don't match their expectation in this area (IEG, 2002 cited in Crompton, 2004). Conversely, Skildum-Reid (2014) insists that measuring sponsorship is not the event manager's job and that it is the sponsor who is 'best placed to measure the sponsor's return, against the sponsor's objectives, from the sponsor's benchmarks'. In Chapter 6 we discussed how measurement of the overall outcomes of the partnership works best as a shared responsibility of the event and its sponsor. In any case, the process necessitates the sharing of information. Pearsall (2010) argues that one of the reasons why this does not take place is because of fear of what the information may initiate: sponsors can use lower than expected results to negotiate more advantageous fees, more concessions from the event or even as a reason not to renew the sponsorship, while the opposite may occur if the results match or exceed expectations. Instead, sponsorship metrics should be considered for how they benefit the partnership, as they serve the purpose of spotting where the sponsorship is under-performing, leading to appropriate interventions to save the partnership (Pearsall, 2010).

One aspect of the sponsorship debate where there appears to be growing consensus is that measurements of sponsorship effectiveness should be discussed as early in the relationship as the proposal stage and that the focus should be on achieving return on objectives (Skildum-Reid, 2014). As Pearsall (2010: 121) puts it, 'properties cannot be expected to help in their partners' efforts if they do not understand the sponsors' priorities'. Crompton (2004: 269) agrees on the important role played by the original specification of sponsorship objectives in evaluation. Kolah (2015: 268) instructs that, irrespective of the methodology utilized, it is important that:

- measurement and evaluation are built on analysing measurable objectives;
- there is a clear research brief;
- the criteria for measurement are properly explained and understood by all those taking part;
- there is an understanding of how this analysis will be used in a constructive (rather than destructive) context.

If objectives have to serve as benchmarks or KPIs against which to assess the success of sponsorship programmes, then it is important that objectives are developed using the SMART criteria. SMART is an acronym first coined by George T Doran in 1981 in a paper entitled 'There's a S.M.A.R.T. way to write management's goals and objectives', and the letters stand for specific, measurable, achievable, relevant and time-bound.

And yet, even when the process of evaluation is informed by the setting of measurable objectives, the vast array of objectives that sponsors seek to achieve through sponsorship pose a major challenge for sponsorship evaluation, as stressed by O'Reilly and Madill (2012), whose review of the literature found 61 distinct sponsorship objectives from the relatively simple such as accessing tickets to an event to the more complex such as building brand equity. Other typical objectives include achieving media exposure, increasing brand awareness, enhancing brand image and growing sales as well as entertaining clients and employee motivation. O'Reilly (2007) and Crompton (1994), among others, insist that unique evaluation methods and types of measures are required for each objective, which in itself illustrates the complexity of the task at hand whereby standardized methods of evaluation across the board do not work. Not surprisingly, according to a survey by the Association of National Advertisers (2013), the trade body representing the marketing community in the US, less than half of marketers have a standardized process for sponsorship/event marketing measurement.

Other challenges in the assessment of the impact of sponsorship according to Meenaghan (1983, cited in Crompton, 1994), are:

- the simultaneous use of other communications mix variables;
- uncontrollable environmental factors;
- the pursuit of multiple objectives.

Indeed, each sponsorship has to be evaluated using as many measures as required to assess the multiple objectives that sponsors seek to achieve through sponsorship programmes, which further complicates the process (Crompton, 2004). Furthermore, a fundamental challenge is what O'Reilly and Madill (2012) define as the issue of attribution, which refers to the ability to attribute specific tangible benefits as having been gained directly as an outcome of sponsorship programmes, rather than other marketing activities and external factors. Crompton (2004: 269) explains: 'even if other promotional tools are not being used simultaneously, there is likely to be some carry-over effect from previous marketing communications efforts that make isolating the impact of a specific sponsorship difficult'. Likewise, changes in sales levels or in the intensity of competition may result from environmental factors, such as changes in economic conditions or disposable income levels (Crompton, 1994).

Traditional types of measurements

Sponsorship can be measured in terms of inputs, outputs and outcomes (Kolah, 2015; Collett and Fenton, 2011). Inputs consist of the initiatives/activities put in place, whereas outputs are the results deriving from these inputs, and outcomes measure how an output benefits the organization, hence is a stronger measure of performance. Kolah (2015: 282) provides this useful breakdown:

- **Inputs** – For example, the number of perimeter boards, the number of news releases issued, the amount of online and offline media exposure, the demographic and psychographic profile of the desired audience and customer segments exposed to the sponsorship campaign, the number of branded marketing materials produced and distributed, the number of attendees/spectators at a sponsorship event, etc.

- **Outputs** – For example, changes in the preference expressed by consumers for the brand, changes in attitudes expressed by consumers for the brand, the number of participants entering the promotion, prize draw or competition, the number of customers signing up to the loyalty programme, improved B2B relationships, etc.

- **Outcomes** – Incremental sales achieved during and after the sponsorship programme, improvements in customer purchase frequency, a reduction in customer churn, higher customer retention rates, a higher level of loyalty, commercial improvement in B2B relationships, cost savings in recruitment, product launch and sales of new product, etc.

As discussed in the previous section, industry practitioners and academics largely agree that sponsorship objectives dictate the types of evaluation methods used to assess the effectiveness of the specific sponsorship programme and that these should be clearly specified at the onset of the sponsorship relationship. This enables the best measures to assess the extent to which the objectives are met to be selected (Crompton, 1994). Pearsall (2010: 119) stresses: 'there is no need for research that does not address the end objectives of the programme'. What we see in practice, though, is a preference for the use of common advertising measurements. Currie (2004) argues that the establishment and universal acceptance of BARB (Broadcasters' Audience Research Board) figures as a benchmark for measuring television advertising and the existence of straightforward rate cards for other media have enabled the advertising sector to provide answers about return on investment, which may in part explain why they have been so promptly adopted in sponsorship evaluation. However, it appears increasingly the case that, as Cameron (2008: 131) puts it, 'traditional measurement approaches of logo counting and sponsor recall are no longer considered sufficient measurements of sponsorship effectiveness'. Exposure-based methods and tracking measures are two of the most commonly utilized ways of measuring sponsorship (Cornwell *et al*, 1998 cited in Glaser and Lum, 2004).

Sponsors seek exposure via the usage of paid, owned and earned media in order to achieve a range of subsequent brand-related effects such as awareness, image, etc (Meenaghan *et al*, 2013). Olson and Thjømøe (2009: 514) explain that the standard way to value exposure is by conversion into media advertising equivalencies (equivalent media value/EMV). Exposure-based methods compare the amount and type of coverage the sponsorship receives, for example sponsor's logo shown on perimeter boards, to the estimated cost of acquiring the same exposure through paid-for media, for example via TV advertising. Tracking measures are used to evaluate sponsor recall, awareness of and attitudes towards sponsors and their products and services (Cornwell *et al*, 1998 cited in Glaser and Lum, 2004).

Available literature abounds with extensive critiques of both these and other metrics commonly utilized (see, for example, Crompton, 2004 and Meenaghan and O'Sullivan, 2013), as discussed in the following Research insight.

Research insight 7: media exposure and sponsorship awareness – a critique

'Media exposure' and 'sponsorship awareness' have traditionally been the two main metrics utilized to evaluate sponsorship effectiveness. Meenaghan and O'Sullivan (2013) critique these practices and warn about their credibility and effectiveness, but also highlight their positive contribution. Ultimately, the authors advise that attention should shift from considering sponsorship in terms of its exposure and awareness value to repositioning the industry in terms of brand experience, engagement and involvement, which are areas in which sponsorship has specific competencies, and urge for the need to establish relevant metrics to capture these effects.

Meenaghan, T and O'Sullivan, P (2013) Metrics in sponsorship research: Is credibility an issue? *Psychology and Marketing*, **30** (5), pp 385–93

Media exposure

Of the three different types of sponsorship impacts, namely inputs, outputs and outcomes, the amount of media coverage that is generated by sponsorship, or the estimated value of that media coverage, is an input (Collett and Fenton, 2011; Meenaghan and O'Sullivan, 2013). Meenaghan and O'Sullivan (2013) explain that this is a measure of publicity rather than a measure of the effects of that publicity. Collett and Fenton (2011: 99) explain that this measure of brand exposure 'does not reveal whether anybody actually noticed the sponsorship, or if it changed the way they thought, or their behaviour'. Moreover, the exposure would need to be weighted to reflect the relative attractiveness and quality of the coverage and its PR value (or credibility multiplier – which is based on the consideration that an editorial is more valuable than paid advertising) (Crompton, 1994; Meenaghan and O'Sullivan, 2013), which shows how this measurement's approach is far from an exact science. What happens frequently is that the value of the coverage is inflated by comparing the article length with advertising space, even if the sponsor is mentioned only a couple of times in the article, or when the maximum rate card value is assumed even though in reality price negotiation may occur and a discounted rate card may be used (Crompton, 2004).

Importantly, media equivalency measurements ignore the fact that there are various ways in which sponsorship is not like advertising. Meenaghan (2013: 388) summarizes these differences as including 'the mutuality of benefit, the consumer interaction process, the comparative nature of the communications process, as well as sponsorship's location at the leisure end of marketing.' Most importantly, media equivalency measures do not assess the effect that event sponsorship can have on attendees' emotional engagement with the brand, which is where sponsorship is more powerful, as stressed at various points in this book when discussing event experiences and their implications for sponsorship.

Awareness

Another popular metric employed by sponsorship practitioners is awareness. Awareness indicates the extent to which the association between the sponsor and the sponsored event has been established in the consumer's mind (Meenaghan and O'Sullivan, 2013). Crompton (2004) believes that the ultimate goal of any communication strategy is to generate sales and stresses that the sponsorship of events is likely to ultimately impact sales if it succeeds in moving the consumer closer to the purchase action. Awareness as a consequence of exposure is important because it represents the critical first stage of the consumer decision process, as illustrated in the production adoption process and various other hierarchy of effects models, which suggest that consumers pass through a series of stages from first becoming aware of the product to finally making a purchase (Crompton, 2004). There are various other adaptations of the hierarchy of effects model first created in 1961 by Robert J Lavidge and Gary A Steiner (awareness, knowledge, liking, preference, conviction and purchase), including the well-known AIDA (awareness, interest, desire, action) model.

Data on sponsorship awareness is collected using consumers' surveys, typically using recognition and recall tests, also known as prompted and unprompted awareness, where the latter is regarded as better reflecting the true knowledge of the sponsor/event association as it indicates the degree to which consumers can remember the brand/sponsor name foremost in their mind (top of the mind awareness) (Meenaghan and O'Sullivan, 2013; Cameron, 2008). Although sponsorship is generally regarded as having a positive impact on brand awareness, a critique of this measure is that recall may result simply from an educated guess. Crompton (2004: 276) explains: 'people are more likely to associate a sponsor with an event based on the brand's popularity, rather than on their remembrance of seeing a company's signage on-site'.

Image

Sponsorship has long been recognized as having the ability to affect the image of the sponsoring brand (Walliser, 2003). Through sponsorship, an event's image may be transferred through association to the sponsoring product in a similar way as 'meaning', ie what the celebrity represents is created through celebrity endorsement (Gwinner, 1997). Gwinner and Eaton (1999: 47) explain that 'the pre-existing associations held in consumers' memories regarding a celebrity or sporting event become linked in memory with the endorsed or sponsoring brand'. Image building is closely linked to the concept of brand equity, which relies on brands having positive associations. It is also acknowledged that, since attitude towards the brand (a measure of sponsorship output) is a component of brand image, it will be also impacted by image transfer (Gwinner, 1997).

Market research using qualitative methods such as in-depth interviews and focus groups are the best ways to gather information on target market perceptions and opinions on the event and brand as well as attitude shifts. These shifts can perhaps also be measured quantitatively by the numbers of people signing up to the brand's loyalty programme (Collett and Fenton, 2011). Gwinner (1997) suggests event managers should conduct research to assess the event image to aid the sponsor recruitment process, while IEG (2017a: 67) recommends to sponsors that 'prior to launching the tie they determine awareness levels, attitudes and image perceptions among their target market'.

Sales

A desirable measure from a sponsor's perspective is the impact that a sponsorship investment has on sales, which, as a measure of sponsorship outcome, is, as Collett and Fenton (2011: 100) describe it, 'the Holy Grail of sponsorship evaluation'.

Impact on sales directly demonstrates the effect of the sponsorship on a company's bottom line; however, it is difficult to attribute specific sales outcomes to sponsorship rather than to other marketing efforts. Not surprisingly, only half of the respondents to the Sponsorship and Event Marketing Measurement Survey conducted by the Association of National Advertisers in 2013 stated that they attempt to isolate the impact for sponsorship activity versus other concurrent marketing communications.

A way for sales increases to be tracked is via the redemption of promotional coupons or other sale promotional efforts, such as ticket discounts given with proof of purchase, or to measure sales for the period surrounding the sponsorship with sales during a comparable period (Crompton, 2004; Collett and Fenton, 2011).

Other metrics

The evaluation practices introduced above, although concerning frequently cited objectives of sponsorship, do not address the increasingly important relational objectives that companies seek to achieve through sponsorship (Donlan and Crowther, 2014). The strength of sponsorship in this respect is seen in its ability to establish a two-way communication with consumers as opposed to other marketing communication methods. Donlan and Crowther (2014) cite the inherent relational, participative and experiential quality of events that make them ideal means to build deeper and more meaningful relationships with consumers. Sponsorship events that engage with consumers in their lifestyle setting, through involvement with their passions, are able to facilitate the creation of an emotional bond. The capacity for events such as these is increasingly recognized and companies use experiential marketing opportunities to drive brand engagement (Meenaghan, 2013).

This development has implications for evaluation measurements, especially considering that traditionally they have paid little attention to assessing the effect of sponsorship activation, an area where the experiential marketing potential of event sponsorship can be fully realized. As Cameron (2008: 133) puts it: 'a billboard does not have the same impact as a well-executed brand experience'.

Meanwhile, social media, as effective platforms for sponsorship activation and for interaction between brands and consumers, have an increasingly important role to play in today's sponsorship measurement and evaluation practices (Meenaghan, 2013; Meenaghan *et al*, 2013), as discussed in the following section.

Web and social media in sponsorship evaluation

According to research carried out by the Association of National Advertisers in 2013, the top metrics used to measure ROI and ROO of sponsorship and/ or event marketing are:

- amount of media exposure generated (70%);
- social media (70%);
- awareness of brand (69%).

As discussed in Chapter 6, it has never been easier to access an audience's information, and especially to communicate with audiences directly before and after an event. Web analytics provide the event manager/marketer with an array of useful insights on the target audience, what they like and dislike, and their opinions and views on a variety of matters. At the same time, analytics also provide the marketer with the ability to find out precisely where and when audiences are active online and when they may be more responsive to marketing messages. This knowledge is invaluable, and the capability of the event organizer to share it with sponsors is an appealing benefit of sponsorship, valued highly by organizations (as research by IEG has confirmed repeatedly in recent years).

In a similar way, social media is increasingly being utilized for sponsorship evaluation purposes, in line with its emerging use as amplification channels and activation platforms (Meenaghan *et al*, 2013). It is easy to see how sites such as Facebook, Twitter and YouTube can be used by event managers and sponsors to gather feedback on the event and information on attendees' views relating to the sponsor. One of the benefits afforded to evaluation via online media is that, thanks to the technologies and algorithms that enable real-time analytics, they permit greater frequency of performance monitoring and measurement (Meenaghan *et al*, 2013). More broadly, Meenaghan *et al* (2013: 445) state, '[t]he attractiveness of new media, originally as conduits to certain key demographics but now more universally employable, relates particularly to their ability to connect with and engage individuals and groups, build communities of interest, and provide a depth of user experience, provides particular appeal to sponsors', and that 'the ability to target and measure communication in real time offers significant possibilities'.

Meanwhile, Steyn (2009) stresses that traditional measurements of the effectiveness of sponsorship are not appropriate in the digital age, as they do not measure online engagement with sponsoring brands. The concept of brand engagement has been receiving considerable attention in recent years within the marketing field and beyond (Shultz, 2007; Brodie *et al*, 2011; Graffigna and Gambetti, 2015). Specifically, consumer brand engagement has been defined as 'establishing a strong and enduring bond between brand and consumers based on an ongoing effort of the brand to activate consumers through interactions, shared values, experiential content and rewards' (Borel and Christodoulides, 2016: 266). Interest in this construct is justified by Brodie *et al* (2011) on the basis of its role in generating increased brand performance such as sales growth, competitive advantage and profitability as a result of the practice of providing referrals and recommendations for products/services/brands by engaged customers as well as in co-creating experiences and value. Thus, not surprisingly, brands increasingly seek methods of creating brand engagement, and social media provides effective platforms (Meenaghan *et al*, 2013; Schivinski *et al*, 2016). Borel and Christodoulides (2016) in fact distinguish between online metrics as follows: 'emails have open and click-through rates. Websites have unique/return visitors, page views, dwell time and conversions. Social media has engagement rate'.

Meenaghan *et al* (2013) indicate that sponsorship monitoring/measurement online should concern buzz (the volume of references in the social media space), sentiment (the extent to which a brand is seen in a positive or negative way), and engagement (the higher order connection between brand and event) as follows:

- Buzz monitoring consists of counting the number of brand mentions and the pattern of brand mentions over time, by market or indeed by channel, and serves to indicate the scale and content of association between a sponsor and an event.

- Sentiment analysis concerns the monitoring of opinion and attitude whether positive or negative towards the brand.

- Engagement metrics include 'likes', 'fans', 'followers' and 'shares', depending on the platform, and can be tracked over time.

Kitchin (2014) warns that these quantitative metrics do not detail the quality of engagement, hence a qualitative investigation is needed for that purpose, including monitoring of online conversations.

Research insight 8: online brand recommendations as a measure of the effect of sponsorship

The importance of measuring electronic word of mouth and of understanding the extent to which customers will promote or demote a sponsor through online channels is emphasized by Steyn (2009). The author proposes online brand recommendations as a more appropriate measurement of sponsorship effectiveness in the digital age, as opposed to traditional awareness measurements. Among the conclusions, the author suggests that brand recommendation though social media is a significant driver of brand equity.

Steyn, PG (2009) Online recommendations as the ultimate yardstick to measure sponsorship effectiveness, *Journal of Sponsorship*, **2** (4), pp 316–29

Third party evaluation

The role played by market research in enabling sponsorship measurement and evaluation is undeniable. Performing evaluation studies, however, can be costly and requires specialist research design expertise. Third party evaluation can avoid bias and ensure objectivity in the interpretation of results. These are some of the reasons why sponsors may choose to appoint external agencies to carry out measurement audits on their behalf. Specialized agencies like IEG and Slingshot exist around the world, while sponsorship consultancy agencies such as Nielsen Sport UK also usually offer data gathering and evaluation packages.

Conclusion

Sponsorship evaluation is undoubtedly one of the most complex aspects of sponsorship. Although its importance is increasingly being recognized, substantial challenges remain. Among the issues that the review of the literature presented in this chapter has highlighted is the use of sponsorship in relation to the achievement of a multitude of objectives, which complicates the process and makes the development of a standardized methodology difficult – if not irrelevant. More likely it is the web and especially social media that are providing a helping hand to marketers undertaking the tasks of gathering information on sponsorship effectiveness. Their widespread use and growing importance in people's lives is leading to a shift in attention away from traditional measurements of effectiveness in sponsorship to a focus on capturing the impact of sponsorship on brand engagement.

Discussion questions and activities

1 What reason would you give for the importance of measurement and evaluation of sponsorship effectiveness? Consider the perspective of both the sponsor and the sponsored event.

2 How would you advise a company who is sponsoring an event for the first time on how to go about the process of sponsorship evaluation?

3 Using an example of your choice, explain how social media can be utilized for sponsorship evaluation purposes.

Further reading

O'Reilly, N and Madill, J (2009) Methods and metrics in sponsorship evaluation, *Journal of Sponsorship*, **2** (3), pp 215–30

This paper combines a review of the literature and expert interviews to identify models, methods and frameworks of sponsorship evaluation between the 1990s and 2005, and concluded that sophisticated metrics are required that are directly related to the sponsors' objectives.

Cahill, J and Meenaghan, T (2013) Sponsorship at the O2 – 'The belief that repaid', *Psychology and Marketing*, **30** (5), pp 431–43

This paper illustrates the strategic use of sponsorship by communication brand O2 in Ireland and how the brand used innovative and creative activation through social networks centred on customers' participation. The authors present the range of metrics utilized by O2 in the sponsorship evaluation process, including sentiment analysis and social media conversation in addition to the more traditional approaches, hence offering a comprehensive approach to measuring sponsorship effectiveness.

Meenaghan, T, McLoughlin, L and McCormack, A (2013) New challenges in sponsorship evaluation actors, new media and the context of praxis, *Psychology and Marketing*, **30** (5), pp 444–60

This paper provides a comprehensive overview of principles and practices in sponsorship evaluation and highlights issues and challenges focused on two main concerns. On the one hand it discusses the measurement of sponsorship performance in social media, focusing on a range of channels. On the other hand it provides a useful outline of the types of benefits that sponsorship can offer to various stakeholders (staff, trade associates/suppliers/distributors, government/ regulators, shareholders and rights holders) to illustrate the emerging concern with delivering on multiple stakeholders' objectives.

Facebook Insights

This is an embedded function that can be accessed by clicking on the relative tab on a Facebook page. It provides data on the performance of your page and your posts as well as useful audience information. More details of how Facebook can be used for marketing and marketing measurement purposes can be found on: https://www. facebook.com/business/

References

Association of National Advertisers (2013) ANA survey uncovers marketers' continuing struggle to validate sponsorship, *Event Marketing* [Online] http://www.ana.net/content/show/id/28377 [Accessed 25/02/18]

Borel, LH and Christodoulides, G (2016) Branding and digital analytics, in *The Routledge Companion to Contemporary Brand Management*, ed F Dall'Olmo Riley, J Singh and C Blankson, pp 255–68, Routledge, London

Brodie, RJ, Hollebeek, LD, Juric, B and Ilic, A (2011) Customer engagement: Conceptual domain, fundamental propositions, and implications for research, *Journal of Service Research*, **14** (3), pp 252–71

Cameron, N (2008) Understanding sponsorship and its measurement implications, *Journal of Sponsorship*, **2** (2), pp 131–39

Collett, P and Fenton, W (2011) *The Sponsorship Handbook: Essential tools, tips and techniques for sponsors and sponsorship seekers*, Jossey-Bass, San Francisco

Cornwell, TB and Maignan, I (1998) An international review of sponsorship research, *Journal of Advertising*, **27** (1), pp 1–21

Crompton, J (1994) Measuring the return on sponsorship investments at major recreation events, *Journal of Park and Recreation Administration*, **12** (2), pp 73–84

Crompton, JL (2004) Conceptualization and alternate operationalizations of the measurement of sponsorship effectiveness in sport, *Leisure Studies*, **23** (3), pp 267–81

Currie, N (2004) The sum of a half measure, *Brand Strategy*, September

Donlan, L and Crowther, P (2014) Leveraging sponsorship to achieve consumer relationship objectives through the creation of 'marketing spaces': An exploratory study, *Journal of Marketing Communications*, **20** (4), pp 291–306

Doran, GT (1981) There's a S.M.A.R.T. way to write management's goals and objectives, *Management Review*, **70** (11), pp 35–36

ESP (2017) Number of companies in ESP's top sponsor rankings shrinks [Online] http://www.sponsorship.com/Report/2017/09/18/Number-Of-Companies-In-ESP-s-Top-Sponsor-Rankings.aspx [Accessed 16/02/18]

Farrelly, F and Quester, P (2003) What drives renewal of sponsorship principal/agent relationship? *Journal of Advertising Research*, **43** (4), pp 353–60

Glaser, EW and Lum, MC (2004) Corporate sponsorship: Measuring its effectiveness, MBA dissertation, Simon Fraser University, Burnaby, Canada

Graffigna, G and Gambetti, RC (2015) Grounding consumer–brand engagement, *International Journal of Market Research*, **57** (4), pp 605–29

Guardian (2012) London 2012 Olympic sponsors list: Who are they and what have they paid? [Online] https://www.theguardian.com/sport/datablog/2012/jul/19/london-2012-olympic-sponsors-list [Accessed 28/01/18]

Gwinner, K (1997) A model of image creation and image transfer in event sponsorship, *International Marketing Review*, **14** (3), pp 145–58

Gwinner, KP and Eaton, J (1999) Building brand image through event sponsorship: The role of image transfer, *Journal of Advertising*, **18** (4), pp 47–57

IEG (International Events Group) (2008) Forecast: Recession slams brakes on sponsorship spending [Online] http://www.sponsorship.com/iegsr/2008/12/22/Forecast--Recession-Slams-Brakes-On-Sponsorship-Sp.aspx [Accessed 26/06/17]

IEG (2016) Sponsorship's big spenders: IEG's top sponsor rankings [Online] http://www.sponsorship.com/iegsr/2016/09/19/Sponsorship-s-Big-Spenders--IEG-s-Top-Sponsor-Rank.aspx [Accessed 9/02/18]

IEG (2017a) *IEG's Guide to Sponsorship* [Online] www.sponsorship.com/IEG/files/59/59ada496-cd2c-4ac2-9382-060d86fcbdc4.pdf [Accessed 25/01/17]

IEG (2017b) *What Sponsors Want and Where Their Dollars Will Go in 2017*, IEG, Chicago, IL

Kitchin, R (2014) *The Data Revolution: Big data, open data, data infrastructures and their consequences*, Sage, Thousand Oaks, CA

Kolah, A (2015) *Improving the Performance of Sponsorship*, Routledge, Oxon

Meenaghan, T (2013) Measuring sponsorship performance: Challenge and direction, *Psychology and Marketing*, **30** (5), pp 385–93

Meenaghan, T and O'Sullivan, P (2013) Metrics in sponsorship research: Is credibility an issue? *Psychology and Marketing*, **30** (5), pp 385–93

Meenaghan, T, McLoughlin, L and McCormack, A (2013) New challenges in sponsorship evaluation actors: New media and the context of praxis, *Psychology and Marketing*, **30** (5), pp 444–60

Olson, EL and Thjømøe, HM (2009) Sponsorship effect metric: Assessing the financial value of sponsoring by comparisons to television advertising, *Journal of the Academy of Marketing Science*, **37**, pp 504–15

O'Reilly, N (2007) Sponsorship evaluation, Doctoral Thesis, Carleton University, Ottawa [Online] https://curve.carleton.ca/system/files/etd/0c3330aa-4c15-4e07-80c3-81df0a4d9bb9/etd_pdf/269380816849b30e7c03067a6e49f045/oreilly-sponsorshipevaluation.pdf [Accessed 29/06/18]

O'Reilly, N and Madill, J (2009) Methods and metrics in sponsorship evaluation, *Journal of Sponsorship*, **2**, (3), pp 215–30

O'Reilly, N and Madill, J (2012) The development of a process for evaluating marketing sponsorships, *Canadian Journal of Administrative Science*, **29** (1) pp 50–66

Pearsall, J (2010) Sponsorship performance: What is the role of sponsorship metrics in proactively managing the sponsor–property relationship? *Journal of Sponsorship*, **3** (2), pp 115–23

Schivinski, B, Christodoulides, G and Dabrowski, D (2016) Measuring consumers' engagement with brand-related social-media content, *Journal of Advertising Research*, **56** (1), pp 64–80.

Schultz, DE (2007) Focus on brand changes rules of engagement, *Marketing News*, **41** (13), pp 7–8

Skildum-Reid, K (2011) Asking the wrong questions: Sponsorship by the numbers [Online] http://powersponsorship.com/asking-the-wrong-questions-sponsorship-by-the-numbers/ [Accessed 25/02/18]

Skildum-Reid, K (2014) What should a sponsee include in a year-end ROI report? [Online] http://powersponsorship.com/year-end-roi-report/ [Accessed 25/06/17]

Steyn, PG (2009) Online recommendations as the ultimate yardstick to measure sponsorship effectiveness, *Journal of Sponsorship*, **2** (4), pp 316–29

Stotlar, DK (2004) Sponsorship evaluation: Moving from theory to practice, *Sport Marketing Quarterly*, **13**, pp 61–64

Urban Kapraun, C (2009) Sponsorship valuation and fair market value, Evaluation and ROI Demystified [Online] http://www.sponsorship.com/About-IEG/Sponsorship-Blog/Carrie-Urban-Kapraun/June-2009/Sponsorship-Valuation-and-Fair-Market-Value,-Evalu.aspx [Accessed 9/01/18]

Walliser, B (2003) An international review of sponsorship research: Extension and update, *International Journal of Advertising*, **22**, pp 5–40

10

Where next for event sponsorship and fundraising?

This chapter explores future trends. Is this the future?

Scenario #1

Simran and Tomi walked onto the Jam & Spoon festival site. The journey had been fun – they'd got to know other festival goers on one of the coaches that had been organized to transport J&S festival goers from the nearest town about five miles away. 'I might have guessed Pelican Transport would be providing the coaches – their logo was all over the website,' said Tomi. Simran smiled wryly, replying, 'I don't mind logos on the website, it's when you start getting loads of spam into your inbox that it gets on my nerves.' 'You forgot to click "opt out" again, didn't you?' laughed Tomi. 'Always too eager to click on the "purchase" button!'

As they left the coach park area and started to make their way to their camping area a bright-faced man seemingly jumped out of nowhere and asked 'Do you want to experience…' but they smiled and kept going as their rucksacks were heavy and they knew if they didn't get to the camping zone and pitch the tent they'd end up with a rubbish spot. 'I know events like this need sponsors to survive but it gets on my nerves when they start paying people to push brands on you,' said Simran. 'Yeah, I know what you mean,' replied Tomi, 'but there's no alternative is there?'

Scenario #2

Clea and Michael walked through the entrance to Marmaladeval, a music and arts festival they'd been going to for several years. Both had performed or volunteered at the festival before. That's what made the event special for them – the opportunity to be involved and participate in creating the event, not buying stuff from market vendors or finding oneself in the middle of an activity that enabled connection with a corporate brand that was sponsoring the event.

As they walked down the main street they checked their phones to see what activity they'd get into first. They knew this year was going to be different. The organizers had been in touch to say that if the festival were to continue new money would need to be found, as ticket sales could not cover the costs, especially with unpredictable weather. Unexpectedly, the organizers had asked all those who'd been to the festival in previous years to vote on which organizations they'd be happy to see sponsoring the event. More importantly, they'd asked how the sponsors should be involved and published the results of the survey.

'I think I'll check out the presentation by that guy who's developing a biodegradeable plastic,' said Clea. 'That's the one sponsored by XTZ isn't it?' said Michael. 'I think it's good that they're actually paying for stuff that's going on here this year – and not just the boring do-gooder stuff!' he added with a smile. 'Can't wait for the main act this evening.' 'Yeah,' said Clea, 'and I like the way there aren't logos everywhere – it still feels like it's our festival, not a sell out.'

So far in this book we have examined a range of issues, processes and concepts that are involved with event sponsorship and fundraising. Through the insights of professionals and thought leaders in the sector it's been possible to see how these are put into practice in real-world scenarios.

As we saw in Chapter 4, event sponsorship and fundraising are motivated by a number of factors. While the importance of entertaining clients and incentivizing retailers, dealers and distributors cannot be denied, looking to the future the main drivers of sponsorship will be increasing brand loyalty, creating awareness and changing or reinforcing an organization's image. These motivations are continuously shifting and evolving as organizations and the personalities within them change. Just as motivations change, event sponsorship and fundraising practices are often subject to abrupt shifts in priorities. Moreover, as we will see, sponsorship and fundraising are particularly sensitive political and economic factors. So it's imperative that organizations seeking sponsorship develop sensitive and agile practices capable of recognizing change and are able to adapt quickly when necessary. This chapter looks to anticipate changes in the sector, and also what may remain the same.

Focus on translation opportunities through brand activation

As noted in Chapter 9, Andrews (2017) suggests that there could be a slow-down in the growth of sponsorship spending by major brands. This is attributed to two key points – increasing activation spend; and uncertainty linked to the UK's exit from the European Union and the election in the United States of Donald Trump.

The predicted slowdown seems to have been confirmed. For the first time no new sponsors were added to the list of biggest US sponsors in 2016 (ESP, 2017). This, according to the ESP report, is due to several factors – competition with other marketing channels, increasing brand activation budgets over sponsorship property fees, and flat sales growth in key companies that have sponsorship as part of their portfolio.

When we read these reports two key points should jump out at us: increasingly, sponsorship is competing with other marketing channels, and, very importantly for event managers, brand activation is receiving more attention from sponsors, which creates a downward pressure on sponsorship property fee spending.

What should we take from this for the future of events sponsorship and fundraising? In Chapter 7 we highlighted Reic's (2017) point that brand activations normally cost two to six times as much as the sponsorship fee. Given this, we suggest that event managers who carefully consider the translation opportunities for brands at their events will be more likely to secure the long-term future of the event in question. A translation opportunity is defined as the moment when we as the consumer and the brand sponsor interact and some change in behaviour or action is suggested, encouraged or invited. The change of behaviour could be low risk and simple – to 'like' a Facebook site or share on social media. At the same time, the translation could be more significant, for example to purchase a new product or service or change some other aspect of behaviour such as taking up a new sport or reducing cholesterol intake.

Translation opportunities are delivered through well-designed and authentic brand activations. To be successful and sustainable in the long term, brand activations should ensure that the overall strategic objectives of the event and the sponsor are aligned.

In doing so the sponsor should be taking into account the customer's needs so that the brand activation is appropriate to the event theme and context, and is personally relevant to the consumer. As we saw in Chapter 3, Poulsson and Kale's (2004) experiential scorecard, in particular the element of personal relevance, is fundamental to the success of a brand activation and the wider sponsorship campaign. If, when the sponsor asks questions like, 'Does the event's target audience, when they take part in our brand activation, have a sense of being true to themselves?' they are able to answer 'yes' then it is likely that the activation will be effective in enabling the target audience to interact positively with the sponsor's product or services and go on to purchase them in the future.

Moreover, a well-executed brand activation that focuses on the translation opportunity will have carefully considered how the inputs, outputs and outcomes of the event will be measured in advance. While measurement has always been important to marketing strategists, the scrutiny of sponsorship as an effective marketing channel has never been as intense as now. Many studies both by industry and academics have shown the positive outcomes of sponsorship campaigns. However, the need to measure the outcomes and return on investment of every sponsorship, brand activation and translation opportunity has become increasingly important. As Nick Adams of Sense London explained in Chapter 3, outputs can be measured through direct and indirect reach.

It goes without saying that translation opportunities need careful consideration if they are to be successful. In Chapter 3 we examined the Expro model (Schmitt, 1999) and the BETTER model (Smilansky, 2009), which focus on how an activation should be designed.

Authenticity – the sponsors' Holy Grail?

In the drive to secure positive returns on investment it is easy for sponsors to lose sight of the reasons why an event is attractive as a property in the first place. Clumsy, insensitive sponsorship campaigns that fail to take into account an event's identity and the audience's values will be less effective, and in the worst case lead to an event being damaged. Ultimately this is a question of authenticity. In Chapter 4 we noted that IEG suggest that sponsorship can be more authentic than other marketing approaches. Event sponsorship campaigns are particularly sensitive when it comes to authenticity. The stakes are high. As we saw in Chapter 2, Gilmore and Pine (2007) suggest that, for the consumer, authenticity is now more important than quality.

For event managers, the need to secure sponsorship for an event may ultimately be the difference between the event's viability and sustainability, and its failure. Given the uncertainty and risk of events due to a range of factors such as the weather, and crowded markets meaning that customers are more likely to decide to buy tickets at the last minute, sponsorship and grant funding can provide vital cash flow which, if not present, would mean bankruptcy. However, there are well-documented instances where events have eschewed sponsorship. A good example of this is the Mardi Gras Carnival in New Orleans. Foley *et al* (2012) observe that at the time of their writing no headline corporate sponsor had been associated with the event and no corporate branding was allowed along any of the main carnival procession routes. This is because the Mayor and administration of New Orleans are mindful of the uniqueness of the Mardi Gras event brand. By associating with a corporate sponsor there is a danger that the event will be perceived as 'selling out'. This is the power of authenticity in event contexts. Despite the financial pressures that the city of New Orleans has faced since Hurricane Katrina, no sponsor has been found.

However, it would not be the whole picture to attribute New Orleans' avoidance of corporate sponsorship to the desire to maintain the event's authenticity. In fact, sponsors were approached to support the carnival and the feedback received was not enthusiastic. This is because of the lack of control that the sponsors (or indeed the organizers) would have over the event and, in particular, the media coverage of the event. Mardi Gras has two faces – a wholesome, family event and a wild, bacchanalian carnival. This dichotomy illustrates the tension between an event's brand identity and the sponsor's need for control, for being at the centre of the event attendee's consciousness just for a moment as opposed to being at the periphery. Likewise, the need to secure funds from public sector bodies may also be very strong.

Physical/virtual (dis)embodied – the role of social media and digital platforms

Human beings are social and want to meet in physical spaces. This is evident in business and leisure contexts with conferences, exhibitions and sporting events of all kinds continuing to flourish. At the same time, the use of virtual and digital gaming technologies has led to significant growth in meetings and corporate events taking place online.

In the meetings, conferences, conventions and exhibitions industries, opportunities for both grants from government and sponsorship from commercial organizations have always existed. For example, FT Live, the global conferences and events division of the Financial Times Group, convenes events across the globe. A recent example is the Kuwait Investment Outreach Roadshow in Singapore, which is in partnership with the Kuwait Direct Investment Promotion Authority (part of the Kuwaiti government). The event also has two sponsors, the Kuwait Financial Centre and Zain, a telecommunications company. The future of such sponsorship markets continues to be positive; as Rogers (2013) observes, there is little appetite for face-to-face meetings to be replaced by virtual events, with technology offering opportunities for hybrid combinations of virtual and face-to-face to reach wider audiences. Such events will be of interest to sponsors, particularly where event managers can demonstrate access to audiences beyond the physical event space.

Another driver of face-to-face meetings over the use of technology in certain business meeting contexts relates to transparency and governance – in particular, the increasing trend in the United States for annual general meetings (AGMs) to be online only. AGMs can be sponsored in much the same way as other business events, with receptions, speakers and items like delegate packs and bottled water being items on the sponsorship properties list. However, Mooney (2017) reports that online AGMs disadvantage shareholders and in particular smaller shareholders because the AGM is often the only opportunity to speak to the company's management team. Critics of online-only AGMs express concern that controversial issues can be ignored as it is much easier to ignore shareholder questions online than at a physical meeting.

There are times when an online-only meeting is best in a business context. Arnfalk and Kogg (2003) found that virtual meetings are best for informative, follow-up, short and/or repetitive meetings. For sponsors, it is important to note that while face-to-face remains the preferred alternative for meetings with complex objectives at present, in the future there will be an increased use of hybrid formats. Therefore, event managers and sponsors will need to identify how best to exploit sponsorship properties such as live streaming sessions in conferences as well as in-kind sponsorship by technology companies who want to demonstrate their information communications technologies to particular target audiences. Live streaming has been very useful in medical association conferences. A recent example is Endoscopy Live, where a medical procedure was performed at a hospital and live streamed so that conference delegates and those not able to attend the event were able to observe and ask questions as the procedure took place.

One new technology that will have a significant impact on the events industry, particularly in relation to streaming and virtual reality, is the introduction of 5G (5th generation) wireless systems. 5G will be potentially 10 times faster than 4G (Sprint Newsroom, 2018) and has the potential to transform live event experiences through improved connectivity and additional revenue streams. While 5G will not be widely available until 2020 it was showcased at the PyeongChang 2018 Winter Olympics. This was a collaboration between a Korean domestic wireless operator called KT and the Games' worldwide sponsor Intel. Several venues were equipped with 5G networks, which enabled live camera feeds from bobsleds and multi-camera views from cross-country skiing and figure skating events. It was also used to deter wild boars, which are a dangerous pest in South Korea (Kim and Kim, 2018)!

New sponsorship opportunities: e-sports – the final frontier?

One of the most interesting areas of new opportunity for sponsors is that of e-sports and online gaming. E-sports, where gamers play popular games such as League of Legends, Call of Duty and Overwatch in front of large, live and online audiences are growing exponentially in popularity. Newzoo, an agency providing market intelligence covering the global games, e-sports, and mobile markets, suggests that the global e-sports economy has grown by 34 per cent year-on-year to US$660 million (£492 million) and will reach $1.5 billion by 2020. Moreover, e-sports attract an audience of 385 million people (Pattenden, 2017). While such figures are exciting, we should not be too quick to accept them. As Malph Mins, Director of Strive Sponsorship, observes, there are differing figures given by different research companies regarding e-sports growth (Coutts, 2017).

Bearing in mind the sector's infancy and the lack of reliable figures, the potential of this sector should be taken seriously. E-sports have rapidly become a hybrid format, with teams playing in front of live, as well as virtual, audiences in major event capitals such as London, Moscow and New York while the Intel Extreme Masters in Katowice, Poland, attracts more than 100,000 fans over three days. Moreover, major live sporting events are recognizing e-sports, with the Olympic Council of Asia introducing them as demonstration sports in 2018, and planning full inclusion in the 2022 Asian Games. The International Olympic Committee recognizes the Asian Games, so there is potential for e-sports to feature in the 2024 Olympic Games in Paris (Ingle, 2017).

The inclusion of e-sports gives insight into the dynamics between sponsors and mega events. In 2017 Alibaba, the Chinese e-commerce, retail and technology conglomerate, became a top-level sponsor of the Olympic Games (Ingle, 2017). This is not just a sponsorship in terms of brand awareness; Alibaba will be involved in transforming how technology is used to support the Olympics in relation to social engagement, and potentially ticketing as well.

The top-line sponsorship deal by Alibaba was preceded by Alibaba Sports Group's announcement in 2016 of a $150m investment in the International e-Sports Federation (IESF). The IESF, based in South Korea, is a long-time advocate for the inclusion of competitive e-gaming in the Olympics (Ingle, 2017). It seems that the International Olympic Committee will be keen to follow the momentum for e-sports to become part of the Olympics, given the involvement of one of their top-level sponsors.

Until recently, e-sports were invested in by brands from the technology sector such as Intel and Alibaba. However, 2017 saw mainstream brands such as Gillette, Mercedes and Jack Jones invest in e-sports (Pattenden, 2017). Gillette is leading the way in hybrid sponsorship in the e-sports sector through its partnership with ESL, a major e-sports event company. Gillette has sponsored e-sport athlete Enrique 'xPeke' Cedeño and the League of Legends team EDward Gaming (EDG) (Gillette Newsroom, 2017a, 2017b). Gillette set up a brand activation at the Intel Extreme Masters in Katowice, Poland, which enabled fans to customize their razor handles using 3-D printers in their RZR MKR Design Studio (Hill+Knowlton Strategies, 2017). Gillette's approach shows an authentic commitment to e-sports from the fan level upwards rather than a superficial engagement though the use of logo placement. This strategy is very important, because the profile of those who play and watch e-sports is approximately 80 per cent males in their mid 20s who are perceived as resistant to advertising (Pattenden, 2017).

While e-sports are growing in popularity, it's important that we recognize there may be a trend towards less use of social media and digital platforms. Observers in the media have in recent years consistently reported on this (Margolis, 2016; Press Association, 2017). In one survey of 5,000 young people aged 14–16, many respondents said that social media was having a negative effect on their mental wellbeing. In particular, lack of sleep was a major concern (Salmons, 2017). Among Millennials (those born between 1980 and 2000), the main issues are around the amount of time social media takes up and the way commercial organizations can use personal information collected through social media.

We can distinguish between online gaming and social media, as these are different activities and platforms. However, the issues highlighted are common to both. Sponsors engaging in either format need to be sensitive to these issues and their consequences. You may be aware of adblocker software and also non-profit, ethical search engines like DuckDuckGo that don't track users' internet use. Such innovations and trends may impact on sponsors' ability to reach target audiences online.

It's not about personalities (is it?)

While it is true to say that the search for sponsorship in an increasingly competitive event environment is about good research into a company's business model and strategic objectives, it's important to remember that this is not the whole story. To illustrate this point, let's examine the Hay Festival, which has grown over the years from a single literature festival to global festival brand with events across the world in countries as diverse as Denmark and Peru.

In the past, the Hay Literature Festival attracted major newspapers as headline sponsors. The *Guardian* newspaper sponsored the festival until 2011, reportedly paying £100,000 in fees (*Evening Standard*, 2016). In 2011 the *Daily Telegraph* outbid the *Guardian*, offering an annual sponsorship fee of £250,000, which continued for several years. However, in 2017 the sponsorship was not renewed and the *Evening Standard* reported that this was in part due to the departure of the *Daily Telegraph*'s Literary Editor, Gaby Wood. For many events this would be a significant blow, and doubtless the Hay Festival organizers were disappointed. However, the event does have a wide portfolio of sponsors. It's important not to overstate the case and conclude from this that individual personalities are more important than sponsorship fit with target audiences, as we discussed in Chapter 4. Nonetheless, it cannot be denied that individuals in senior positions within organizations make the decisions on which sponsorship properties will be invested in. Therefore, a wise sponsorship executive will take time to identify and understand the personality profiles of key decision makers for companies that they are prospecting. Analysis of an executive's social media platforms and media interviews will enable those seeking sponsorship to tailor sponsorship proposals and develop better rapport in face-to-face meetings.

Fundraising insight 1: keep on networking...

All fundraisers recall a few particularly satisfying success moments when things come together to achieve a significant result. Sometimes this can be from a chance conversation, or serendipitous moment. Tom Lunt recalls one such moment from his first job as a Promotions and Development Organizer for a major UK charity.

As part of his job Tom attended numerous networking events and venue show-rounds. One such event took place at Lord's Cricket Ground in London. 'I went to the event to see if there was a possibility that we might be able to get a charity cricket match at Lord's,' Tom recalls. 'I asked one of the account managers there and he said there was very little chance of the charity I represented getting a charity match at Lord's, but almost as a throw-away comment at the end the manager said, "Why don't you try writing to JP Getty? I think he'd like your ideas."

'I went back to the office and did some research, and then sent off a proposal. A few weeks later back came a letter with a cheque, which was a great start. Over time I wrote with more ideas and a shopping list of different projects. We started getting more cheques back, some of them for five figures.

'It's so important in fundraising to network, talk to people and be open to suggestions, ideas and opportunities, no matter how unlikely they may seem. More than that, following up with research and developing a good relationship can reap significant rewards. For me personally, I got a promotion in part because of the work I did to prospect and successfully engage with the Getty Fund. And it all came about from a chance conversation at a venue show-round.'

Ethics – is there a skeleton in the closet?

In Chapter 7 some examples of ethical issues were highlighted in relation to corporate social responsibility. In particular, we identified that the reputation of an organization sponsoring an event property may come under scrutiny. This is particularly the case where the event has a high media profile. However, this doesn't mean that relatively low-profile events such as local or regional charity fundraisers are immune from scrutiny. It may not be the media that scrutinize the sponsors of an event but the host community and event attendees. If a sponsor is deemed by either of these stakeholders to be inappropriate then there may be negative consequences in terms of loss of local support and decreased attendance. The event will be perceived as 'selling out' to a commercial interest.

Another important aspect in the relationship between the sponsor and event property is the performer. If the performers – artists, musicians, actors or similar – object to the sponsor of an event that they are performing in this may have serious consequences both in terms of media coverage and ultimately the event's viability.

When selecting sponsors, those managing event properties should ensure that before entering into a contract the following questions are asked:

- What is the history of this organization – has it received any negative media coverage, and if so what was the issue?
- Who among our supporters might object to this sponsor?
- Are we being true to the event's vision and values by accepting this sponsorship?

Creativity

Sponsorship relations with events follow a cycle. As with the example of the *Telegraph* and the Hay Festival, it is quite normal for brands to terminate sponsorship arrangements and move to new events or other marketing activities. New opportunities present themselves and priorities change. For event managers involved in sourcing sponsorship it is important to recognize that creativity can engage the sponsor and prolong the life of the sponsor's support.

The Nocturne cycle event is a good example of the need for creative innovation – for example, the use of technology, but also, and perhaps more importantly, content is king. By including features like the penny-farthing race and the Brompton races, the Nocturne created fun and exciting content that involved a range of cycling enthusiasts to create a spectacle that attracts crowds of onlookers. This, of course, is what sponsors are looking for. What is so important to recognize is that creativity often comes from the participants and attendees of the event rather than being something that is done for attendees as passive consumers. Creativity can become an important part of a proposal to a potential sponsor. Successful proposals will try to look at the event through the sponsor's eyes. It is important for us not to interpret this as a simple question of 'How can the sponsor make money or increase exposure at the event?' A more nuanced approach is needed that explores how sponsors can become part of the event, creating and facilitating content. As set out in Chapter 6, Skinner and Rukavina (2003) suggest five key aspects of a sponsorship proposal. However, above these a proposal must show how the sponsor can become part of the creativity of the festival, conference, exhibition or other event. Sponsor and grant-maker contributions can be in several forms, but what will differentiate them and lead to positive perceptions among target audiences is how they are able to generate creative content either through funding a range of artistic performances or through translation opportunities that offer experiences where audiences feel they are getting involved in something they want to engage with, and that enhances their experience. Crude activations that focus on selling products or capturing data are likely to be detrimental to the event in the long term.

Another aspect of creativity that should not be overlooked is the choice of sponsorship property. The example of the cough sweet company that sponsored the Sydney Opera House illustrates this point well – a tangential and humorous focal point demonstrates creative empathy with both artists and audience.

Scenario #3

'What a great weekend,' sighed Simran, as she and Tomi settled down in the coach back to the station from the festival. 'Such a lot happened, time seemed to go fast and slow at the same time. The bands were great, the food was great and the party on Saturday night at that little bar was so much fun!'

'Yes, it was awesome!' yawned Tomi. 'I mean, those guys playing and performing at the bar, I don't even know what band they were, they just seemed to come out of nowhere.'

'The spontaneous stuff is the best,' said Simran, as she pulled on her eye mask emblazoned with Pelicans. 'The bands were great and some of the other stuff was good too, I'm loving this eye mask.'

And with that both girls dozed as the coach drove them back to the station.

Scenario #4

'Well, I am not sure I'll be going back next year,' said Clea as she heaved her rucksack onto the train. 'The words SOLD and OUT apply, in that order!'

'Yeah, I know what you mean,' sighed Michael, as he squeezed into a seat beside his friend. 'But you've got to give the organizers a chance. Do we want a festival or not? If we do someone's got to pay the bills.'

'I know, I know, but that was ridiculous. There were logos here, there and everywhere. And when that guy got up and started shouting about XTZ being greenwash and their track record in Africa... and the organizers virtually frogmarched him out – it's like a police state!' 'Sure,' said Michael, 'but this was the first time. Some stuff did get out of control. I think the organizers are going to get a lot of feedback and will make changes.'

'I think the organizers should start to look more closely at the vision and objectives of the event and try to align with grant makers and other organizations that are more educational and not so driven by the need to put their logo everywhere,' said Clea. 'Easier said than done, I reckon. Those kinds of funds are hard to come by and you have to account for every penny spent,' Michael replied.

Clea looked thoughtful. 'Maybe they could do a crowdfunder or something and set up a pot of money that is for difficult times of year. I'd put £10 in,' she suggested. 'So charitable!' laughed Michael. 'By the way did you see they're looking for a trustee with expertise in sponsorship and fundraising – sounds right up your street.' 'Are they really?' said Clea, as she tapped on her phone, navigating to the Marmaladeval website.

Conclusion

In answering the question 'Is this the future?' posed at the start of the chapter it is our suggestion that there will be as many futures as there are events, sponsors and other sources of funding. In the imagined scenarios we attempt to draw together some of the main themes of this book: commodification, authenticity, fit/congruence, ethics and engagement. It is our hope that you will be able to apply them to other event contexts.

In the final scenario we are left wondering whether Clea will apply for and be appointed to the role of trustee at the Marmaladeval Festival. Will she be able to develop new sources of income for the event through sponsorship and fundraising? Our aspiration for this book is that, if you are coming to this area of events management for the first time, you will be inspired to go further and pursue a career in this area. There are many ways to get experience and there are few feelings to compare with the sense of achievement on agreeing and signing off a sponsorship contract. The afterword provides some useful guidance. If you are already in the field it is our hope that you will have found some useful material in this book that will help you in your work and that you'll be encouraged to offer opportunities to the next generation of event professionals as they seek to find their way in our exciting and challenging industry.

References

Andrews, J (2017) *What Sponsors Want and Where the Dollars Will Go in 2017*, Industry Insight, ESP Properties, Chicago, pp 1–13

Arnfalk, P and Kogg, B (2003) Service transformation: Managing a shift from business travel to virtual meetings, *Journal of Cleaner Production* (Product Service Systems and Sustainable Consumption), **11** (8), pp 859–72

Coutts (2017) How e-sports are taking over the world, Coutts Bank [Online] https://www.coutts.com/insight-articles/news/2017/how-esports-are-taking-over-the-world.html [Accessed 04/01/18]

ESP (2017) Number of companies in ESP's top sponsor rankings shrinks [Online] http://www.sponsorship.com/Report/2017/09/18/Number-Of-Companies-In-ESP-s-Top-Sponsor-Rankings.aspx [Accessed 16/02/18]

Foley, M, McGillivray, D and McPherson, G (2012) *Event Policy: From theory to strategy*, Routledge, Abingdon

Gillette Newsroom (2017a) Gillette bolsters its esports roster with EDward Gaming (EDG) team partnership [Online] http://news.gillette.com/press-release/sports/gillette-bolsters-its-esports-roster-edward-gaming-edg-team-partnership [Accessed 04/01/18]

Gillette Newsroom (2017b) Gillette enters esports through global partnership with ESL as sponsor of the Intel Extreme Masters World Championship Katowice 2017 [Online] http://news.gillette.com/press-release/sports/gillette-enters-esports-through-global-partnership-esl-sponsor-intel-extreme-ma [Accessed 04/01/18]

Gilmore, J and Pine, BJ (2007) *Authenticity: What consumers really want*, Harvard Business Review Press, Cambridge, MA

Hill+Knowlton Strategies (2017) What we've been up to in London – 3rd March 2017 [Online] http://www.hkstrategies.com/en-uk/weve-london-3rd-march-2017/ [Accessed 04/01/18]

IMG (no date) Our story [Online] http://img.com/story/ [Accessed 22/02/18]

Ingle, S (2017) Chinese company Alibaba signs deal to be major sponsor of Olympic Games, *Guardian*, 19 January [Online] http://www.theguardian.com/sport/2017/jan/19/chinese-e-commerce-company-alibaba-major-olympic-games-sponsor [Accessed 04/01/18]

Kim, S and Kim, S (2018) 5G is making its global debut at Olympics, and it's wicked fast, Bloomberg [Online] https://www.bloomberg.com/news/articles/2018-02-12/5g-is-here-super-speed-makes-worldwide-debut-at-winter-olympics [Accessed 13/03/18]

Margolis, J (2016) More Millennials switch off social media, *Financial Times*, 11 October [Online] https://www.ft.com/content/5477680e-8ece-11e6-a72e-b428cb934b78 [Accessed 08/01/18]

Mooney, A (2017) Nuns tell companies to get real over virtual AGMs, *Financial Times*, 20 October

Pattenden, M (2017) 'They see the potential': Why J-Lo and Gillette want a piece of the eSports action, *Guardian*, 25 December. [Online] http://www.theguardian.com/games/2017/dec/25/esports-jennifer-lopez-gillette-audi-mercedes-benz-a-piece-of-the-action [Accessed 04/01/18]

Poulsson, SHG and Kale, SH (2004) The experience economy and commercial experiences, *The Marketing Review*, **4** (3), pp 267–77

Press Association (2017) Growing social media backlash among young people, survey shows, *Guardian*, 4 October [Online] http://www.theguardian.com/media/2017/oct/05/growing-social-media-backlash-among-young-people-survey-shows [Accessed 08/01/18]

Reic, I (2017) *Events Marketing Management: A consumer perspective*, Routledge, London

Rogers, T (2013) *Conferences and Conventions: A global industry*, 3rd edn, Butterworth-Heinemann, Oxon

Salmons, H (2017) Parent/pupil digital behaviour poll – media briefing, HMC, 23 April [Online] http://www.hmc.org.uk/blog/parentpupil-digital-behaviour-poll-media-briefing/ [Accessed 08/01/18]

Schmitt, B (1999) *Experiential Marketing: How to get customers to sense, feel, think, act, relate to your company and brands*, The Free Press, New York

Skinner, BE and Rukavina, V (2003) *Event Sponsorship*, Wiley, Hoboken, NJ

Smilansky, S (2009), *Experiential Marketing: A practical guide to interactive brand experiences*, Kogan Page, London

Sprint Newsroom (2018) Sprint unveils six 5G-ready cities: Significant milestone toward launching first 5G mobile network in the US, Sprint [Online] http://newsroom.sprint.com/sprint-unveils-5g-ready-massive-mimo-markets.htm [Accessed 13/03/18]

Practical templates 11
to kick-start your
event sponsorship
and fundraising

Developing a sponsorship campaign

This chapter sets out a process that I find useful when developing a sponsorship or fundraising campaign. The process is for the event manager, event sponsorship manager, fundraising committee or volunteer fundraiser looking to build support for a new or established event. The framework helps to build a case for support and develop strong, tailored proposals to use when approaching prospective sponsors.

Phase one: research

1 Who are the event's target audiences?

The answer to this question will include the size and nature of each audience. Objective measures such as age and gender, and inferred measures such as life stage and psychographic profiles can be used (see Chapter 4).

2 What does the event need money for?

Each sponsorship or funding proposal will need to clearly state the amount of money required. And what kind of financial support is needed? Is it for operating costs or capital expenditure? 'In-kind' sponsorship should also be considered.

3 What properties does the event have to offer?

This is sometimes called getting the event 'sponsor ready'. List all the parts of the event that can be sponsored – the stage, website, opening reception, programme, event database and hospitality opportunities are just a few elements of an event that can be sponsored. In-kind sponsorship should also be considered (eg media sponsor, or a product sponsor such as providing bottled water for a running event).

4 Which companies, organizations, grant making trusts and public bodies will be interested in the event?

This question is about examining the target audience of an event from two perspectives:

1 Identifying synergies between the strategic aims and objectives of a range of funding organizations and the event in question. For example, if a local government is trying to attract tourists – take a look at the Margaret River Pro surfing event in Western Australia: https://www.margaretriver.com/event/the-margaret-river-pro/

2 Matching target audiences of an event with a range of companies offering products and services that will be attractive to the event's target audience. A good example of this Sense London's work for the Guitar Hero computer game: https://www.senselondon.com/project/guitar-hero-live-amp/

Structuring the sponsorship portfolio of sponsorship opportunities is an important strategic decision when preparing to approach sponsors. The question here is, should the sponsorship be:

- sole sponsorship;
- hierarchical packaging (for example, tiers of gold, silver, bronze);
- a pyramid structure (whereby each sponsor level below the principal sponsor jointly spends the amount invested by the top sponsor, with proportional benefits);
- a level playing field (all sponsors negotiate and leverage their own benefits);
- an ad hoc approach?

The size of the event will influence the approach taken to the sponsorship portfolio. Increasingly, the consensus is to offer sponsors a level playing field or an ad hoc approach that allows them to customize their sponsorship benefits. The consequence of this is that whoever is managing the sponsorship will have to be very mindful of not allowing overlap between sponsors or overexposure of particular aspects of the event.

The size of the event will also influence the cost of the sponsorship. This is a commercially sensitive area, and the amounts paid are normally kept secret. Even in the case of public bodies the costs may be kept secret. This is so that sponsors are not outbid by competitors.

From the event manager's point of view the best approach is to prepare a fully costed budget for the event and then calculate how much sponsorship income is needed. Other factors that can be objectively priced are the size of a database and the media value, for example if the event is reported in the press the amount of coverage can be calculated as advertising equivalent value (AEV).

Funding databases can help in the search for appropriate sponsors and funding bodies. Well-known examples in the UK are Pearlfinders (https://www.home.pearlfinders.com/) and those offered by the Directory of Social Change (https://www.dsc.org.uk/funding-websites/).

Phase 2: pitching to funders and sponsors

Approaching sponsors should normally take place 6–18 months prior to the event. Approaches should be coordinated by category of sponsorship. Ideally the sequence for conversion of prospective sponsors will be:

Step 1: initial contact and a preliminary discussion will have taken place based on the presentation of the pre-proposal and event prospectus.

Step 2: If the initial discussions are positive a full proposal will be submitted.

Step 3: If the proposal is agreed then a contract will be prepared and signed off by both parties.

Phase 3: implementation of the sponsorship agreement

The event manager's involvement in this phase of the sponsorship framework will vary depending on the client. However, it is important that the event manager is able to contribute to the following:

4 What are the sponsor's aims?

As part of the contract the sponsor will have stated their aims. At the beginning of phase 3 it's important to make sure everyone involved understands them. These can be expressed either as SMART objectives or as KPIs. Once established, it helps to ensure that all parties are mindful of each other's requirements.

The sponsor may wish to achieve some of the following:

- increased brand awareness;
- distribution of a certain number of samples;
- collection of names and addresses for future marketing communications;
- social media activity, eg likes on Facebook, retweets, etc.

5 What do you want the target audience to experience?

Sense	Feel	Think	Act	Relate

(Based on Schmitt's Strategic Experiential Modules, 1999)

Based on the table above, the event sponsor should be able to clearly state what they want the target audience to do based on their involvement with the event. This is where the importance of thinking through the translation opportunity that is facilitated through a brand activation is so important.

6 The target audience should engage with the brand in the following way:

7 Having engaged with the brand, the target audience should:

Once the translation opportunity has been clearly expressed a timeline should be established for its implementation.

8 What is the project timeline?

Stage	Date	Named individual(s) responsible
Contracts signed off		
Translation opportunities agreed and signed off		
Activation developed		
On-site set up and testing		
Event		

Phase 4: evaluation

It is important not to see phase 4 as coming last in the sponsorship frame-work. Post-event evaluation is important, but decisions on what to evaluate and how must be agreed in phase 2 when the sponsorship is agreed and the contract negotiated and signed.

Moreover, the use of SMART objectives and KPIs will help to focus the evaluation of the event into phases before, during and after the event. They can also be categorized as inputs (eg number of perimeter boards), outputs (eg changes in preference expressed by the target audience) and outcomes (eg increases in sales volume or frequency).

Evaluation stage	Activity	Measure (input/output/ outcome)
Pre-event	Social media activity	Likes, posts, tweets, impressions
	Ticket sales	Numbers
	Hits on sponsor's website via the event's website, Facebook page, etc	Number of redirects Mentions in media
	New releases	
During the event	Social media activity	
	Sponsor awareness among attendees	
	Samples handed out	
	Data gathered	
Post-event	Product or service sales	Increase in company profits
	Customer lifetime value	Increase in customer loyalty

Example of information required by a corporate sponsor

Contact information

Name of event
Name of company
Website
Contact name
Email
Company address
Telephone number

Have you established contact with someone at this organization regarding this sponsorship?

Contact name:
Contact email:
Contact telephone number:

Sponsorship details

Event category:

- community events;
- festivals, fairs and annual events;
- arts;
- entertainment, tours and attractions;
- technology and education events;
- associations and membership organizations;
- other;
- sports (specify: motor sport, soccer/rugby/American football, hockey, cycling, other);
- movie request;
- product placement;
- use of logo.

Event category (other)

Cost of sponsorship

Would a gift in kind (use of our products/services) be acceptable instead of cash/fees?

Will this sponsorship be category exclusive?

Length of sponsorship opportunity:

- 1 year;
- 2–3 years;
- 3–5 years;
- more than 5 years.

When do you need a decision by?

Describe the sponsorship opportunity

In no more than 300 words, describe the sponsorship opportunity. Include the following information:

- How does the sponsorship benefit and provide value to X?
- How does the sponsorship positively increase X's brand awareness?
- How will the sponsorship money be used?
- How will X be referred to in the sponsorship?

Measuring effectiveness

List all the metrics that will be used to measure the sponsorship of your event's effectiveness.

Select the level of exposure the event sponsorship has:

- local;
- regional;
- national;
- international.

Have we sponsored your organization or event before?

If yes when and for how long?

Are our local dealers/outlets/shops involved with this opportunity?

If yes give their contact details.

How many sponsors will the event have?

What is the estimated total attendance for the event?

What is the estimated total viewership/audience for the event?

Average demographic information of the event participants

Age:

under 16

under 21

22–30

31–45

46–65

66+

Gender:

male;

female;

other.

Income per annum:

under £10,000

£10,000 to 20,000

£21,000 to 35,000

£36,000 to 50,000

£51,000 to 75,000

£76,000 to 100,000

£101,000 to 150,000

£151,000+

Education:

secondary school;

undergraduate;

post graduate;

doctorate.

Example of information required by a grant funder

Eligibility

The following organizations can apply:

- voluntary or community organization;
- registered charity;
- constituted group or club;
- not-for-profit company or community interest company;
- social enterprise;
- school;
- statutory body (including town, parish and community council).

The following may not apply:

- individuals;
- sole traders;
- companies that are aimed at generating profits primarily for private distribution;
- organizations based outside the country;
- applications made by one organization on behalf of another.

What are we looking for?

To be successful in applying organizations must meet at least one of our funding priorities and show in the application process how one or more of the following priorities are met:

- bringing people together and building strong relationships in and across communities;
- improving the places and spaces that matter to communities;
- enabling more people to fulfil their potential by working to address issues at the earliest possible stage.

The project or activity is led by people

It's important that you involve your community in the design, development and delivery of the activities you're planning. In our experience of funding projects it's likely that your project or activity will be more successful as a result.

What can grants be spent on?

We can fund:

- equipment;
- one-off events;
- small capital projects;
- staff costs;
- training costs;
- transport;
- utilities/running costs;
- volunteer expenses.

We can't fund:

- alcohol;
- contingency costs, loans, endowments or interest;
- electricity generation and feed-in tariff payments;
- paying someone else to write your application;
- political or religious activities;
- profit-making/fundraising activities;
- recoverable VAT;
- statutory activities.

Contact details

Give the names, contact details and dates of birth of two unconnected people from your organization, one of whom will be the legally responsible contact for any grant awarded. Unconnected means not related by blood or marriage, in a long-term relationship or living together at the same address.

Organization details

Give the type of organization that's applying for a grant. Provide the full legal name and address including postcode.

Accounting details

Provide the organization's accounting year-end date and total annual income. To be eligible for funding the organization must present its annual accounts unless the organization is new (started in the last 15 months) and has not yet produced them.

Bank statement

To be eligible to apply the organization must have a bank account and when applying must include a copy of a recent (within the last three months) bank statement. It must show the:

- organization's legal name;
- address the statements are sent to;
- bank name;
- account number and sort code;
- date.

About the event/project

The application must state:

- the name of the project;
- when the project will start (this must be at least 12 weeks from when you submit your application);
- where the project will take place;
- all the costs involved in the project;
- whether the project targets a specific group of people and, if so, who.

What the event project will do

In around 500 words state what the project will do. There are two key areas that influence funding decisions – ensure this section focuses on these as much as possible:

1 The event project must meet at least one of our funding priorities, which are:

- bringing people together and building strong relationships in and across communities;

- improving the places and spaces that matter to communities;

- enabling more people to fulfil their potential by working to address issues at the earliest possible stage.

2 You involve your community in the design, development and delivery of the activities you're planning. Tell us how you've done this.

Afterword – building your career in sponsorship and fundraising

There are a number of career pathways in events sponsorship. Here are some of the leading organizations that offer careers in sponsorship.

Organizations involved in sponsorship

Sponsorship agencies are the high-profile players in the sector. One of the most well-established is IMG (img.com), which was founded in 1960 with a deal involving Arnold Palmer, an American golfer. Today IMG operates in over 30 countries, representing famous sports and fashion figures as well as staging hundreds of live events and branded entertainment experiences.

Sponsorship agencies sometimes describe themselves as management consultancies that specialize in sponsorship management. An example of this is Onside, based in Ireland. The company specializes in developing sponsorship strategy, contract negotiations, market research, activation, management and evaluation for brands and rights holders.

Slingshot Sponsorship (www.slingshotsponsorship.com/) is another example of an agency that works with rights holders from a variety of industries. Slingshot specializes in developing partnerships between brands and rights holders and offers a range of services including:

- sponsorship strategy – which includes competitor evaluation and identifying prospective sponsors;
- asset audit and valuation – where a rights holder's assets are identified and valued with a view to preparation of sponsorship packages that can be offered to prospective sponsors;

- sponsorship sales – Slingshot has a team of sales people who can focus on selling a client's sponsorship property to potential brands;
- proposal creation – the agency's creative team will develop tailored proposals to send to prospective sponsors;
- brand consultancy – through its extensive network Slingshot is able to put brands in contact with a range of sponsorship rights holders;
- sponsorship training – with extensive knowledge and experience, Slingshot offer workshops that cover the sponsorship lifecycle.

Roles and responsibilities in sponsorship

So, who fulfils the services that agencies like IMG, Onside and Slingshot offer? The European Sponsorship Association (no date) provides a useful guide to the roles and responsibilities of different positions within a sponsorship agency. The business model of a sponsorship agency varies and will often involve a range of marketing communications activities such as brand activation and event management. IMG is unique in that it is a multifaceted business that goes well beyond sponsorship management to include venue management, talent management (athletes endorsing products) and distribution of sport content to broadcasters.

Sponsorship agencies compete with each other to win and retain client accounts. A client account could be a project to develop and deliver a sponsorship campaign across a number of events or one particular aspect of a campaign, such as to create brand activations for a sponsor at a particular event.

Senior positions in a sponsorship agency are normally titled senior account director and/or account director. Individuals with these roles will normally have 10 or more years' experience in account management and take a more strategic overview of the business. Account directors are ultimately responsible for ensuring that the aim, objectives and scope of work defined and agreed with the client are achieved and that the client is satisfied with the outcome. In this way the account director will take on a consulting role with the client, aiming to become a valued and trusted contributor to the client at a senior level.

Senior account directors are responsible for a portfolio of accounts and will set budgets, identify when accounts demand additional staff with new skills and recruit accordingly. Account directors will be the main point of contact both for the client and agency staff. They ensure that agency staff are completing tasks on time and to the highest standard.

The account manager's role is to ensure that each client's account is delivered in a timely, efficient and effective way. Account managers will work with the account director and client at the project briefing stage and contribute creatively with original ideas. Once the budget has been set it will be the account manager who will ensure that costs are controlled and the project comes in on budget. Account managers need to be resourceful and, within the bounds of the role's authority, take the initiative in running the client's account.

The account executive is the entry-level position for many people starting work at sponsorship agencies. The role involves research, for example monitoring the media response to a particular campaign, and also administrative duties, such as ensuring that the paperwork for an account, invoices, minutes of meetings, etc are properly organized. Account executives will also help to plan and execute client events. The role gives insight into all aspects of sponsorship management and equips an individual with the skills, knowledge and confidence to progress to account manager and, in time, account director level.

Sponsorship agencies have a research function within their business. This area is often called 'research and intelligence'. Agencies will employ a head of research intelligence, research and intelligence manager and research and intelligence executive. These roles focus on delivering high-quality business insights and demand strong numeracy, knowledge of quantitative and qualitative research techniques and project management skills.

As we have seen, some sponsorship agencies include sponsorship sales as part of the service they offer. However, some major rights holders such as conferences, sporting events and also venues will employ sponsorship sales people to sell sponsorship packages, which generate vital income for the property.

Sponsorship sales roles such as head of sponsorship, sponsorship sales manager or sponsorship sales executive are often described as account managers and there is often a significant element of sales within an account management role. Individuals who succeed in sponsorship sales will be open-minded and have great collaborative and investigative skills. In sponsorship sales patience, resilience and adaptability are important, as is the ability to thrive under the pressure of a deadline-driven environment. Progression in sponsorship sales is meritocratic. Individuals who prove themselves capable of selling significant sponsorship packages, sometimes into six figures, can expect to earn high basic salaries with bonuses.

GLOSSARY

Ambush marketing   A promotional activity that seeks to benefit from a sponsorship property in a way that has not been agreed through a sponsorship contract.

Amplification   A term used to describe how a live event's audience can be increased through other marketing channels such as TV and social media.

Audience   A particular group of people that a sponsor wishes to communicate and engage with, often referred to as a target audience made up of particular market segments.

Authenticity   The quality of truthfulness or realness. Authenticity can be seen from three perspectives: objective – a product or service is the real thing; constructed – a product or service is seen as real because it projects an individual's beliefs or values; and existentialist – where consumers believe that by consuming a product they are upholding the values and traditions they see as important in their lives.

Brand   A name, term, sign, symbol, design or combination of these which identify the products or services of one seller or group of sellers in order to differentiate their offer from competing sellers.

Brand activation   The process of engaging target audiences with a brand through some form of live experience. This can be straightforward sampling where a product is handed out to an audience at an event or it can be more sophisticated, combining the experience with social media, public relations and other marketing channels. For some good examples see Sense London's catalogue: https://www.senselondon.com/project/

Brand ambassador   An individual who is paid to promote a particular brand. In the past this has often been done by resting actors or drama students. More recently brands have recognized that people who actually use the product can be employed as very effective, authentic brand ambassadors even when they have never done so before.

Brand communities   A group whose members focus on activities and relationships around a particular brand.

Business ethics   A set of moral principles and values that guide the actions of businesses and relate to acceptable behaviour, particularly when business decisions lead to actions that have negative or harmful outcomes for stakeholders.

Case for support   A fundraising document written for the donor (in this instance sponsor), it sets out the organization's mission and vision for the future. The case for support makes clear why funding is needed and what outcomes will result from the sponsor's investment. The case for support offers strong reasons why prospective sponsors should sponsor your organization.

Co-creation   A high-quality interaction between a consumer and a company that creates unique experiences and unlocks new sources of competitive advantage. The creation of value becomes a shared activity between the producer and consumer.

Collective effervescence   The state of togetherness of thought and action experienced by a group of individuals. In the context of event-led experiential marketing it is the time when consumers interact with a brand and with each other utilizing, understanding and enjoying its benefits.

Community of practice   A theory of learning that suggests that communities encourage social relationships and knowledge sharing. From this, the individual knowing how to perform socially does not pre-exist social experiences, but results from participation in a community of practice.

Consumer tribes   A group whose members identify with one another, share experiences and emotions and socialize together using a range of brands, products, activities and services.

Contract   A legally binding agreement made between two parties, usually to exchange goods, services or money. It can be made orally or in writing, or even by actions alone.

Core funding   Term referring to grants that will cover salaries, offices/equipment and other direct expenses of day-to-day work.

Congruency   Can be used synonymously with the term 'fit' (see below) along with relevancy. A key criterion in driving successful event sponsorships.

Expectancy   A term used to describe the extent to which the consumer could have predicted a particular brand would be a sponsor of a particular event.

Experiential marketing events   Can take many forms and can be utilized by a wide range of different industry sectors. What these events have in common is their physicality, interactivity and embodied nature, which defines them as experiential marketing events (see 'brand activation').

Fit   The similarity or the logic of association between a sponsor and an event. Fit is based on a variety of factors including whether and to what degree a sponsor's products are used by event participants, the match between the sponsors and the event's target audiences, attitudes and geographic location.

Goody bag   A bag handed out to event attendees, normally on arrival at an event. The contents are normally promotional items such as samples and offers for products and services related to the event theme.

Hyperreality   A term used to describe a false reality that engineers an illusion of fake nature that satisfies visitors' daydreams and fantasies.

Integrated marketing communications mix (IMC mix)   A concept that deals with planning and coordinating marketing communications to incorporate a wider, more comprehensive and holistic approach that takes in both communication of the benefits of products and services to customers but also communication of an organization's brand to internal and external audiences.

In-kind sponsorship/contra sponsorship   Supply of goods or services rather than cash as a sponsorship offering. An example would be a computer services company supplying information technology for an events team to use to run their event.

(Il)logicality of association   The degree to which an audience sees a sponsor as part of an event. This may be influenced by the sponsor's products being used by event participants, the match between the sponsors and the event's target audiences, attitudes and geographic location. Illogicality of association relates to a sponsor of an event where the match between the product or service offered is not immediately seen as a fit by the target audience but through experience or over time the match becomes clear.

Media equivalency   Used to calculate the value of a piece of media, eg a newspaper article or TV interview. The size of the coverage, its placement and what the equivalent amount of space would cost, if paid for as advertising, are used in the calculation. Media equivalency has been seen as unethical and inaccurate as it doesn't take into account whether the media coverage is negative and/or includes mentions of competitors. Moreover, in relation to sponsorship, media equivalency measures do not assess the effect that event sponsorship can have on attendees' emotional engagement with the brand.

Postmodern   Describes a society in which individuals are no longer prepared to believe in, or sign up to, ideas, doctrines and faiths as their predecessors once did.

Promissory estoppel   A legal term that refers to the principle used to stop one party from enforcing their legal rights when they have given their word that they will not.

Pseudo event   The phenomenon of events created by the media and, in some cases, used to deceive and influence an audience.

Public liability insurance   Covers the cost of a claim made by a member of the public that has been injured or had their property damaged as a result of a business or a product it has supplied. This means that it protects against the cost of compensation to be paid out, as well as the legal expenses incurred by the claims process.

Reach   Any kind of contact a sponsorship campaign has with its audience where the intended message is communicated. Reach can be subdivided into direct and indirect reach. Direct reach relates to physical interactions between a consumer and a sponsor. Indirect reach relates to individuals who did not go to the event but were told about the sponsor's message through word of mouth, social media or advertising.

Relevancy   One of the most important factors driving good sponsor/event property fit. Refers to the consumer's reaction to and understanding of a brand's involvement and message through an event sponsorship.

Return on investment   A method of evaluation that takes the gain from investment minus the cost of investment and divides by the cost of investment. Normally expressed as a percentage.

Return on outcomes   A method of evaluation that recognizes that the desirable outcomes from an event are not just financial. Recognized as a more appropriate evaluation method for sponsorship.

Market segmentation   The identification of groups of people with specific characteristics in common (age, gender, lifestyle, life stage, etc). These groups or audiences may then be targeted with particular products and services or communicated with in particular ways.

Sponsor   An organization that provides financial or other support to an event in return for association with the event and other agreed benefits.

Sponsee   In the event context, an event that receives support from a sponsor.

Sponsorship   A commercial agreement by which a sponsor, for the mutual benefit of the sponsor and sponsored party, contractually provides financing or other support in order to establish an association between the sponsor's image, brand, products and a sponsorship property in return for rights to promote this association and/or for the granting of pertained/agreed direct or indirect benefits.

Sponsor ready   The process of quantifying what opportunities there are for brands to sponsor a particular event. This is also known as developing an event sponsorship portfolio, which may be tiered, a hierarchy of opportunities based on cost, or tailored where sponsors can purchase a range of opportunities based on their preference.

Third party insurance   A general term that covers public liability insurance. It is where the insured (the first party) buys insurance from an insurer (the second party) to protect against the claims of another (the third party).

Translation opportunity   The moment when the consumer and the brand sponsor interact and some change in behaviour or action is suggested, encouraged or invited.

REFERENCES

Aaker, JL (1999) The malleable self: The role of self-expression in persuasion, *Journal of Marketing Research*, **36** (1), pp 45–57

American Express (2011) American Express global customer service barometer [Online] http://about.americanexpress.com/news/pr/2011/csbar.aspx [Accessed 03/01/17]

Andersson, T, Getz, D, Mykletun, J, Jæeger, K and Dolles, H (2013) Factors influencing grant and sponsorship revenue for festivals, *Events Management*, **17** (3), pp 195–212

Andreason, A and Belk, R (1980) Predictors of attendance at the performing arts, *Journal of Consumer Research*, **7** (2), pp 112–20

Andrews, J (2017) *What Sponsors Want and Where the Dollars Will Go in 2017*, Industry Insight, ESP Properties, Chicago, pp 1–13.

Arcodia, C and Barker, T (2003) The employability prospects of graduates in event management: Using data from job advertisements, in *Riding the Wave of Tourism and Hospitality Research*, CAUTHE, pp 19–34, Southern Cross University, Lismore, NSW

Arnfalk, P and Kogg, B (2003) Service transformation: Managing a shift from business travel to virtual meetings, *Journal of Cleaner Production* (Product Service Systems and Sustainable Consumption), **11** (8), pp 859–72

Arts and Business (2005) *Sponsorship Manual*, 5th edn, Arts and Business, London

Arts Council England (no date) [Online] https://www.artscouncil.org.uk/ [Accessed 06/08/18]

Association of National Advertisers (2013) ANA survey uncovers marketers' continuing struggle to validate sponsorship, *Event Marketing* [Online] http://www.ana.net/content/show/id/28377 [Accessed 25/02/18]

Bagozzi, RP (1974) Marketing as an organized behavioral system of exchange, *Journal of Marketing*, **38** (4), pp 77–81

Baudrillard, J (1988) *Selected Writings*, Polity, Cambridge

Baylis, C (2016) Sponsorship inventory and asset development essentials, The Sponsorship Collective, 3 June [Online] https://sponsorshipcollective.com/sponsorship-inventory-asset-development-essentials/ [Accessed 02/07/18]

BBC (2011) Emirates sponsors Thames cable car [Online] http://www.bbc.co.uk/news/uk-england-london-15217173 [Accessed 27/03/17]

Boorstin, DJ (1964) *The Image: A guide to pseudo-events in America*, Harper & Row, New York

Borel, LH and Christodoulides, G (2016) Branding and digital analytics, in *The Routledge Companion to Contemporary Brand Management*, ed F Dall'Olmo Riley, J Singh and C Blankson, pp 255–68, Routledge, London

Bovaird, T and Bovaird, N (1997) *Arts Sponsorship: The case for and against*, Birmingham, Aston Business School Research Institute

Bowen, JT (1998) Market segmentation in hospitality research: No longer a sequential process, *International Journal of Contemporary Hospitality Management*, **10** (7), pp 289–96

Bowdin, G, Allen, J and Harris, R (2006) *Events Management*, 2nd edn, Butterworth-Heinemann, Oxford

Bowdin, G, Allen, J and Harris, R (2011) *Events Management*, 3rd edn, Butterworth-Heinemann, Oxford

Brodie, RJ, Hollebeek, LD, Juric, B and Ilic, A (2011) Customer engagement: Conceptual domain, fundamental propositions, and implications for research, *Journal of Service Research*, **14** (3), pp 252–71

Brown, M (2016) BP ends sponsorship of Edinburgh International Festival after 34 years, *Guardian*, 6 April [Online] https://www.theguardian.com/culture/2016/apr/06/bp-ends-34-year-edinburgh-international-festival-sponsorship [Accessed 28/06/18]

Cameron, N (2008) Understanding sponsorship and its measurement implications, *Journal of Sponsorship*, **2** (2), pp 131–39

Carú, A and Cova, B (2003) Revisiting consumption experience: A more humble but complete view of the concept, *Marketing Theory*, **3** (2), pp 267–86

Caterpillar Foundation (no date) [Online] http://www.cybergrants.com/pls/cybergrants/quiz.check_answer [Accessed 15/06/17]

Caywood, C, Schultz, DE, and Wang, P (1991) Integrated marketing communications, Northwestern University Medill School of Journalism, Evanston, Illinois

Chadwick, S and Burton, N (2011) The evolving sophistication of ambush marketing: A typology of strategies, *Thunderbird International Business Review*, **53** (6), pp 709–19

Close, A, Krishen, A and Latour, M (2009) This event is me! How consumer event self-congruity leverages sponsorship, *Journal of Advertising Research*, **49** (3), pp 271–84

Cobbs, J, Groza, M and Rich, G (2015) Brand spillover effects within a sponsor portfolio: The interaction of image congruence and portfolio size, *Marketing Management Journal*, **25** (2), pp 107–22

Collett, P and Fenton, W (2011) *The Sponsorship Handbook: Essential tools, tips and techniques for sponsors and sponsorship seekers*, Jossey-Bass, San Francisco

Cornwell, TB (1995) Sponsorship-linked marketing development, *Sport Marketing Quarterly*, **4** (4), pp 13–24

Cornwell, TB and Maignan, I (1998) An international review of sponsorship research, *Journal of Advertising*, **27** (1), pp 1–21

Cornwell, TB, Roy, DP and Steinard, EA (2001) Exploring managers' perceptions of the impact of sponsorship on brand equity, *Journal of Advertising*, **30** (2), pp 41–51

Coulton, A (1997) With sports alliances, cards make big play for fans, *American Banker* [Online] https://www.highbeam.com/doc/1G1-19834689.html [Accessed 24/11/16]

Coutts (2017) How e-sports are taking over the world, Coutts Bank [Online] https://www.coutts.com/insight-articles/news/2017/how-esports-are-taking-over-the-world.html [Accessed 04/01/18]

Cova, B and Cova, V (2002) Tribal marketing: The tribalisation of society and its impact on the conduct of marketing, *European Journal of Marketing*, **36** (5/6), pp 595–620

Cova, B and White, T (2010) Counter-brand and alter-brand communities: The impact of Web 2.0 on tribal marketing approaches, *Journal of Marketing Management*, **26** (3–4), pp 256–70

Cowan, A (2012) *Starting a Tech Business: A practical guide for anyone creating or designing applications or software*, Wiley, Hoboken, New Jersey

Crompton, J (1993) Sponsorship of sport by tobacco and alcohol companies: A review of the issues, *Journal of Sport & Social Issues*, **17** (3), pp 148–67

Crompton, J (1994) Benefits and risks associated with sponsorship of major events, *Festival Management and Event Tourism*, **2** (2), pp 65–74

Crompton, J (1994) Measuring the return on sponsorship investments at major recreation events, *Journal of Park and Recreation Administration*, **12** (2), pp 73–84

Crompton, J (1995) Factors that have stimulated the growth of sponsorship of major events, *Festivals Management and Event Tourism*, **3** (2), pp 97–105

Crompton, J (1996) The potential contribution of sports sponsorship in impacting the product adoption model, *Managing Leisure*, **1** (4), pp 199–212

Crompton, JL (2004) Conceptualization and alternate operationalizations of the measurement of sponsorship effectiveness in sport, *Leisure Studies*, **23** (3), pp 267–81

Currie, N (2004) The sum of a half measure, *Brand Strategy*, September

Daellenbach, K (2012) Understanding the decision making process for art sponsorship, *International Journal of Nonprofit and Voluntary Sector Marketing*, **17** (4), pp 363–74

Daft, R, Kendrick, M and Vershinina, N (2010) *Management: International edition*, 10th edn, Cengage Learning EMEA, Hampshire

Deloitte (2016) *Technology, Media and Telecommunication Prediction 2016* [Online] www2.deloitte.com/content/dam/Deloitte/global/Documents/Technology-Media-Telecommunications/gx-tmt-prediction-2016-full-report.pdf [Accessed 23/01/17]

Donlan, L and Crowther, P (2014) Leveraging sponsorship to achieve consumer relationship objectives through the creation of 'marketing spaces': An exploratory study, *Journal of Marketing Communications*, **20** (4), pp 291–306

Doran, GT (1981) There's a S.M.A.R.T. way to write management's goals and objectives, *Management Review*, **70** (11), pp 35–36

Durkheim, É (1912) *The Elementary Forms of Religious Life*, Allen and Unwin, London

eMarketer (2016) Worldwide ad spending growth revised downward [Online] www.emarketer.com/Article/Worldwide-Ad-Spending-Growth-Revised-Downward/1013858 [Accessed 20/01/17]

Enciclopedia Treccani (no date) *Mecenate* [Online] http://www.treccani.it/enciclopedia/mecenate/

Encyclopaedia Britannica (2007) *Gaius Maecenas: Roman Diplomat and Patron* [Online] https://www.britannica.com/biography/Gaius-Maecenas [Accessed 13/02/17]

Escalas, JE and Bettman, JR (2017) Connecting with celebrities: How consumers appropriate celebrity meanings for a sense of belonging, *Journal of Advertising*, **46** (2), pp 297–308

ESP (2017) Number of companies in ESP's top sponsor rankings shrinks [Online] http://www.sponsorship.com/Report/2017/09/18/Number-Of-Companies-In-ESP-s-Top-Sponsor-Rankings.aspx [Accessed 16/02/18]

European Commission (2017) Ban on cross-border tobacco advertising and sponsorship [Online] https://ec.europa.eu/health/tobacco/advertising_en [Accessed 15/02/17]

European Sponsorship Association (no date) Roles & responsibilities [Online] https://sponsorship.org/careers/roles-responsibilities/ [Accessed 23/02/18]

European Sponsorship Association (2016) *Sponsorship Market Overview 2016*, European Sponsorship Association

Evening Standard (2016) The Hay Festival of Literature and Arts needs to plough a new sponsor furrow, London Evening Standard [Online] https://www.standard.co.uk/news/londoners-diary/londoners-diary-hay-needs-to-plough-a-new-sponsor-furrow-a3312821.html [Accessed 14/11/17]

Eventbrite (2016) *The New Rules of Event Sponsorship*, Eventbrite

Eventbrite (2017) *Guide to Event Sponsorship: The current trends and best practices for success*, Eventbrite

EventScotland (no date) Event management guide – EventScotland [Online] http://www.eventscotland.org/development/our-key-publications/event-management-a-practical-guide/ [Accessed 26/0218]

EventScotland (no date) About Scotland The Perfect Stage, EventScotland [Online] http://www.eventscotland.org/about/ [Accessed 27/02/18]

EventScotland (no date) International events programme, EventScotland [Online] http://www.eventscotland.org/funding/international-programmes/ [Accessed 27/02/18]

EventScotland (2017) A spotlight on Scotland The Perfect Stage 2017, EventScotland [Online] http://www.eventscotland.org/assets/show/5689 [Accessed 27/02/18]

Farrelly, F and Quester, P (2003) What drives renewal of sponsorship principal/agent relationship? *Journal of Advertising Research*, **43** (4), pp 353–60

Ferdinand, N and Kitchin, P (2012) *Events Management: An international approach*, Sage, London

Ferrier, S, Waite, K and Harrison, T (2013) Sports sponsorship perceptions: An exploration, *Journal of Financial Services Marketing*, **18** (2), pp 78–90

Firat, F and Shultz II, C (1997) From segmentation to fragmentation: Markets and marketing strategy in the postmodern era, *European Journal of Marketing*, **31** (3/4), pp 183–207

Fishel, D (1993) *Arts Sponsorship Handbook*, Directory of Social Change, London

Fitzgerald, K (2000) Events offer new level of brand immersion, *Advertising Age*, **71** (17) [Online] http://adage.com/article/news/events-offer-level-brand-immersion/58677/ [Accessed 25/06/18]

Fleck, ND and Quester, P (2007) Birds of a feather flock together… definition, role and measure of congruence: An application to sponsorship, *Psychology and Marketing*, **24** (11), pp 975–1000

Foley, M, McGillivray, D and McPherson, G (2012) *Event Policy: From theory to strategy*, Routledge, Abingdon

Frank, R, Massey, W and Wind, Y (1972) *Market Segmentation*, Prentice Hall, Upper Saddle River, NJ

Frericks, M (2016) Which sponsor will win Wimbledon? *Media Monitoring*, 8 July [Online] https://bis.lexisnexis.co.uk/blog/posts/which-sponsor-will-win-wimbledon [Accessed 25/06/17]

Gabriel, Y and Lang, T (2008) New faces and new masks of today's consumer, *Journal of Consumer Culture*, **8** (3), pp 321–40

Ganassali, S and Didellon, L (1996) Le transfert comme principe central du parrainage, *Recherche et Applications en Marketing*, **11** (1), pp 37–48

Gardner, MP and Shuman, P (1988) Sponsorship and small businesses, *Journal of Small Business Management*, **26** (4), pp 44–52

GE (2008) GE launches marketing initiatives for London 2012 Olympic Games, GE Newsroom [Online] http://www.genewsroom.com/Press-Releases/GE-Launches-Marketing-Initiatives-For-London-2012-Olympic-Games-235162 [Accessed 12/11/16]

Gerald, E and Sinclair, L (2003) *The Sponsorship Manual: Sponsorship made easy*, 2nd edn, Sponsorship Unit, Victoria, Australia

Getz, D (2007) *Event Studies: Theory, research and policy for planned events*, Events Management Series, Elsevier Butterworth-Heinemann, Amsterdam and London

Gillette Newsroom (2017a) Gillette bolsters its esports roster with EDward Gaming (EDG) team partnership [Online] http://news.gillette.com/press-release/sports/gillette-bolsters-its-esports-roster-edward-gaming-edg-team-partnership [Accessed 04/01/18]

Gillette Newsroom (2017b) Gillette enters esports through global partnership with ESL as sponsor of the Intel Extreme Masters World Championship Katowice 2017 [Online] http://news.gillette.com/press-release/sports/gillette-enters-esports-through-global-partnership-esl-sponsor-intel-extreme-ma [Accessed 04/01/18]

Gilmore, J and Pine, BJ (2007) *Authenticity: What consumers really want*, Harvard Business Review Press, Cambridge, MA

Glaser, FW and Lum, MC (2004) Corporate sponsorship: Measuring its effectiveness, MBA dissertation, Simon Fraser University, Burnaby, Canada

Goffman, E (1959) *The Presentation of Self in Everyday Life*, Penguin Books, Harmondsworth

Goulding, C, Canniford, R and Shankar, A (2013) Learning to be tribal: Facilitating the formation of consumer tribes, *European Journal of Marketing*, 47 (5/6), pp 813–32

Graffigna, G and Gambetti, RC (2015) Grounding consumer–brand engagement, *International Journal of Market Research*, 57 (4), pp 605–29

Gregory, P (1984) Sponsoring et mécénat: instruments de communication institutionnelle, *Revue Francaise de Gestion* (September–October), pp 163–75

Guardian (2012) London 2012 Olympic sponsors list: Who are they and what have they paid? [Online] https://www.theguardian.com/sport/datablog/2012/jul/19/london-2012-olympic-sponsors-list [Accessed 28/01/18]

Gupta, S (2003) Event marketing: Issues and challenges, *IIMB Management Review* (Indian Institute of Management Bangalore), 15 (2), pp 87–96

Gwinner, K (1997) A model of image creation and image transfer in event sponsorship, *International Marketing Review*, 14 (3), pp 145–58

Gwinner, KP and Eaton, J (1999) Building brand image through event sponsorship: The role of image transfer, *Journal of Advertising*, **18** (4), pp 47–57

Hackley, C and Tiwsakul, R (2006) Entertainment marketing and experiential consumption, *Journal of Marketing Communicatios*, **14** (3), pp 145–58

Hakala, H, Nummelin, L and Kohtamäki, M (2017) Online brand community practices and the construction of brand legitimacy, *Marketing Theory*, **17** (4), pp 537–58

Hanlon, P (2012) Face slams: Event marketing takes off, *Forbes* [Online] http://www.forbes.com/sites/patrickhanlon/2012/05/09/face-slams-event-marketing-takes-off/ [Accessed 05/11/16]

Hart, S (2012) London 2012 Olympics: Watchdog commissioner resigns over Games' sponsorship link with Dow Chemical, *Daily Telegraph*, 25 January [Online] http://www.telegraph.co.uk/sport/olympics/9039749/London-2012-Olympics-watchdog-commissioner-resigns-over-Games-sponsorship-link-with-Dow-Chemical.html [Accessed 15/06/17]

Hibbert, C (1979) *The Rise and Fall of the House of Medici*, Penguin Books, London

Hill+Knowlton Strategies (2017) What we've been up to in London – 3rd March 2017 [Online] http://www.hkstrategies.com/en-uk/weve-london-3rd-march-2017/ [Accessed 04/01/18]

Hogg, MK, Cox, AJ and Keeling, K (2000) The impact of self-monitoring on image congruence and product/brand evaluation, *European Journal of Marketing*, **34** (5/6), pp 641–67

Holbrook, MB (2006) The consumption experience—something new, something old, something borrowed, something sold: Part 1, *Journal of Macromarketing*, **26** (2), pp 259–66

Holbrook, MB and Hirschman, EC (1982) The experiential aspects of consumption: Consumer fantasies, feelings, and fun, *Journal of Consumer Research*, **9** (2), pp 132–40

IEG (International Events Group) (no date) IEG's sponsorship contract checklist [Online] http://www.sponsorship.com/iegsr/2014/04/07/IEG-s-Sponsorship-Contract-Checklist.aspx [Accessed 03/07/18]

IEG (2008) Forecast: Recession slams brakes on sponsorship spending [Online] http://www.sponsorship.com/iegsr/2008/12/22/Forecast–Recession-Slams-Brakes-On-Sponsorship-Sp.aspx [Accessed 26/06/17]

IEG (2013) The key to sponsor servicing: Post-event fulfillment reports [Online] http://www.sponsorship.com/iegsr/2013/04/15/The-Key-To-Sponsor-Servicing–Post-Event-Fulfillme.aspx [Accessed 26/06/17]

IEG (2016) *What Sponsors Want and Where Their Dollars Will Go in 2016*, IEG, Chicago, IL

IEG (2016) Sponsorship's big spenders: IEG's top sponsor rankings [Online] http://www.sponsorship.com/iegsr/2016/09/19/Sponsorship-s-Big-Spenders–IEG-s-Top-Sponsor-Rank.aspx [Accessed 9/02/18]

IEG (2017) *IEG's Guide to Sponsorship* [Online] www.sponsorship.com/IEG/files/59/59ada496-cd2c-4ac2-9382-060d86fcbdc4.pdf [Accessed 25/01/17]

IEG (2017) *What Sponsors Want and Where Their Dollars Will Go in 2017*, IEG, Chicago, IL

IMG (no date) Our story [Online] http://img.com/story/ [Accessed 22/02/18]

Ingle, S (2017) Chinese company Alibaba signs deal to be major sponsor of Olympic Games, *Guardian*, 19 January [Online] http://www.theguardian.com/sport/2017/jan/19/chinese-e-commerce-company-alibaba-major-olympic-games-sponsor [Accessed 04/01/18]

International Chamber of Commerce (2003) *ICC International Code on Sponsorship* [Online] http://www.abfi.ie/Sectors/ABFI/ABFI.nsf/vPagesABFI/Responsibilities~sponsorship/$File/ICC+International+Code+on+Sponsorship.pdf [Accessed 23/01/17]

Keller, KL (1993) Conceptualizing, measuring, managing customer-based brand equity, *Journal of Marketing*, 57 (1), pp 1–22

Keller, KL (2016) Unlocking the power of integrated marketing communications: How integrated is your IMC program? *Journal of Advertising*, 45 (3), pp 286–301

Keller, KN (2003) *Strategic Brand Management: Building measuring, and managing brand equity*, 2nd edn, Pearson Education International, New Jersey

Key Note (2016) Sport sponsorship [Online] www.keynote.co.uk [Accessed 21/01/17]

Khomami, N (2016) Mark Rylance heads list of artists calling for end to BP cultural sponsorship, *Guardian*, 2 August [Online] https://www.theguardian.com/environment/2016/aug/02/mark-rylance-heads-list-of-artists-calling-for-end-to-bp-cultural-sponsorship [Accessed 28/06/18]

Kim, S and Kim, S (2018) 5G is making its global debut at Olympics, and it's wicked fast, Bloomberg [Online] https://www.bloomberg.com/news/articles/2018-02-12/5g-is-here-super-speed-makes-worldwide-debut-at-winter-olympics [Accessed 13/03/18]

Kitchin, R (2014) *The Data Revolution: Big data, open data, data infrastructures and their consequences*, Sage, Thousand Oaks, CA

Kjeldgaard, D and Bode, M (2017) Broadening the brandfest: Play and ludic agency, *European Journal of Marketing*, 51 (1), pp 23–43

Koenigstorfer, J and Uhrich, S (2017) Consumer attitudes toward sponsors' counterambush marketing ads, *Psychology & Marketing*, **34** (6), pp 631–47

Kolah, A (2015) *Improving the Performance of Sponsorship*, Routledge, Oxon

Kotler, P and Andreason, A (2003) *Strategic Marketing for Nonprofit Organizations*, 6th edn, Prentice Hall, Upper Saddle River, NJ

Kotler, P and Armstrong, G (2014) *Principles of Marketing*, 15th edn, Global Editions, Boston, MA; Pearson, London

Lagae, W (2005) *Sports Sponsorship and Marketing Communication: A European perspective*, Prentice Hall, Harlow

Lave, J and Wenger, E (1997) *Situated Learning: Legitimate peripheral participation*, Cambridge University Press, Cambridge

Lee, H-K (2014) Transnational cultural fandom, in *The Ashgate Research Companion to Fan Cultures*, ed L Duits, L Zwaan and K Reijnders, pp 195–208, Ashgate, Surrey

Li, M, Huang, Z and Cai, LA (2009) Benefit segmentation of visitors to a rural community-based festival, *Journal of Travel & Tourism Marketing*, **26** (5–6), pp 585–98

Luonila, M (2016) Sponsorship thinking: A creator for collaborative undertakings in the festival context, *Event Management*, **20** (2), pp 267–84

Lyotard, J-F (1984) *The Postmodern Condition: A report on knowledge*, tr G Bennington and B Massumi, Manchester University Press, Manchester

McAlexander, JH, Schouten, JW and Koenig, HF (2002) Building brand community, *Journal of Marketing*, **66** (1), pp 38–54

McAlexander, JH, Kim, SK and Roberts, SD (2003) Loyalty: The influences of satisfaction and brand community integration, *Journal of Marketing Theory and Practice*, **11** (4), pp 1–11

MacCannell, D (1973) Staged authenticity: Arrangements of social space in tourist settings, *American Journal of Sociology*, **79** (3), pp 589–603

McDonnell, A and Moir, M (2013) *Event Sponsorship*, Routledge, London

Magnay, J (2012) London 2012 Olympics: Dow Chemical puts blame for ongoing crisis in Bhopal at Indian government's door, *Daily Telegraph*, 8 March [Online] https://www.telegraph.co.uk/sport/olympics/9130231/London-2012-Olympics-Dow-Chemical-puts-blame-for-ongoing-crisis-in-Bhopal-at-Indian-governments-door.html [Accessed 28/06/18]

Margolis, J (2016) More Millennials switch off social media, *Financial Times*, 11 October [Online] https://www.ft.com/content/5477680e-8ece-11e6-a72e-b428cb934b78 [Accessed 08/01/18]

Martensen, A, Grønholdt, L, Bendtsen, L and Juul Jensen, M (2007) Application of a model for the effectiveness of event marketing, *Journal of Advertising Research*, **47** (3), pp 283–301

Masterman, G (2004) *Strategic Sports Event Management: An international approach*, Elsevier Butterworth-Heinemann, Oxford

Masterman, G (2007) *Sponsorship for a Return on Investment*, Butterworth-Heinemann, Oxford

Meenaghan, JA (1983) Commercial sponsorship, *European Journal of Marketing*, 17 (7), pp 1–73

Meenaghan, T (1991) Sponsorship: Legitimising the medium, *European Journal of Marketing*, 25 (11), pp 5–10

Meenaghan, T (2001) Understanding sponsorship effects, *Psychology & Marketing*, 18 (2), pp 95–122

Meenaghan, T (2013) Measuring sponsorship performance: Challenge and direction, *Psychology and Marketing*, 30 (5), pp 385–93

Meenaghan, T and O'Sullivan, P (2013) Metrics in sponsorship research: Is credibility an issue? *Psychology and Marketing*, 30 (5), pp 385–93

Meenaghan, T, McLoughlin, L and McCormack, A (2013) New challenges in sponsorship evaluation actors: New media and the context of praxis, *Psychology and Marketing*, 30 (5), pp 444–60

Mida, F and Zaiem, I (2015) Emotion and sponsorship: Case of television sponsorship, *International Journal of Management, Accounting & Economics*, 2 (4), pp 325–38

Mintel (2016) *Music Concerts and Festivals – UK – 2016*, Mintel

Mooney, A (2017) Nuns tell companies to get real over virtual AGMs, *Financial Times*, 20 October

More, G (2008) The rights holder guide to successful sponsorship sales, *Journal of Sponsorship*, 2 (1), pp 67–76

Morgan, M and Watson, P (2007) *Resource Guide in Extraordinary Experiences: Understanding and managing the consumer experience in hospitality, leisure, events, sports and tourism*, Project Report, Higher Education Academy, York

Morhart, F, Malär, L, Guèvremont, A, Girardin, F and Grohmann, B (2015) Brand authenticity: An integrative framework and measurement scale, *Journal of Consumer Psychology*, 25 (2), pp 200–18

Mostert, F (2017) China clamps down on pirate trademark ransoms for famous brands, *Financial Times*, 29 June [Online] https://www.ft.com/content/3f580c34-4c70-11e7-a3f4-c742b9791d43 [Accessed 28/06/18]

Musgrave, J and Woodward, S (2016) Ecological systems theory approach to corporate social responsibility: Contextual perspectives from meeting planners, *Event Management*, 20 (3), pp 365–81

National Lottery (2017) Life changing [Online] https://www.national-lottery.co.uk/life-changing/where-the-money-goes [Accessed 06/05/18]

Olson, EL and Thjømøe, HM (2009) Sponsorship effect metric: Assessing the financial value of sponsoring by comparisons to television advertising, *Journal of the Academy of Marketing Science*, 37, pp 504–15

Olson, E and Thjømøe, H (2011) Explaining and articulating the fit construct in sponsorship, *Journal of Advertising*, **40** (1), pp 57–70

O'Reilly, N (2007) Sponsorship evaluation, Doctoral Thesis, Carleton University, Ottawa [Online] https://curve.carleton.ca/system/files/etd/0c3330aa-4c15-4e07-80c3-81df0a4d9bb9/etd_pdf/269380816849b30e7c03067a6e49f045/oreilly-sponsorshipevaluation.pdf [Accessed 29/06/18]

O'Reilly, N and Huybers, T (2015) Servicing in sponsorship: A best–worst scaling empirical analysis, *Journal of Sports Management*, **29**, pp 155–69

O'Reilly, N and Madill, J (2009) Methods and metrics in sponsorship evaluation, *Journal of Sponsorship*, **2** (3), pp 215–30

O'Reilly, N and Madill, J (2012) The development of a process for evaluating marketing sponsorships, *Canadian Journal of Administrative Science*, **29** (1) pp 50–66

Osterwalder, A and Pigneur, Y (2010) *Business Model Generation: A handbook for visionaries, game changers, and challengers*, John Wiley and Sons, Hoboken, NJ

Otker, T (1998) Exploitation: The key to sponsorship success, *European Research*, **16** (2), pp 77–85

O'Toole, W (2011) *Events Feasibility and Development: From strategy to operations*, Butterworth-Heinemann, London

O'Toole, W and Mikolaitis, P (2002) *Corporate Events Project Management*, Wiley, New Jersey

Pattenden, M (2017) 'They see the potential': Why J-Lo and Gillette want a piece of the eSports action, *Guardian*, 25 December. [Online] http://www.theguardian.com/games/2017/dec/25/esports-jennifer-lopez-gillette-audi-mercedes-benz-a-piece-of-the-action [Accessed 04/01/18]

Pearsall, J (2010) Sponsorship performance: What is the role of sponsorship metrics in proactively managing the sponsor–property relationship? *Journal of Sponsorship*, **3** (2), pp 115–23

Pentecost, R and Spence, M (2004) Exploring the dimensions of fit within sports sponsorship, *ANZMAC 2004 Marketing Accountabilities and Responsibilities*, ANZMAC

Perry, M, Foley, P and Rumpf, P (1996) Events management: An emerging challenge in Australian higher education, *Festival Management and Event Tourism*, **4** (3), pp 85–93

Pine, BJ and Gilmore, JH (1998) Welcome to the experience economy, *Harvard Business Review*, **76** (4), pp 97–105

Poulsson, SHG and Kale, SH (2004) The experience economy and commercial experiences, *The Marketing Review*, **4** (3), pp 267–77

Press Association (2017) Growing social media backlash among young people, survey shows, *Guardian*, 4 October [Online] http://www.theguardian.com/media/2017/oct/05/growing-social-media-backlash-among-young-people-survey-shows [Accessed 08/01/18]

Reic, I (2017) *Events Marketing Management: A consumer perspective*, Routledge, London

Repucom (2015) *Live Music Sponsorship* [Online] http://nielsensports.com/wp-content/uploads/2014/09/Repucom-Live-Music-Report-2015.pdf [Accessed 21/01/17]

Rogers, T (2013) *Conferences and Conventions: A global industry*, 3rd edn, Butterworth-Heinemann, Oxon

Rowley, J and Williams, C (2008) The impact of brand sponsorship of music festivals, *Marketing Intelligence and Planning*, **6** (7), pp 781–96

Ryan, A and Fhay, J (2012) Evolving priorities in sponsorship: From media management to network management, *Journal of Marketing Management*, **28** (9–10), pp 1132–58

Salmons, H (2017) Parent/pupil digital behaviour poll – media briefing, HMC, 23 April [Online] http://www.hmc.org.uk/blog/parentpupil-digital-behaviour-poll-media-briefing/ [Accessed 08/01/18]

Sam, MP, Batty, R and Dean, RGK (2005) A transaction cost approach to sport sponsorship, *Sport Management Review*, **8**, pp 8–17

Sandler, D and Shani, D (1989) Olympic sponsorship vs ambush marketing: Who gets the gold?' *Journal of Advertising Research*, **29** (4), pp 9–14

Sanghak, L (2009) The commencement of modern sport sponsorship in 1850s–1950s, paper given at Sponsorship Marketing Association Conference, 2009

Schau, HJ, Muñiz, AM and Arnould, EJ (2009) How brand community practices create value, *Journal of Marketing*, **73** (5), pp 30–51

Schivinski, B, Christodoulides, G and Dabrowski, D (2016) Measuring consumers' engagement with brand-related social-media content, *Journal of Advertising Research*, **56** (1), pp 64–80.

Schmitt, B (1999) *Experiential Marketing: How to get customers to sense, feel, think, act, relate to your company and brands*, The Free Press, New York

Schmitt, BH, Brakus, J and Zarantonello, L (2014) The current state and future of brand experience, *Journal of Brand Management*, **21** (S9), pp 727–33

Schultz, DE (2007) Focus on brand changes rules of engagement, *Marketing News*, **41** (13), pp 7–8

Schultz, DE and Kitchen, PJ (2000) *Communicating Globally: An integrated marketing approach*, Palgrave, Basingstoke

Sense London (2015) *Real World Ideas: A guide to modern experiential marketing*, Sense Marketing Services Ltd, London

Shani, D and Sandler, DM (1998) Ambush marketing: Is confusion to blame for the flickering of the flame? *Psychology and Marketing*, **15** (4), pp 367–82

Sherry, J, Kozinets, RV and Borghini, S (2007) Agents in paradise: Experiential co-creation through emplacement, ritualization and community, in Consuming Experience, ed A Carú and B Cova, Routledge, London/New York

Simmons, G (2008) Marketing to postmodern consumers: Introducing the internet chameleon, *European Journal of Marketing*, **42** (3/4), pp 299–310

Simmons, R (2017) Paddy Power under fire after Wimbledon publicity stunt [Online] https://www.gamblinginsider.com/news/3626/paddy-power-under-fire-after-wimbledon-publicity-stunt [Accessed 08/01/18]

Skildum-Reid, K (2011) Asking the wrong questions: Sponsorship by the numbers [Online] http://powersponsorship.com/asking-the-wrong-questions-sponsorship-by-the-numbers/ [Accessed 25/02/18]

Skildum-Reid, K (2012) How to shift a sponsor's mindset on measurement [Online] http://powersponsorship.com/how-to-shift-a-sponsors-mindset-on-measurement/ [Accessed 25/06/17]

Skildum-Reid, K (2014) Can't keep up? 5 ways to simplify sponsorship servicing [Online] http://powersponsorship.com/cant-keep-up-5-ways-to-simplify-sponsorship-servicing/ [Accessed 26/06/17]

Skildum-Reid, K (2014) What should a sponsee include in a year-end ROI report? [Online] http://powersponsorship.com/year-end-roi-report/ [Accessed 25/06/17]

Skildum-Reid, K (2016) Don't send a sponsorship proposal until you read this [Online] http://powersponsorship.com/dont-send-a-sponsorship-proposal/ [Accessed 17/06/17]

Skinner, BE and Rukavina, V (2003) *Event Sponsorship*, Wiley, Hoboken, NJ

Smilansky, S (2009), *Experiential Marketing: A practical guide to interactive brand experiences*, Kogan Page, London

Smith, MK (2009) *Issues in Cultural Tourism*, Routledge, London

Spanier, G (2017) O2 has renewed the naming rights for The O2, the world's most successful entertainment arena, in a ten-year partnership with the London venue, *Campaign Magazine*, 23/02 [Online] https://www.campaignlive.co.uk/article/o2-renews-naming-rights -o2-greenwich-10-year-deal/1425091 [Accessed 05/05/18]

Sprint Newsroom (2018) Sprint unveils six 5G-ready cities: Significant milestone toward launching first 5G mobile network in the US, Sprint [Online] http://newsroom.sprint.com/sprint-unveils-5g-ready-massive-mimo-markets.htm [Accessed 13/03/18]

Steyn, PG (2009) Online recommendations as the ultimate yardstick to measure sponsorship effectiveness, *Journal of Sponsorship*, **2** (4), pp 316–29

Stotlar, DK (2004) Sponsorship evaluation: Moving from theory to practice, *Sport Marketing Quarterly*, **13**, pp 61–64

Stotlar, DK (2005) *Developing Successful Sport Sponsorship Plans*, Fitness Information Technology, Morgantown, WV

Sweeny, M (2012) Ryder Cup 2012: Paddy Power tees up ambush plan, *Guardian*, 1 October [Online] https://www.theguardian.com/media/2012/sep/29/ryder-cup-2012-paddy-power-ambush [Accessed 28/06/18]

Tang, H-WV (2014) Constructing a competence model for international professionals in the MICE industry: An analytic hierarchy process approach, *Journal of Hospitality, Leisure, Sport & Tourism Education*, **15**, pp. 34–49

Uhlik, KS (1995) Partnership, step by step: A practical model of partnership formation, *Journal of Park and Recreation Administration*, **13** (4), pp 13–24

Ukman, L (2012) 11 basics of successful sponsorship sales [Online] http://www.sponsorship.com/About-IEG/Sponsorship-Blogs/Lesa-Ukman/June-2012/11-Basics-Of-Successful-Sponsorship-Sales.aspx [Accessed 20/06/17]

Urban Kapraun, C (2009) Sponsorship valuation and fair market value, Evaluation and ROI Demystified [Online] http://www.sponsorship.com/About-IEG/Sponsorship-Blog/Carrie-Urban-Kapraun/June-2009/Sponsorship-Valuation-and-Fair-Market-Value,-Evalu.aspx [Accessed 9/01/18]

VilaóLópez, N and Rodríguez–Molina, M (2013) Event–brand transfer in an entertainment service: Experiential marketing, *Industrial Management & Data Systems*, **113** (5), pp 712–31

Virgin Money London Marathon (2016) Latest news: Lucozade extends Virgin Money London Marathon partnership [Online] https://www.virginmoneylondonmarathon.com/en-gb/news-media/latest-news/item/lucozade-extends-virgin-money-london-marathon-partnership/ [Accessed 27/06/17]

Walliser, B (2003) An international review of sponsorship research: Extension and update, *International Journal of Advertising*, **22**, pp 5–40

Walmsley, B and Franks, A (2011) *The audience experience: Changing roles and relationships, in Key Issues in the Arts and Entertainment Industry*, ed B Walmsley, Goodfellow

Wang, RT and Kaplanidou, K (2013) I want to buy more because I feel good: The effect of sport-induced emotion on sponsorship, *International Journal of Sports Marketing and Sponsorship*, **15** (1), pp 52–66

Welsh, J (2003) Reinventing sponsorship [Online] https://jcwelsh.wordpress.com/2010/03/11/reinventing-sponsorship/ [Accessed 24/05/17]

Wenger, E. (2000) Communities of Practice and Social Learning Systems, *Organization*, 7(2), pp. 225–246. doi: 10.1177/135050840072002

Wimbledon (2017) Official suppliers [Online] http://www.wimbledon.com/en_GB/atoz/official_suppliers.html# [Accessed 27/06/17]

Wood, EH (2009) Evaluating event marketing: Experience or outcome? *Journal of Promotion Management*, **15** (1–2), pp 247–68

World Federation of Advertisers (2017) What is WFA? [Online] https://www.wfanet.org/about/who-we-are/ [Accessed 20/01/17]

FURTHER READING

Chapter 1

The following articles, albeit not recent, should prove useful as a foundation for understanding sponsorship and its evolution.

Cornwell, TB and Maignan, I (1998) An international review of sponsorship research, *Journal of Advertising*, **27** (1), pp 1–21

This article, by prominent authors Bettina Cornwell and Isabelle Maignan, has long been the most relied upon review of the literature investigating sponsorship as a marketing communication method. It identifies 80 articles published up to 1996, which are grouped into five research streams: the nature of sponsorship; managerial aspects of sponsorship; measurement of sponsorship effects; strategic use of sponsorship; and legal/ethical considerations. This provides a useful categorization for further exploration of the key aspects of sponsorship.

Walliser, B (2003) An international review of sponsorship research: Extension and update, *International Journal of Advertising*, **22**, pp 5–40

Building on and expanding Cornwelll and Maignan's work, Walliser's review of the literature adds a further 153 articles to the analysis. In addition to covering an additional six years of published material, it makes a greater effort to include international research to complement the mostly Ango-Saxon body of literature included in the 1998 review.

Crompton, J (1995) Factors that have stimulated the growth of sponsorship of major events, *Festivals Management and Event Tourism*, **3**, pp 97–105

John L Crompton has written extensively about sponsorship. We have referred to this article earlier in this book when examining reasons that have led to sponsorship's growth in importance.

Chapter 2

Donlan, L and Crowther, P (2014) Leveraging sponsorship to achieve consumer relationship objectives through the creation of 'marketing spaces': An exploratory study, *Journal of Marketing Communications*, **20** (4), pp. 291–306

This is an insightful research paper that examines how sponsorship managers are starting to set relational objectives for their campaigns. The authors then consider how relational objectives can be achieved and, importantly, evaluated.

Grohs, R (2016) Drivers of brand image improvement in sports-event sponsorship, *International Journal of Advertising*, **35** (3), pp 391–420

This is a wide-ranging research paper that examines the last 20 years of research on what influences brand image improvement in sports event sponsorship. The author suggests a way to measure image change in sponsorships.

Holbrook, MB and Hirschman, EC (1982) The experiential aspects of consumption: Consumer fantasies, feelings, and fun, *Journal of Consumer Research*, **9** (2), pp 132–40

This is a tough article to read, *but* it is one of the most important and authoritative articles on experience as a driver of consumer decision making. The authors identify the prevalent mode of analysing consumer decision making, which sees the individual as rational and making decisions based on information. In contrast, the experiential view put forward in this paper suggests that consumption is primarily subjective and is driven by 'fantasies, feelings and fun'.

Keller, KL (2016) Unlocking the power of integrated marketing communications: How integrated is your IMC program? *Journal of Advertising*, **45** (3), pp 286–301

This article examines integrated marketing communications in the light of the widening range of digital platforms available to marketers. The author sets out seven criteria that marketers should use to inform the design of their IMC programmes.

Chapter 3

Novais, MA and Arcodia, C (2013) Measuring the effects of event sponsorship: theoretical frameworks and image transfer models, *Journal of Travel & Tourism Marketing*, **30** (4), pp 308–34

This article is very useful in that it summarizes the main research areas relating to events and sponsorship, including leveraging sponsorship at events. This is an important article that reviews a significant amount of up-to-date research on events and sponsorship. The authors also make suggestions for future research in this area.

Schmitt, B (1999) *Experiential Marketing: How to get customers to sense, feel, think, act, relate to your company and brands*, The Free Press, New York

This book was written nearly 20 years ago and so some of the examples are a bit dated. However, the ideas and concepts are very useful for sponsors and event managers who are looking to activate brands. In particular Chapters 4–8 set out the Sense, Feel, Think, Act and Relate experiences and how to create them.

Smilansky, S (2009), *Experiential Marketing: A practical guide to interactive brand experiences*, Kogan Page, London

This book gives practical, how-to advice on putting together interactive experiences that will enable brands to engage with their target audiences. There are useful chapters on setting experiential marketing objectives, recruiting brand ambassadors and insights from leading experiential marketers in the form of Q&A interviews.

Chapter 4

Cova, B and White, T (2010) Counter-brand and alter-brand communities: The impact of Web 2.0 on tribal marketing approaches, *Journal of Marketing Management*, **26** (3–4), pp 256–70

This research paper does not focus specifically on sponsorship but it does cover important developments in theory relating to brand tribes and communities. In particular, it is important for event managers and sponsors to understand the identification of groups of consumers that oppose and contest how their favourite brands are managed, in relation to their own practices.

Gwinner, K (1997) A model of image creation and image transfer in event sponsorship, *International Marketing Review*, **14** (3), pp 145–58

While this research paper is over 20 years old it is important as it sets out the similarities between the process of celebrity endorsement of products and event image associations transferring to sponsoring brands.

International Events Group (IEG) (2017) *IEG's Guide to Sponsorship* [Online] www.sponsorship.com/IEG/files/59/59ada496-cd2c-4ac2-9382-060d86fcbdc4.pdf

This comprehensive guide covers a wide range of important topics, including why companies sponsor, deal making and leveraging sponsorship, best practice and why sponsorships fail.

Wang, RT and Kaplanidou, K (2013) I want to buy more because I feel good: The effect of sport-induced emotion on sponsorship, *International Journal of Sports Marketing and Sponsorship*, **15** (1), pp 52–66

This important research paper examines how spectators' emotions relate to their attitudes towards sponsors. This is particularly important considering that in sport there is always a winning and a losing side, so sponsors need to be able to appeal to spectators who are experiencing both positive and negative emotions.

Chapter 5

Close, A, Krishen, A and Latour, M (2009) This event is me! How consumer event self-congruity leverages sponsorship, *Journal of Advertising Research*, **49** (3), pp 271–84

This research paper examines sponsored promotional events in shopping centres. The theory of self-congruity is examined and defined as when consumers, in their search for self-esteem, compare themselves to products to determine the products' consistency with their self-image. The paper offers both theoretical and practical insights that are helpful to both students and professionals.

Kwon, E, Ratneshwar, S and Kim, E (2016) Brand image congruence through sponsorship of sporting events: A reinquiry of Gwinner and Eaton (1999), *Journal of Advertising*, **45** (1), pp 130–38

As the title suggests, this article tests the findings of Gwinner and Eaton's (1999) research paper from both a methodological and findings perspective. This is particularly useful as it allows the reader to examine a robust academic critique of an influential piece of research. It will be interesting to see whether Gwinner and Eaton respond!

Olson, E and Thjømøe, H (2011) Explaining and articulating the fit construct in sponsorship, *Journal of Advertising*, **40** (1), pp 57–70

This article offers a comprehensive review of literature relating to sponsorship fit before moving on to present three pieces of novel research in this area that draw on three different research methods: cognitive mapping, survey based experiment and conjoint analysis. The three pieces of research are linked in that the constructs generated in the first qualitative study are then tested in the following two quantitative studies.

IEG's website (www.sponsorship.com) has a wealth of resources and up-to-date information on the sponsorship industry.

Chapter 6

Daellenbach, K, Davies, J and Ashill, N (2006) Understanding sponsorship and sponsorship relationships: Multiple frames and multiple perspectives, *International Journal of Nonprofit and Voluntary Sector Marketing*, **11** (1), pp 73–87

This paper reviews and applies multiple organizational behaviour frameworks, namely lifecycle theory, resource based view of the firm, resource dependency theory, institutional theory and social network theory, to examine the role of sponsorship relationships.

Farelly, F and Quester, P (2003) The effects of market orientation on trust and commitment: The case of the sponsorship business-to-business relationship, *European Journal of Marketing*, 37 (3/4)

Here agency theory is utilized to examine the relationship between the sponsor and the sponsored party, especially focusing on the effects of market orientation, trust and commitment, and whether they drive sponsorship renewal.

Eventbrite: eventbrite.com and eventbrite.co.uk

The world's fastest growing registration and ticketing platform also serves as an event management services website. Among its varied content it includes a wealth of practical information on how to go about seeking event sponsorship. Free resources available include prospectus and proposals templates, guides and original research on the sector.

Chapter 7

IEG: www.sponsorship.com

This website is very useful for getting up-to-date information on sponsorship, insights, trends and events.

Mullins, LJ (2013) *Management and Organisational Behaviour*, FT Publishing International, London

This is a general management text that covers a range of issues including a comprehensive and thorough discussion of ethics and corporate social responsibility in Chapter 17.

Chapter 8

Chadwick, S and Burton, N (2011) The evolving sophistication of ambush marketing: A typology of strategies, *Thunderbird International Business Review*, 53 (6), pp 709–19

This is a comprehensive article that examines the genesis of ambush marketing, how it is defined and the ways in which it can be managed. The authors present a typology of different ambush marketing techniques and provide examples from major sport events.

Duxbury, R (2015) *Contract Law*, 10th edn, Sweet and Maxwell, London

Hiscox Insurance website: www.hiscox.co.uk/event-insurance

This website gives good advice on securing event insurance. There are draft policies and application forms for conferences, exhibitions and special events to download.

Ofcom: www.ofcom.org.uk

The government agency Office of Communications website sets out the OFCOM Broadcasting Code, which includes the Crosspromotion Code and Commercial References on TV.

Eventbrite: https://www.eventbrite.co.uk/blog/event-insurance-explained-ds00/

Eventbrite has a range of useful advice guides and interviews with experts on a range of important event management topics, including event insurance. There is a good interview with Martin Linfield, Head of Hiscox's Event Insurance on this link.

Chapter 9

O'Reilly, N and Madill, J (2009) Methods and metrics in sponsorship evaluation, *Journal of Sponsorship*, **2** (3), pp 215–30

This paper combines a review of the literature and expert interviews to identify models, methods and frameworks of sponsorship evaluation between the 1990s and 2005, and concluded that sophisticated metrics are required that are directly related to the sponsors' objectives.

Cahill, J and Meenaghan, T (2013) Sponsorship at the O2 – 'The belief that repaid', *Psychology and Marketing*, **30** (5), pp 431–43

This paper illustrates the strategic use of sponsorship by communication brand O2 in Ireland and how the brand used innovative and creative activation through social networks centred on customers' participation. The authors present the range of metrics utilized by O2 in the sponsorship evaluation process, including sentiment analysis and social media conversation in addition to the more traditional approaches, hence offering a comprehensive approach to measuring sponsorship effectiveness.

Meenaghan, T, McLoughlin, L and McCormack, A (2013) New challenges in sponsorship evaluation actors, new media and the context of praxis, *Psychology and Marketing*, **30** (5), pp 444–60

This paper provides a comprehensive overview of principles and practices in sponsorship evaluation and highlights issues and challenges focused on two main concerns. On the one hand it discusses the measurement of sponsorship performance in social media, focusing on a range of channels. On the other hand it provides a useful outline of the types of benefits that sponsorship can offer to various stakeholders (staff, trade associates/suppliers/distributors, government/regulators, shareholders and rights holders) to illustrate the emerging concern with delivering on multiple stakeholders' objectives.

Facebook Insights

This is an embedded function that can be accessed by clicking on the relative tab on a Facebook page. It provides data on the performance of your page and your posts as well as useful audience information. More details of how Facebook can be used for marketing and marketing measurement purposes can be found on: https://www.facebook.com/business/

INDEX

CPSIA information can be obtained
at www.ICGtesting.com
Printed in the USA
BVHW020543041218
534641BV00028B/1590/P